Lenin 2017

Lenin 2017

*Remembering, Repeating,
and Working Through*

V. I. LENIN

Edited and Introduced
by Slavoj Žižek

V E R S O
London • New York

First published by Verso 2017
Introduction and Afterword © Slavoj Žižek 2017
The works of V. I. Lenin collected here derive
from the Marxists Internet Archive

1 3 5 7 9 10 8 6 4 2

Verso
UK: 6 Meard Street, London W1F 0EG
US: 20 Jay Street, Suite 1010, Brooklyn, NY 11201
versobooks.com

Verso is the imprint of New Left Books

ISBN-13: 978-1-78663-188-6
ISBN-13: 978-1-78663-189-3 (US EBK)
eISBN-13: 978-1-78663-187-9 (UK EBK)

British Library Cataloguing in Publication Data
A catalogue record for this book is available from the British Library

Library of Congress Cataloging-in-Publication Data
A catalog record for this book is available from the Library of Congress

Typeset in Sabon by MJ&N Gavan, Truro, Cornwall
Printed in the UK by CPI Mackays Ltd

Contents

Introduction: Remembering, Repeating and Working Through

Slavoj Žižek

Remembering and Repeating

The title of Freud's short text from 1914, 'Remembering, Repeating and Working Through', provides the best formula for the way we should relate – today, 100 years later – to the event called the October Revolution. The three concepts Freud mentions form a dialectical triad: they designate the three phases of the analytical process, and resistance intervenes in every passage from one phase to the next. The first step consists in remembering the repressed past traumatic events, in bringing them out, which can also be done by hypnosis. This phase immediately runs into a deadlock: the content brought out lacks its proper symbolic context and thus remains ineffective; it fails to transform the subject and resistance remains active, limiting the amount of content revealed. The problem with this approach is that it stays focused on the past and ignores the subject's present constellation which keeps this past alive, symbolically active. Resistance expresses itself in the form of transference: what the subject cannot properly remember, she repeats, transferring the past constellation onto a present (e.g., she treats the analyst as if he were her father). What the subject cannot properly remember, she acts out, re-enacts – and when the analyst points this out, her intervention is met with resistance. Working through is working through the resistance, turning it from the obstacle into the very resort of analysis, and this turn is self-reflexive in a properly Hegelian sense: resistance is a link between object and subject, between past and present, proof that we are not only fixated on the past but that this fixation is an effect of the present deadlock in the subject's libidinal economy.

With regard to 1917, we also begin by remembering, by recalling, the true history of the October Revolution and, of course, its reversal into Stalinism. The great ethico-political problem of the communist regimes can best be captured under the title 'founding fathers, founding crimes'. Can a communist regime survive the act of openly confronting its violent past in which millions were imprisoned and killed? If so, in what form and to what degree? The first paradigmatic case of such a confrontation was, of course, Nikita Khrushchev's 'secret' report on Stalin's crimes to the 20th Congress of the Soviet Communist Party in 1956. The first thing that strikes one in this report is the focus on Stalin's personality as being the key factor in the crimes, and the concomitant lack of any systematic analysis of what made those crimes possible. The second feature is its strenuous effort to keep the Origins clear: not only is the condemnation of Stalin limited to his arrest and killing of high-ranking Party members and military officers in the 1930s (where rehabilitations were very selective: Bukharin, Zinoviev, etc., continued to be non-persons, not to mention Trotsky), ignoring the great famine of the late 1920s; but the report is also presented as announcing the return of the Party to its 'Leninist roots', so that Lenin emerges as the pure Origin spoiled or betrayed by Stalin. In his belated but perspicuous analysis of the report, written in 1970, Sartre noted that

it was *true* that Stalin had ordered massacres, transformed the land of the revolution into a police state; he was *truly* convinced that the USSR would not reach communism without passing through the socialism of concentration camps. But as one of the witnesses very rightly points out, when the authorities find it useful to tell the truth, it's because they can't find any better lie. Immediately this truth, coming from official mouths, becomes a lie corroborated by the facts. Stalin was a wicked man? Fine. But how had Soviet society perched him on the throne and kept him there for a quarter of a century.[1]

Indeed, is not Khrushchev's later fate (he was deposed in 1964) proof of Oscar Wilde's quip that if one tells the truth, one will sooner or later be caught out? Sartre's analysis nonetheless falls short on one crucial point: even if Khrushchev was 'speaking in the name of the system' – 'the machine was sound, but its chief operator was not; this saboteur had relieved the world of his presence, and everything was going to run smoothly again'[2] – his report *did* have a traumatic impact, and his intervention set in motion a process that ultimately brought down the system itself – a lesson worth remembering today. In this precise sense, Khrushchev's 1956 speech denouncing Stalin's crimes was a true political act – after which, as William Taubman put it, 'the Soviet regime never fully recovered, and neither did he'.[3] Although the opportunist motives for this daring move are plain enough, there was clearly more than mere calculation to it, a kind of reckless excess which cannot be accounted for by strategic reasoning. After the speech, things were never the same again, the fundamental dogma of infallible leadership had been fatally undermined; no wonder then, that, in reaction to the speech, the entire *nomenklatura*

---

1 Quoted in Ian H. Birchall, *Sartre against Stalinism*, New York: Berghahn Books, 2004, p. 166.

2 Ibid.

3 William Taubman, *Khrushchev: The Man and His Era*, London: Free Press, 2003, p. 493.

sank into temporary paralysis. During the speech itself, a dozen or so delegates suffered nervous breakdowns and had to be carried out and given medical help; a few days later, Boleslaw Bierut, the hard-line general secretary of the Polish Communist Party, died of a heart attack, and the model Stalinist writer Alexander Fadeyev shot himself. The point is not that they were 'honest communists' – most of them were brutal manipulators who harboured no subjective illusions about the nature of the Soviet regime. What broke down was their 'objective' illusion: the figure of the 'big Other' that had provided the background against which they were able to pursue their ruthless drive for power. The Other onto which they had transposed their belief, which as it were believed on their behalf, their subject-supposed-to-believe, disintegrated.

Khrushchev's wager was that his (limited) confession would strengthen the communist movement – and in the short term he was right. One should always remember that the Khrushchev era was the last period of authentic communist enthusiasm, of belief in the communist project. When, during his visit to the United States in 1959, Khrushchev made his famous defiant statement to the American public that 'your grandchildren will be communists', he effectively spelled out the conviction of the entire Soviet *nomenklatura*. After his fall in 1964, a resigned cynicism prevailed, up until Gorbachev's attempt at a more radical confrontation with the past (the rehabilitations then included Bukharin, but – for Gorbachev at least – Lenin remained the untouchable point of reference, and Trotsky continued to be a non-person).

With Deng Xiaoping's 'reforms', the Chinese proceeded in a radically different, almost opposite, way. While at the level of the economy (and, up to a point, culture) what is usually understood as 'communism' was abandoned, and the gates were opened wide to Western-style 'liberalisation' (private property, profit-making, hedonist individualism, etc.), the

Party nevertheless maintained its ideologico-political hegemony – not in the sense of doctrinal orthodoxy (in the official discourse, the Confucian reference to the 'Harmonious Society' practically replaced any reference to communism), but in the sense of maintaining the unconditional political hegemony of the Communist Party as the only guarantee of China's stability and prosperity. This required a close monitoring and regulation of the ideological discourse on Chinese history, especially the history of the last two centuries: the story endlessly varied by the state media and textbooks is one of China's humiliation from the Opium Wars onwards, which ended only with the communist victory in 1949, leading to the conclusion that to be patriotic is to support the rule of the Party. When history is given such a legitimising role, of course, it cannot tolerate any substantial self-critique; the Chinese had learned the lesson of Gorbachev's failure: full recognition of the 'founding crimes' will only bring the entire system down. Those crimes thus have to remain disavowed: true, some Maoist 'excesses' and 'errors' are denounced (the Great Leap Forward and the devastating famine that followed; the Cultural Revolution), and Deng's assessment of Mao's role (70 per cent positive, 30 per cent negative) is enshrined as the official formula. But this assessment functions as a formal conclusion which renders any further elaboration superfluous: even if Mao was 30 per cent bad, the full symbolic impact of this admission is neutralised, so he can continue to be celebrated as the founding father of the nation, his body in a mausoleum and his image on every banknote. We are dealing here with a clear case of fetishistic disavowal: although we know very well that Mao made errors and caused immense suffering, his figure is kept magically untainted by these facts. In this way, the Chinese communists can have their cake and eat it: the radical changes brought about by economic 'liberalisation' are combined with the continuation of the same Party rule as before.

Yang Jisheng's massive and meticulously documented study, *Tombstone: The Untold Story of Mao's Great Famine*, offers an exemplary case of remembering: the result of nearly two decades of research, it puts the number of 'prematurely dead' between 1958 and 1961 at 36 million.[4] (The official stance is that the disaster was due 30 per cent to natural causes and 70 per cent to mismanagement – an exact inversion of Deng's judgement on Mao).[5] With the privileges afforded a senior Xinhua journalist, Yang was able to consult state archives around the country and form the most complete picture of the great famine that any researcher, foreign or local, has ever managed. He was helped by scores of collaborators within the system – demographers who had toiled quietly for years in government agencies to compile accurate figures on the loss of life; local officials who had kept ghoulish records of the events in their districts; the keepers of provincial archives who were happy to open their doors, with a nod and a wink, to a trusted comrade pretending to be researching the history of China's grain production. The reaction? In Wuhan, a major city in central China, the office of the Committee of Comprehensive Management of Social Order put *Tombstone* on a list of 'obscene, pornographic, violent and unhealthy books for children', to be confiscated on sight. Elsewhere, the Party killed *Tombstone* with silence, banning any mention of it in the media but refraining from attention-grabbing attacks

---

4   Yang Jisheng, *Tombstone: The Untold Story of Mao's Great Famine*, London: Penguin, 2012 (*Mubei – Zhongguo Liushi Niandai Da Jihuang Jishi*, Hong Kong: Cosmos Books, 2008).

5   To this day, the Chinese government has never said how many people it thinks died, although it commissioned a study in the mid-1980s for internal circulation. The academic who prepared that study had spent most of his life as a lecturer in automated production systems in Xi'an before studying demography for barely a year in India. He came up with a figure of 17 million premature deaths. The study has been widely dismissed because it looked mainly at recorded deaths.

on the book itself. But Yang still lives in China, retired, unmolested, publishing occasionally in scientific journals. Among other important insights, Yang establishes that one reason for the famine lay in the application of bad science: the central government decreed several changes in agricultural techniques based on the ideas of the Ukrainian pseudo-scientist Trofim Lysenko. One of these ideas was close planting, where the density of seedlings is first tripled and then doubled again. Transposing class solidarity onto nature, the theory was that plants of the same species would not compete with but would help each other – in practice, of course, they did compete, which stunted growth and resulted in lower yields.[6]

This is how a combination of false remembering and repetition operates with regard to the communist past, but such falsity is in no way limited to communists who refuse to settle accounts with their past and thus condemn themselves to repeat it. The standard liberal or conservative demonisation of the October Revolution also misses the emancipatory potential clearly discernible therein, reducing it to a brutal takeover of state power. The tension between these two dimensions of the Revolution does not mean that the Stalinist turn was a secondary deviation, since one can well argue that the latter was a possibility inherent in the Bolshevik project, meaning it was doomed from the very beginning. This is why the project was genuinely tragic: an authentic emancipatory vision condemned to failure by its very victory.

This is where the working through enters as the radical rethinking of communism, re-actualising it for today. And this is why only those faithful to communism can deploy a truly

---

6 The main critical point made against Yang's study is comparative; for example, there are well-argued claims that the extra-mortality in India from regular deprivation in 'normal' times is much greater than the extra-mortality in China. With this point, one cannot but agree, although it does not in any way diminish the horror of the Chinese famine.

radical critique of the sad reality of Stalinism and its offspring. Let's face it: today, Lenin and his legacy are perceived as hopelessly dated, belonging to a defunct 'paradigm'. Not only was Lenin understandably blind to many of the problems that are now central to contemporary life (ecology, struggles for emancipated sexuality, etc.), but also his brutal political practice is totally out of sync with current democratic sensitivities, his vision of the new society as a centralised industrial system run by the state is simply irrelevant, etc. Instead of desperately attempting to salvage the authentic Leninist core from the Stalinist alluvium, would it not be more advisable to forget Lenin and return to Marx, searching in his work for the roots of what went wrong in the twentieth-century communist movements?

Nevertheless, was not Lenin's situation marked precisely by a similar hopelessness? It is true that today's left is facing the shattering experience of the end of an entire epoch of the progressive movement, an experience which compels it to reinvent the most basic coordinates of its project. But an exactly homologous experience was what gave birth to Leninism. Recall Lenin's shock when, in the autumn of 1914, all the European social-democratic parties (with the honourable exception of the Russian Bolsheviks and the Serbian Social Democrats) opted to toe the 'patriotic line'. When the German Social Democrats' daily newspaper *Vorwärts* reported that social democrats in the Reichstag had voted for the military credits, Lenin even thought that it must have been a forgery by the Russian secret police designed to deceive the Russian workers. In an era of a military conflict that cut the European continent in half, how difficult it was to refuse the notion that one should take sides and to reject the 'patriotic fervour' in one's own country! How many great minds (including Freud) succumbed to the nationalist temptation, even if only for a couple of weeks!

The shock of 1914 was – to put it in Alain Badiou's terms – a *désastre*, a catastrophe in which an entire world disappeared: not only the idyllic bourgeois faith in progress, but *also* the socialist movement that accompanied it. Even Lenin himself lost his footing – there is, in his desperate reaction in *What Is to Be Done?*, no satisfaction, no 'I told you so!' *This* moment of *Verzweiflung, this* catastrophe, opened up the site for the Leninist event, for breaking with the evolutionary historicism of the Second International – and Lenin was the only one at the level of this opening, the only one to articulate the Truth of the catastrophe. Born in this moment of despair was the Lenin who, via the detour of a close reading of Hegel's *Logic*, was able to discern the unique chance for revolution.

Today, the left is in a situation that uncannily resembles the one that gave birth to Leninism, and its task is to repeat Lenin. This does *not* mean a *return* to Lenin. *To repeat Lenin is to accept that 'Lenin is dead'*, that his particular solution failed, even failed monstrously. To repeat Lenin means that one has to distinguish between what Lenin actually did and the field of possibilities that he opened up, to acknowledge the tension in Lenin between his actions and another dimension, what was 'in Lenin more than Lenin himself'. To repeat Lenin is to repeat not what Lenin *did*, but what he *failed to do*, his *missed* opportunities.

Goodbye Lenin in Ukraine

The last time Lenin made headlines in the West was during the Ukrainian uprising of 2014 that toppled the pro-Russian president Yanukovych: in TV reports on the mass protests in Kiev, we saw again and again scenes of enraged protesters tearing down statues of Lenin. These furious attacks were understandable in so far as the statues functioned as a symbol of Soviet oppression, and Putin's Russia is perceived as a continuation of the Soviet policy of subjecting non-Russian nations to Russian domination. We should also recall the precise historical moment when statues of Lenin began to proliferate in their thousands across the Soviet Union: only in 1956, after Khruschev's denunciation of Stalin at the 20th Congress, were statues of Stalin replaced en masse by those of Lenin. The latter was literally a stand-in for the former, as was also made clear by a weird thing that happened in 1962 on the front page of *Pravda*:

> Lenin appeared on the masthead of *Pravda* in 1945 (one might speculatively suggest that he appeared there to reassert Stalin's authority over the Party – in light of the potentially disruptive force of returning soldiers, who have seen both death and bourgeois Europe, and in light of circulating myths that Lenin had warned against him on his deathbed). In 1962 – when, at the 22nd Congress of the Communist Party, Stalin was publicly denounced – two images of Lenin suddenly appear on the masthead, as if the strange double-Lenin covered the missing 'other leader' who was actually never there![7]

Why, then, were two identical profiles of Lenin printed side by side? In this strange repetition, Stalin was, in a way, more present than ever in his absence, since his shadowy presence was the answer to the obvious question: 'why Lenin twice, why not just a single Lenin?' There was nonetheless a deep irony in watching Ukrainians tearing down Lenin statues as a sign of their will to break with Soviet domination and assert their national sovereignty: the golden era of Ukraine's national identity was not tsarist Russia (in which Ukrainian self-assertion as a nation had been thwarted), but the first decade of the Soviet Union when they established their full national identity. As even the Wikipedia passage on Ukraine in the 1920s notes:

---

7 Personal communication from Xenia Cherkaev.

The Civil War that eventually brought the Soviet government to power devastated Ukraine. It left over 1.5 million people dead and hundreds of thousands homeless. In addition, Soviet Ukraine had to face the famine of 1921. Seeing an exhausted Ukraine, the Soviet government remained very flexible during the 1920s. Thus, under the aegis of the Ukrainisation policy pursued by the national Communist leadership of Mykola Skrypnyk, Soviet leadership encouraged a national renaissance in literature and the arts. The Ukrainian culture and language enjoyed a revival, as Ukrainisation became a local implementation of the Soviet-wide policy of *Korenisation* (literally *indigenisation*). The Bolsheviks were also committed to introducing universal health care, education and social-security benefits, as well as the right to work and housing. Women's rights were greatly increased through new laws designed to wipe away centuries-old inequalities. Most of these policies were sharply reversed by the early 1930s after Joseph Stalin gradually consolidated power to become the de facto communist party leader.

This 'indigenisation' followed the principles formulated by Lenin in quite unambiguous terms:

> The proletariat cannot but fight against the forcible retention of the oppressed nations within the boundaries of a given state, and this is exactly what the struggle for the right of self-determination means. The proletariat must demand the right of political secession for the colonies and for the nations that 'its own' nation oppresses. Unless it does this, proletarian internationalism will remain a meaningless phrase; mutual confidence and class solidarity between the workers of the oppressing and oppressed nations will be impossible.[8]

---

8 V.I. Lenin, 'The Socialist Revolution and the Right of Nations to Self-Determination' (January–February 1916), *Collected Works*, Vol. 22, Moscow: Progress, 1966, p. 147.

Lenin remained faithful to this position to the end. Immediately after the October Revolution he engaged in a polemic with Rosa Luxemburg, who advocated allowing small nations to be given full sovereignty only if progressive forces predominated in the new state, while Lenin was for the unconditional right to secede, even if the 'bad guys' would take power. In his final struggle against Stalin's project for a centralised Soviet Union, Lenin again advocated for the unconditional right of small nations to secede (in this case, Georgia was at stake), insisting on the full sovereignty of the national entities that composed the Soviet state; no wonder that, on 27 September 1922, in a letter to the members of the Politburo, Stalin openly accused Lenin of 'national liberalism'. The direction in which Stalin was already blowing is clear from how he proposed to enact the decision to proclaim the government of the RSFSR also the government of the other five republics (Ukraine, Belarus, Azerbaijan, Armenia and Georgia):

> If the present decision is confirmed by the Central Committee of the RCP, it will not be made public, but communicated to the Central Committees of the Republics for circulation among the Soviet organs, the Central Executive Committees or the Congresses of the Soviets of the said Republics before the convocation of the All-Russian Congress of the Soviets, where it will be declared to be the wish of these Republics.[9]

The interaction of the Central Committee (CC) with its base was thus not merely abolished, so that the higher authority simply imposed its will; to add insult to injury, it was also restaged as its opposite: the CC itself now decided what the base would ask the higher authority to enact as if it were its own wish. (But note also that Lenin himself, by imposing the

---

9 Quoted in Moshe Lewin, *Lenin's Last Struggle*, Ann Arbor: University of Michigan Press, 2005, p. 61.

prohibition of Party factions a year earlier, had opened up the very process he was now fighting.) Recall the most conspicuous case of such restaging when in 1939 the three Baltic states freely asked to join the Soviet Union, which granted their wish. What Stalin did in the early 1930s thus amounted simply to a return to tsarist foreign and national policy. For example, as part of this turn, the Russian colonisation of Siberia and Muslim Asia was no longer condemned as imperialist expansion but was celebrated as an introduction of progressive modernisation that would challenge the inertia of these traditional societies.

Today, Putin's foreign policy is a clear continuation of this tsarist-Stalinist line. According to him, after the Revolution, it was the turn of the Bolsheviks to aggrieve Russia: 'The Bolsheviks, for a number of reasons – may God judge them – added large sections of the historical South of Russia to the Republic of Ukraine. This was done with no consideration for the ethnic makeup of the population, and today these areas form the southeast of Ukraine.'[10] In January 2016, Putin again made the same point in his characterisation of Lenin's greatest mistake:

> Ruling with your ideas as a guide is correct, but that is only the case when that idea leads to the right results, not like it did with Vladimir Ilyich. In the end that idea led to the ruin of the Soviet Union. There were many of these ideas such as providing regions with autonomy, and so on. They planted an atomic bomb under the building that is called Russia and which would later explode.[11]

---

10 Address by President of the Russian Federation, 18 March 2014, available at en.kremlin.ru.

11 'Russia's Putin Accused Lenin of Ruining the Soviet Union', *Newsweek*, 22 January 2016, available at europe.newsweek.com.

In short, Lenin was guilty of taking seriously the autonomy of the different nations that composed the Russian empire, and thus of questioning Russian hegemony. No wonder we see portraits of Stalin again during Russian military parades and public celebrations, while Lenin is obliterated. In a big opinion poll conducted a couple of years ago, Stalin was voted the third-greatest Russian of all time, while Lenin was nowhere to be seen. Stalin is not celebrated today as a communist, but as the restorer of Russia's greatness after Lenin's anti-patriotic 'deviation'. For Lenin, 'proletarian internationalism' goes hand in hand with a defence of the rights of small nations against the big nations: for a 'great' nation dominating others, giving full rights to smaller nations is the key indicator of the seriousness of their professed internationalism.

Violence, Terror, Discipline

However, even if Lenin can be redeemed with regard to national liberation, what about his advocacy (and practice) of brutal violence, inclusive of terror? In the history of radical politics, violence is usually associated with the so-called Jacobin legacy, which, for that very reason, is dismissed as something that should be abandoned if we are truly to begin from the beginning again. Even many contemporary (post-) Marxists are embarrassed by the so-called Jacobin legacy of centralised state terror, from which they want to distance Marx himself – it was Lenin, so the story goes, who (re)introduced the Jacobin legacy into Marxism, thus falsifying Marx's libertarian spirit. But is this really true? Let us take a closer look at how the Jacobins effectively opposed the recourse to a majority vote, on behalf of those who talk of an eternal Truth (how 'totalitarian' …). How could the Jacobins, the partisans of unity and of the struggle against factions and divisions, justify this rejection? 'The entire difficulty resides in how to distinguish between the voice of truth, even if it is minoritary, and the factional voice which seeks only to divide artificially to conceal the truth.'[12] Robespierre's answer is that the truth is irreducible to numbers (counting); it can be experienced also in solitude: those who proclaim a truth they have experienced should not be considered as factionalists, but as sensible and courageous people. In this case of attesting the truth, Robespierre said in the National Assembly on 28 December 1792, any invocation of majority or minority is nothing but a means to 'reduce to silence those whom one designated by this term [minority]': 'Minority has everywhere an eternal right: to render audible the *voice of truth*.' It is deeply significant that Robespierre made this statement in the course of the Assembly apropos the trial of the king. The Girondins proposed a 'democratic' solution: in such a difficult case, it was necessary to make an 'appeal to the people', to convoke local assemblies across France and ask them to vote on how to deal with the king – only such a move would give legitimacy to the trial. Robespierre's answer was that such an 'appeal to the people' effectively cancels the sovereign will of the people which, through insurrection and revolution, had already made itself known and changed the very nature of the French state, bringing about the Republic. What the Girondins were effectively insinuating was that the revolutionary insurrection was 'only an act of a part of the people, even of a minority, and that one should solicit the speech of a kind of silent majority'. In short, the Revolution had already decided the matter, the very fact of the Revolution (if it was just and not a crime) meant that the king was guilty, so to put that guilt to the vote would mean putting the Revolution itself into question.

Robespierre's argument effectively points forward to Lenin, who, in his writings of 1917, saves his most acerbic irony

---

12   Sophie Wahnich, 'Faire entendre la voix de la vérité, un droit révolutionnaire éternel', manuscript, June 2010. All further non-attributed quotations are from this outstanding text.

for those who engaged in an endless search for some kind of 'guarantee' for the revolution. This guarantee assumed two main forms: either the reified notion of social Necessity (we should not risk the revolution too early; we must wait for the right moment, when the situation is 'mature' with regard to the laws of historical development; 'it is too early for the socialist revolution, the working class is not yet advanced enough') or a normative notion of 'democratic' legitimacy ('the majority of the population is not on our side, so the revolution would not really be democratic') – as if, before the revolutionary agent risks the seizure of the state power, it needs to secure permission from some figure of the big Other (e.g., organise a referendum to be sure that the majority supports the revolution). With Lenin, as with Lacan, the revolution *ne s'autorise que d'elle-même*: we must assume the revolutionary *act* as not being covered by the big Other – the fear of taking power 'prematurely', the search for the guarantee, is the fear of the abyss of the act. Therein lies the ultimate dimension of what Lenin incessantly denounces as 'opportunism', and his wager is that 'opportunism' is a position which is inherently false, masking the fear of accomplishing the act with a protective screen of 'objective' facts, laws or norms. This is why the first step in combating it is to *announce* it clearly: 'What, then, is to be done? We must *aussprechen was ist*, 'state the facts', admit the truth that there is a tendency, or an opinion, in our Central Committee.'[13]

When we are dealing with 'strong truths' (*les vérités fortes*), shattering insights, asserting them entails symbolic violence. When *la patrie est en danger*, Robespierre said, one should fearlessly state the fact that 'the nation is betrayed. This truth is now known to all Frenchmen': 'Lawgivers, the danger is immanent; the *reign of truth* has to begin: we are courageous

---

13 V.I. Lenin, *Collected Works*, Vol. 33, Moscow: Progress, 1965, p. 422.

enough to tell you this; be courageous enough to hear it.' In such a situation, there is no space for a neutral third position. In his speech celebrating the dead of 10 August 1792, Abbé Gregoire declared: 'there are people who are so good that they are worthless; and in a revolution which engages in the strug- gle of freedom against despotism, a neutral man is a pervert who, without any doubt, waits for how the battle will turn out to decide which side to take'. Before we dismiss these lines as 'totalitarian', let us recall a later time when the French *patrie* was again *en danger*, the situation after the French defeat in 1940, when none other than General de Gaulle, in his famous radio address from London, announced to the French people the 'strong truth': France is defeated, but *the war is not over*; against the Pétainist collaborators one must insist that the struggle goes on. The exact conditions of this statement are worth recalling: even Jacques Duclos, the second-strongest figure in the French Communist Party, admitted in a private conversation that if, at that moment, free elections had been held in France, Marshal Pétain would have won with 90 per cent of the vote. When de Gaulle, in his historic act, refused to acknowledge the capitulation to the Germans and continued to resist, he claimed that it was only he, not the Vichy regime, who spoke on behalf of the true France (*on behalf of France as such, not only on behalf of the 'majority of the French'!*). What he was saying was deeply true even if, 'democratically', it was not only without legitimisation but also clearly opposed to the opinion of the majority of the French people. (And the same goes for Germany: it was the tiny minority actively resisting Hitler that stood for Germany, not the active Nazis or the undecided opportunists.) This is not a reason to despise democratic elections; the point is only to insist that they are not per se an indication of Truth – as a rule, they tend to reflect the predominant *doxa* determined by the hegemonic ideology. There *can* be democratic elections which enact an event of Truth – elections in which, against the sceptic–cynical inertia, the majority momentarily 'awakens' and votes against the hegemonic ideological opinion – the exceptional status of such a surprising electoral result proves that elections as such are not a medium of Truth.

This position of a minority which stands for All is more than ever relevant today, in our post-political epoch in which a plurality of opinions reigns: under such conditions, the universal Truth is by definition a minority position. As Sophie Wahnich has pointed out, in a democracy corrupted by media, what 'the freedom of the press without the duty to resist' amounts to is 'the right to say anything in a political relativist manner' instead of defending the 'demanding and sometimes even lethal ethics of truth'. In such a situation, the uncompromising insistent voice of truth (about ecology, about biogenetics, about the excluded ...) cannot but appear as 'irrational' in its lack of consideration for the opinions of others, in its refusal of the spirit of pragmatic compromise, in its apocalyptic finality. Simone Weil offered a simple and poignant formulation of this partiality of truth:

> There is a class of people in this world who have fallen into the lowest degree of humiliation, far below beggary, and who are deprived not only of all social consideration but also, in everybody's opinion, of the specific human dignity, reason itself – and these are the only people who, in fact, are able to tell the truth. All the others lie.[14]

The slum dwellers are indeed the living dead of global capitalism: alive, but dead in the eyes of the *polis*.

The term 'eternal Truth' should be read here in a properly dialectical way, as referring to eternity grounded in a unique

---

14 Simone Weil, *Seventy Letters*, Oxford: Oxford University Press, 1965, p. 200.

temporal act (as in Christianity, where the eternal Truth can only be experienced and enacted by endorsing the temporal–historical singularity of Christ). What grounds a truth is the experience of suffering and courage, sometimes in solitude, not the size or force of a majority. This, of course, does not mean that there are infallible criteria for determining the truth: its assertion involves a kind of wager, a risky decision; one has to cut out its path, sometimes even enforce it, and at first those who tell the truth are as a rule not understood, they struggle (with themselves and others), looking for the proper language in which to express it. It is the full recognition of this dimension of risk and wager, of the absence of any external guarantee, that distinguishes an authentic truth-engagement from any form of 'totalitarianism' or 'fundamentalism'.

But, again: how are we to distinguish this 'demanding and sometimes even lethal ethics of truth' from sectarian attempts to impose one's own position on everyone else? How can we be sure that the voice of the minoritarian 'part of no-part' is indeed the voice of universal truth and not merely that of a particular grievance? The first thing to bear in mind here is that the truth we are dealing with is not 'objective', but a self-relating truth about one's own subjective position; as such, it is an engaged truth, measured not by its factual accuracy but by the way it affects the subjective position of enunciation. In his (unpublished) Seminar 18 on 'a discourse which would not be that of a semblance', Lacan provided a succinct definition of the truth of interpretation in psychoanalysis: 'Interpretation is not tested by a truth that would decide by yes or no, it unleashes truth as such. It is only true inasmuch as it is truly followed.' There is nothing 'theological' in this precise formulation, only an insight into the properly dialectical unity of theory and practice in (not only) psychoanalytic interpretation: the 'test' of the analyst's interpretation lies in the truth-effect it unleashes in the patient. This is how one should also (re)read Marx's Thesis XI: the 'test' of Marxist theory is the truth-effect it unleashes in its addressees (the proletarians), in transforming them into revolutionary subjects.

The problem, of course, is that today there is no revolutionary discourse able to produce such a truth-effect – so what are we to do? The quintessential text here is Lenin's wonderful short essay 'On Ascending a High Mountain', written in 1922,[15] when, after winning the Civil War against all odds, the Bolsheviks had to retreat into the New Economic Policy, giving a much wider scope to the market economy and private property. Lenin uses the simile of a climber who has to return to the valley after his first attempt to reach a new mountain peak in order to describe what a retreat means in a revolutionary process, i.e., how one retreats without opportunistically betraying one's fidelity to the Cause:

> Let us picture to ourselves a man ascending a very high, steep and hitherto unexplored mountain. Let us assume that he has overcome unprecedented difficulties and dangers and has succeeded in reaching a much higher point than any of his predecessors, but still has not reached the summit. He finds himself in a position where it is not only difficult and dangerous to proceed in the direction and along the path he has chosen, but positively impossible. He is forced to turn back, descend, seek another path, longer, perhaps, but one that will enable him to reach the summit. The descent from the height that no one before him has reached proves, perhaps, to be more dangerous and difficult for our imaginary traveller than the ascent – it is easier to slip; it is not so easy to choose a foothold; there is not that exhilaration that one feels in going upwards, straight to the goal, etc. ... The voices from below ring with malicious joy. They do not conceal it; they chuckle gleefully

---

15   Written in February 1922; see below, p. 29.

and shout: 'He'll fall in a minute! Serves him right, the lunatic!' Others try to conceal their malicious glee and behave mostly like Judas Golovlyov. They moan and raise their eyes to heaven in sorrow, as if to say: 'It grieves us sorely to see our fears justified! But did not we, who have spent all our lives working out a judicious plan for scaling this mountain, demand that the ascent be postponed until our plan was complete? And if we so vehemently protested against taking this path, which this lunatic is now abandoning (look, look, he has turned back! He is descending! A single step is taking him hours of preparation! And yet we were roundly abused when time and again we demanded moderation and caution!), if we so fervently censured this lunatic and warned everybody against imitating and helping him, we did so entirely because of our devotion to the great plan to scale this mountain, and in order to prevent this great plan from being generally discredited!'

After enumerating the achievements of the Soviet state, Lenin then goes on to focus on what was *not* done:

But we have not finished building even the foundations of socialist economy and the hostile powers of moribund capitalism can still deprive us of that. We must clearly appreciate this and frankly admit it; for there is nothing more dangerous than illusions (and vertigo, particularly at high altitudes). And there is absolutely nothing terrible, nothing that should give legitimate grounds for the slightest despondency, in admitting this bitter truth; for we have always urged and reiterated the elementary truth of Marxism – that the joint efforts of the workers of several advanced countries are needed for the victory of socialism. We are still alone and in a backward country, a country that was ruined more than others, but we have accomplished a great deal. More than that – we have preserved intact the army of the revolutionary proletarian forces; we have preserved its manoeuvring ability; we have kept clear heads and can soberly calculate where, when and how far to retreat (in order to leap further forward); where, when and how to set to work to alter what has remained unfinished. Those Communists are doomed who imagine that it is possible to finish such an epoch-making undertaking as completing the foundations of socialist economy (particularly in a small-peasant country) without making mistakes, without retreats, without numerous alterations to what is unfinished or wrongly done. Communists who have no illusions, who do not give way to despondency, and who preserve their strength and flexibility 'to begin from the beginning' over and over again in approaching an extremely difficult task, are not doomed (and in all probability will not perish).

This is Lenin at his Beckettian best, echoing the line from *Worstward Ho*: 'Try again. Fail again. Fail better.'[16] Lenin's conclusion – 'to begin from the beginning over and over again' – makes it clear that he is not talking merely of slowing down in order to defend what has already been achieved, but precisely of *descending back to the starting point*: one should 'begin from the beginning', not from where one had managed to get to in the previous effort. In Kierkegaard's terms, a revolutionary process is not a gradual progress, but a repetitive movement, a movement of *repeating the beginning* again and again. This is exactly where we are today, after the 'obscure disaster' of 1989. As in 1922, the voices from below ring with malicious joy all around us: 'Serves you right, you lunatics who wanted to enforce their totalitarian vision on society!' Others try to conceal their malicious glee, raising their eyes to heaven in sorrow, as if to say: 'It grieves us sorely to see our fears justified! How noble was your vision of creating a just society! Our heart beat in sympathy with you, but our reason told us that your noble plans could end only in misery

---

16 Samuel Beckett, *Nohow On*, London: Calder, 1992, p. 101.

and new forms of servitude!' While rejecting any compromise with these seductive voices, we certainly now have to 'begin from the beginning', not 'building on the foundations of the revolutionary epoch of the twentieth century' (from 1917 to 1989 or, more precisely, 1968), but 'descending' to the starting point in order to choose a *different* path.

If the communist project is to be renewed as a true alternative to global capitalism, we must make a clear break with the twentieth-century communist experience. One should always bear in mind that 1989 represented the defeat not only of communist state socialism but also of Western social democracy. Nowhere is the misery of today's left more palpable than in its 'principled' defence of the social-democratic welfare state. In the absence of a feasible radical leftist project, all the left can do is to bombard the state with demands for the expansion of the welfare state, knowing full well that the state will not be able to deliver. This necessary disappointment will then serve as a reminder of the basic impotence of the social-democratic left and thus push the people towards a new radical revolutionary left. Needless to say, such a politics of cynical 'pedagogy' is destined to fail, since it is fighting a losing battle: in the present politico-ideological constellation, the reaction to the inability of the welfare state to deliver will be rightist populism. In order to avoid this reaction, the left will have to propose its own positive project beyond the confines of the social-democratic welfare state. This is also why it is totally erroneous to pin one's hopes on strong sovereign nation-states that can defend the welfare state against transnational bodies like the European Union which, so the story goes, serve as the instruments of global capital to dismantle whatever remains of the welfare state.[17] From here, it is only

---

17 One of the crazy consequences of this stance is that some leftists supported the Czech liberal-conservative President Václav Klaus, a staunch Eurosceptic: his ferocious anti-communism and opposition to the

a short step to accepting a 'strategic alliance' with the nationalist right worried about the dilution of national identity in transnational Europe. (As has de facto already happened with the Brexit victory in the UK.)

The walls which are now being thrown up all around the world are not of the same nature as the Berlin Wall, the icon of the Cold War. Today's walls appear not to belong to the same notion, since the same wall often serves multiple functions: as a defence against terrorism, illegal immigrants or smuggling, as a cover for colonial land-grabbing, etc. In spite of this appearance of multiplicity, however, Wendy Brown is right to insist that we are dealing with the same phenomenon, even though its examples are usually not perceived as cases of the same notion: today's walls are a reaction to the threat to national sovereignty posed by the ongoing process of globalisation: 'Rather than resurgent expressions of nation-state sovereignty, the new walls are icons of its erosion. While they may appear as hyperbolic tokens of such sovereignty, like all hyperbole, they reveal a tremulousness, vulnerability, dubiousness, or instability at the core of what they aim to express – qualities that are themselves antithetical to sovereignty and thus elements of its undoing.'[18] The most striking thing about

---

'totalitarian' welfare state is dismissed as a cunning strategy to render his anti-Europeanism acceptable ... Among further leftist stupidities is a weird form of critique of Really Existing Socialism: although these regimes were basically progressive, they 'neglected' democracy and personal freedom ... Not to mention the idea that central planning did not really fail, since it was never fully tested (exactly the same logic as that of market liberals who claim that the latest financial crisis is not the result of neoliberal politics, but of the fact that pure market liberalism was never fully realised in practice). One cannot help but recall here the logic of the joke quoted by Lacan: 'My fiancée is never late for an appointment, because the moment she is late, she is no longer my fiancée!' – the market never fails, since if it fails, that only proves it was not a pure market. A model of what Hegel calls 'abstract reasoning' if there ever was one.

18 Wendy Brown, *Walled States, Waning Sovereignty*, New York: Zone Books, 2010, p. 24.

these walls is their theatrical, and rather inefficient, nature: basically, they consist of old-fashioned materials (concrete and metal), representing a weirdly medieval countermeasure to the immaterial forces which effectively threaten national sovereignty today (digital and commercial mobility, advanced cyberweaponry). Brown is also right to highlight the role of organised religion, alongside globalisation, as a major trans-statal agency posing a threat to state sovereignty. For example, one can argue that China, in spite of its recent softening towards religion as an instrument of social stability, so ferociously opposes some religions (Tibetan Buddhism, the Falun Gong movement) precisely in so far as it perceives them to be a threat to national sovereignty and unity (Buddhism yes, but under the Chinese state control; Catholicism yes, but the bishops nominated by the Pope must be screened by the Chinese authorities ...).

One of the trickiest forms of false fidelity to twentieth-century communism is the rejection of all Really Existing Socialisms on behalf of some authentic working-class movement waiting to explode. Back in 1983, Georges Peyrol wrote a piece entitled 'Thirty Ways of Easily Recognising an Old Marxist', a wonderfully ironic portrait of a traditional Marxist certain that – sooner or later, we just have to be patient – an authentic revolutionary workers' movement will rise up again, victoriously sweeping away capitalist rule along with the corrupt official leftist parties and trade unions ... Frank Ruda has pointed out that Georges Peyrol is one of the pseudonyms of Alain Badiou:[19] the target of his attack were those surviving Trotskyists who continued to keep the faith that, out of the crisis of the Marxist left, a new authentic revolutionary working-class movement would somehow emerge.[20] How,

19 In his introduction to the German translation of Badiou's *Peut-on penser la politique?*.
20 Jaruzelski's *coup d'état* in 1981 also saved Solidarity from the

then, to break out of this deadlock? What if we risk taking a fateful step further and reject not only state and market regulation but also their utopian shadow: the idea of a direct transparent regulation 'from below' of the social process of production, as the economic counterpart to the dream of the 'immediate democracy' of workers' councils?

Leninist Freedom

What, then, of freedom? Here is how Lenin states his position in a polemic against the Menshevik and Socialist-Revolutionaries' critique of Bolshevik power in 1922:

> Indeed, the sermons which ... the Mensheviks and Socialist-Revolutionaries preach express their true nature – 'The revolution has gone too far. What you are saying now we have been saying all the time, permit us to say it again.' But we say in reply: 'Permit us to put you before a firing squad for saying that. Either you refrain from expressing your views, or, if you insist on expressing your political views publicly in the present circumstances, when our position is far more difficult than it was when the whiteguards were directly attacking us, then you will have only yourselves to blame if we treat you as the worst and most pernicious whiteguard elements.'[21]

This Leninist freedom of choice – not 'Life or money!' but 'Life or critique!' – combined with Lenin's dismissive attitude towards the 'liberal' notion of freedom, accounts for his bad reputation among liberals. Their case largely rests on

disappointment of its political profanation: had it been allowed to function freely in the 1980s, it would have lost its magic as an all-national force and decomposed into political factions, each of them pursuing pragmatic politics under the Catholic-conservative hegemony (which is what happened ten years later).

21 V.I. Lenin, 'Political Report of the Central Committee of the R.C.P.(B.)' (27 March 1922), *Collected Works*, Vol. 33, p. 283.

their rejection of the standard Marxist–Leninist opposition of 'formal' and 'actual' freedom: as even leftist liberals like Claude Lefort emphasise again and again, freedom is in its very notion 'formal', so that 'actual freedom' equals the lack of freedom.[22] In other words, with regard to freedom, Lenin is best remembered for his famous retort 'Freedom – yes, but for WHOM? To do WHAT?' – for him, in the above-quoted case of the Mensheviks, their 'freedom' to criticize the Bolshevik government effectively amounted to the 'freedom' to undermine the workers' and peasants' government on behalf of the counter-revolution. After the terrifying experience of Really Existing Socialism, is it not all too obvious today where the fault of this reasoning resides? First, it reduces a historical constellation to a closed, fully contextualised situation in which the 'objective' consequences of one's acts are fully determined ('independently of your intentions, what you are doing now objectively serves …'); second, the position of enunciation of such statements usurps the right to decide what your acts 'objectively mean', so that their apparent 'objectivism' (the focus on 'objective meaning') is the form of appearance of its opposite, a thorough *subjectivism*: I decide what your acts objectively mean, since I define the context of the situation (for example, if I conceive of my power as the immediate equivalent/expression of the power of the working class, then everyone who opposes me is 'objectively' an enemy of the working class). Against this full contextualisation, one should emphasise that freedom is 'actual' precisely and only as the capacity to 'transcend' the coordinates of a given situation, to 'posit the presuppositions' of one's activity (as Hegel would have put it), i.e., to redefine the very situation within which one is active. Furthermore, as many a critic pointed out, the very term 'Really Existing Socialism', though it was coined

---

22   See Claude Lefort, *Democracy and Political Theory*, Minneapolis: Minnesota University Press, 1988.

in order to assert socialism's success, is in itself a proof of socialism's utter failure, of the failure of the attempt to legitimise socialist regimes – the term appeared at that historical moment when the only legitimising reason for socialism was the mere fact that it existed.[23]

Is this, however, the whole story? How does freedom actually function in liberal democracies themselves? In spite of all compromises, Obama's healthcare reform amounted to a kind of *act*, at least in today's conditions, since it was based on a rejection of the hegemonic notion of the need to curtail big government expenditure and administration – in a way, it 'did the impossible'. No wonder, then, that it triggered such opposition – bearing witness to the material force of the ideological notion of 'free choice'. That is to say, although the great majority of so-called 'ordinary people' were not properly acquainted with the reform programme, the medical lobby (twice as strong as the infamous defence lobby!) succeeded in imposing on the public the fundamental idea that, with universal healthcare, free choice (in matters concerning medicine) would be somehow threatened. Against this purely fictional reference to 'free choice', every appeal to the 'hard facts' (in Canada, healthcare is less expensive and more effective, with no less 'free choice', etc.) proved useless.

At the very nerve centre of liberal ideology is the idea of freedom of choice grounded in the notion of the 'psychological' subject endowed with potentials she strives to realise. And this holds all the more so today, in the era of the so-called 'risk society',[24] when the ruling ideology endeavours to sell us

23 To put it in Badiou's terms of the opposition of Being and Event, the rise of the term 'Really Existing Socialism' signalled the final and full reinscription of the communist regimes into the positive order of Being: even the minimal utopian potential still discernible in the wildest Stalinist mobilisation and, later, in the Khrushchevian 'thaw', definitively disappeared.

24 See Ulrich Beck, *Risk Society: Towards a New Modernity*, London: Sage, 1992.

the very insecurity caused by the dismantling of the welfare state as an opportunity for new freedoms: you have to change your job every year, relying on short-term contracts instead of a long-term stable appointment? Why not see this as a liberation from the constraints of a fixed job, as the chance to reinvent yourself again and again, to become aware of and then realise the hidden potentials of your personality? You can no longer rely on the standard healthcare and retirement plans, so you have to take out additional insurance? Why not see this as another opportunity to choose: either a better life now or long-term security? And if this predicament causes you anxiety, the postmodern ideologist will immediately accuse you of wanting to 'escape from freedom' by clinging mindlessly to the old stable forms.

Phenomena like these make it all the more necessary today to *reassert* the opposition of 'formal' and 'actual' freedom in a new, more precise, sense. What we need is a 'Leninist' *traité de la servitude libérale*, a new version of la Boetie's *Traité de la servitude volontaire* that would fully justify the apparent oxymoron 'liberal totalitarianism'. In experimental psychology, Jean-Léon Beauvois took the first step in this direction with his precise exploration of the paradoxes that arise when the freedom to choose is conferred on the subject.[25] Repeated experiments established the following paradox: if, *after* getting two groups of volunteers to agree to participate in the experiment, one informs them that it will involve something unpleasant, against their ethical principles even, and if, at this point, one tells the first group that they are free to refuse to participate but says nothing to the other group, then in *both* groups the *same* (very high) percentage will agree to continue their participation. In other words, *conferring the formal freedom of choice does not make any difference to the*

25   See Jean-Léon Beauvois, *Traité de la servitude libérale: Analyse de la soumission*, Paris: Dunod, 1994.

outcome: those given the freedom to choose will do the same thing as those (implicitly) denied it. This, however, does not mean that the reminder or bestowal of that freedom makes no difference at all: those given it will not only tend to choose the same as those denied it, on top of that they will be inclined to 'rationalise' their 'free' decision to continue to participate in the experiment: unable to endure the so-called cognitive dissonance (their awareness that they have *freely* acted against their interests, propensities, tastes or norms), they will tend to *change their opinion* about the act they were asked to accomplish. Let us say that an individual agrees to participate in an experiment that concerns changing eating habits in order to fight against famine; once in the laboratory, he is then asked to swallow a live worm, with the explicit reminder that, if he finds this repulsive, he can, of course, say no, since he has the full freedom to choose. In most cases, he will agree to do it, and then rationalise it by saying to himself something like: 'What I am being asked to do *is* disgusting, but I am not a coward, I should display some courage and self-control, otherwise the scientists will see me as a weak person who pulls out at the first minor obstacle! In any case, a worm does have a lot of proteins so it could effectively be used to feed the poor – who am I to hinder such an important experiment because of my petty sensitivity? And maybe my disgust at worms is just a prejudice, maybe a worm isn't so bad – and wouldn't tasting it be a new and daring experience? What if it enables me to discover an unexpected, if slightly perverse, dimension of myself of which I was hitherto unaware?'

In analysing what motivates people to accomplish such an act that runs against their perceived propensities and/or interests, Beauvois identifies three distinct modes: *authoritarian* (the pure command 'You should do it because I say so, without questioning it!', sustained by a reward if the subject does it and punishment if he does not); *totalitarian* (with reference to some higher Cause or common Good which is greater than the subject's perceived interest: 'You should do it because, even if it is unpleasant, it serves our Nation, the Party, Humanity!'); and *liberal* (with reference to the subject's inner nature itself: 'What is asked of you may appear repulsive, but look deep into yourself and you will find that it's in your true nature to do it, you will find it attractive, you will become aware of new, unexpected, dimensions of your personality!'). But Beauvois's categorisation needs to be corrected: a direct authoritarianism is practically nonexistent – even the most oppressive regime *publicly* legitimises its demands with reference to some higher Good, and, ultimately, 'you have to obey because I say so' reverberates only as its obscene supplement discernible between the lines. If it is the specificity of standard authoritarianism to refer to some higher Good, 'totalitarianism', like liberalism, interpellates the subject on behalf of *his own* good ('what may appear to you as an external pressure is really the expression of your objective interests, of what you *really want* without being aware of it!'). The difference between the two resides elsewhere: 'totalitarianism' imposes on the subject her own good, even if it is against her will – recall the (in)famous statement made by Charles I to the Earl of Essex: 'If any shall be so foolishly unnatural as to oppose their king, their country and their own good, we will make them happy, by God's blessing – even against their wills.' Here we encounter already the later Jacobin theme of happiness as a political factor, as well as the Saint-Justian idea of forcing people to be happy. Liberalism, in contrast, tries to avoid (or rather cover up) this paradox by clinging to the fiction of the subject's immediate free self-perception ('I don't claim to know better than you what you want – just look deep into yourself and decide freely!').

Beauvois's line of argumentation is faulty because he fails to recognise how the abyssal tautological authority (the 'It is so because I say so!' of the Master) does not work simply because of the sanctions (punishments or rewards) it implicitly or explicitly evokes. What, then, actually makes a subject freely choose to do something imposed on her against her interests and/or propensities? Here, the empirical inquiry into 'pathological' (in the Kantian sense) motivations is not sufficient: the enunciation of an injunction that imposes on its addressee a symbolic commitment evinces an inherent force of its own, so that what seduces us into obeying it is the very feature that may appear to be an obstacle – the absence of a reason 'why'. Here, Lacan can be of some help: the Lacanian 'Master Signifier' designates precisely this hypnotic force of the symbolic injunction which relies only on its own act of enunciation – it is here that we encounter 'symbolic efficacy' at its purest. The three ways of legitimising the exercise of authority ('authoritarian', 'totalitarian', 'liberal') are simply three ways to cover up, to blind us to the seductive power of, the abyss of this empty call. In a way, liberalism is even the worst of the three, since it *naturalises* the reasons for obedience, incorporating them into the subject's internal psychological structure. The paradox, then, is that 'liberal' subjects are in a way the least free: in changing their own opinion or perception of themselves, accepting what is *imposed* on them as originating in their 'nature', they are no longer even *aware* of their subordination.

Take the situation in the Eastern European countries around 1990, when Really Existing Socialism was falling apart: all of a sudden, people were faced with the 'freedom of political choice'. But were they *really* at any point asked the fundamental question of what kind of new order they actually wanted? Was it not rather that they found themselves in the exact situation of the subject-victim in a Beauvois-style experiment? They were first told that they were entering the promised land of political freedom; soon afterwards, they were informed that this freedom involved unrestrained privatisation, the dismantling of social security, and so on and so forth. They still had the freedom to choose, so, if they wanted, they could refuse to take this path; but, no, our heroic Eastern Europeans did not want to disappoint their Western tutors, so they stoically persisted in the choice they had never made, convincing themselves that they should behave as mature subjects who were aware that freedom has its price. This is why the notion of the psychological subject endowed with natural propensities, who has to realise its true Self and its potential, and who is, consequently, ultimately responsible for its own failure or success, is the key ingredient of liberal freedom.

This is where one should insist on reintroducing the Leninist opposition of 'formal' and 'actual' freedom: in an act of actual freedom, one dares precisely to *break* this seductive power of symbolic efficacy. Therein resides the moment of truth of Lenin's acerbic retort to his Menshevik critics: the truly free choice is a choice in which I do not merely choose between two or more options *within* a pre-given set of coordinates; rather I choose to change this set of coordinates itself. The catch of the 'transition' from Really Existing Socialism to capitalism was that the Eastern Europeans never had the chance to choose the *ad quem* of this transition – all of a sudden, they were (almost literally) 'thrown' into a new situation in which they were presented with a new set of given choices (pure liberalism, nationalist conservatism ...). What this means is that 'actual freedom', as the act of consciously changing this set, occurs only when, in the situation of a forced choice, one *acts as if the choice is not forced* and 'chooses the impossible'. This is what Lenin's obsessive tirades against 'formal' freedom are all about, and therein lies the 'rational kernel' that is worth saving today: when he insists that there is no 'pure' democracy, that we should always ask apropos of any freedom, whom does it serve, what is its role in the class struggle, his point is precisely to maintain the possibility of a *true* radical choice.

This is what the distinction between 'formal' and 'actual' freedom ultimately amounts to: the former refers to freedom of choice *within* the coordinates of the existing power relations, while the latter designates the site of an intervention that undermines these very coordinates. In short, Lenin's aim is not to limit freedom of choice, but to maintain the fundamental Choice – when he asks about the role of a freedom within the class struggle, what he is asking is precisely: 'Does this freedom contribute to or constrain the fundamental revolutionary Choice?'

Which brings us back to Jacobin revolutionary terror, wherein we should not be afraid to identify the emancipatory kernel. Let us recall the rhetorical turn often taken as proof of Robespierre's 'totalitarian' manipulation of his audience.[26] This took place during Robespierre's speech in the National Assembly on 11 Germinal Year II (31 March 1794); the previous night, Danton, Camille Desmoulins and others had been arrested, so many members of the Assembly were understandably afraid that they would be next. Robespierre directly addressed the moment as pivotal, 'Citizens, the moment has come to speak the truth', and went on to evoke the fear in the room: 'One wants [*on veut*] to make you fear abuses of power, of the national power you have exercised … One wants to make us fear that the people will fall victim to the Committees … One fears that the prisoners are being oppressed.'[27] The opposition here is between the impersonal 'one' (the instigators of fear are not personified) and the collective thus put under pressure, which almost imperceptibly shifts from the plural second-person 'you' (*vous*) to the first-person 'us' (Robespierre gallantly includes himself in the collective). However, the final formulation introduces an ominous twist:

---

26 See the detailed analysis in Lefort, 'The Revolutionary Terror', in *Democracy and Political Theory*, pp. 50–88.

27 Quoted in ibid., p. 63.

it is no longer that 'one wants to make you/us fear', but that 'one fears', which means that the enemy stoking the fear is no longer outside 'you/us', the members of the Assembly; it is here, among us, among 'you' addressed by Robespierre, corroding our unity from within. At this precise moment, Robespierre, in a true masterstroke, assumed full subjectivisation – waiting a moment for the ominous effect of his words to sink in, he then continued in the first person *singular*: 'I say that anyone who trembles at this moment is guilty; for innocence never fears public scrutiny.'[28] What could be more 'totalitarian' than this closed loop of 'your very fear of being found guilty makes you guilty' – a weird superego-twisted version of the well-known motto 'the only thing we have to fear is fear itself'? We should nonetheless reject the easy dismissal of this rhetorical strategy as one of 'terrorist culpabilisation', and discern its moment of truth: at the crucial moment of a revolutionary decision there are no innocent bystanders, because, in such a moment, innocence itself – exempting oneself from the decision, going on as if the struggle one is witnessing is not really one's concern – *is* indeed the highest treason. That is to say, the fear of being accused of treason *is* my treason, because, even if I 'did nothing against the revolution', this fear itself, the fact that it emerged in me, demonstrates that my subjective position is external to the revolution, that I experience 'revolution' as an external force threatening me.

But what is going on in this unique speech is even more revealing: Robespierre directly addresses the touchy question that must have arisen in the mind of his audience – how can he be sure that he won't be next in line to be accused? He is not the master exempted from the collective, the 'I' outside 'we' – after all, he was once very close to Danton, a powerful figure now under arrest, so what if, tomorrow, that fact will be used against him? In short, how can Robespierre be

28 Quoted in ibid., p. 65.

sure that the process he himself unleashed will not swallow him up too? It is here that his position takes on a sublime greatness – he fully assumes that the danger that now threatens Danton will tomorrow threaten him. The reason he is so serene, unafraid of his fate, is not that Danton was a traitor while he is pure, a direct embodiment of the people's Will; it is that he, Robespierre, *is not afraid to die* – his eventual death will be a mere accident that counts for nothing: 'What does danger matter to me? My life belongs to the Fatherland; my heart is free from fear; and if I were to die, I would do so without reproach and without ignominy.'[29] Consequently, in so far as the shift from 'we' to 'I' can effectively be determined as the moment when the democratic mask falls off and Robespierre openly asserts himself as a 'Master' (up to this point, we follow Lefort's analysis), the term Master has to be given here its full Hegelian weight: the Master is the figure of sovereignty, the one who is not afraid to die, who is ready to risk everything. In other words, the ultimate meaning of Robespierre's first-person-singular 'I' is: I am not afraid to die. What authorises him is just this, not any kind of direct access to the big Other, i.e., he does not claim that it is the people's Will which speaks through him.

Another 'inhuman' dimension of the Virtue–Terror couple promoted by Robespierre is the rejection of habit (in the sense of the agency of realistic compromises). Every legal order, or every order of explicit normativity, has to rely on a complex 'reflexive' network of informal rules which tells us how we are to relate to and apply the explicit norms; to what extent we're meant to take them literally; how and when we're allowed, solicited even, to disregard them; etc. – this is the domain of habit. To know the habits of a society is to know the meta-rules of how to apply its norms: think of the polite offer-that-is-meant-to-be-refused – it is 'habitual' to refuse

---

29 Quoted in ibid., p. 64.

such an offer, and anyone who accepts it commits a vulgar blunder. The same goes for many political situations in which a choice is given us only on condition that we make the right decision: we are solemnly reminded that we can say no – but we are expected to reject this offer and enthusiastically say yes. With many sexual prohibitions, the situation is the opposite: the explicit 'no' effectively functions as the implicit injunction 'do it, but in a discreet way!' Measured against this background, revolutionary egalitarian figures from Robespierre to John Brown are (potentially at least) figures without habits: they refuse to take into account the habits that qualify the functioning of a universal rule. As Robespierre himself explained:

> Such is the natural dominion of habit that we regard the most arbitrary conventions, sometimes indeed the most defective institutions, as absolute measures of truth or falsehood, justice or injustice. It does not even occur to us that most are inevitably still connected with the prejudices on which despotism fed us. We have been so long stooped under its yoke that we have some difficulty in raising ourselves to the eternal principles of reason; anything that refers to the sacred source of all law seems to us to take on an illegal character, and the very order of nature seems to us a disorder. The majestic movements of a great people, the sublime fervours of virtue often appear to our timid eyes as something like an erupting volcano or the overthrow of political society; and it is certainly not the least of the troubles bothering us, this contradiction between the weakness of our morals, the depravity of our minds, and the purity of principle and energy of character demanded by the free government to which we have dared aspire.[30]

---

30 Maximilien Robespierre, *Virtue and Terror*, London: Verso, 2007, p. 103.

To break the yoke of habit means, for example, that if all men are equal, then all men are to be effectively treated as equal; if blacks are also human, then they should be immediately treated as such. Recall the early stages of the struggle against slavery in the US, which, even prior to the Civil War, culminated in the armed insurrection led by the unique figure of John Brown:

> African Americans were caricatures of people, they were characterized as buffoons and minstrels, they were the butt-end of jokes in American society. And even the abolitionists, as antislavery as they were, the majority of them did not see African Americans as equals. The majority of them, and this was something that African Americans complained about all the time, were willing to work for the end of slavery in the South but they were not willing to work to end discrimination in the North ... John Brown wasn't like that. For him, practicing egalitarianism was a first step toward ending slavery. And African Americans who came in contact with him knew this immediately.[31]

For this reason, John Brown is a key political figure in the history of the US: in his fervently Christian 'radical abolitionism', he came closest to introducing a Jacobin logic into the US political landscape: 'John Brown considered himself a complete egalitarian. And it was very important for him to practice egalitarianism on every level ... He made it very clear that he saw no difference, and he didn't make this clear by saying it, he made it clear by what he did.'[32] Even today, long after the abolition of slavery, Brown is a divisive figure in American collective memory. Those whites who supported

---

31 Margaret Washington, historian, on Brown's egalitarianism, available at pbs.org.
32 Ibid.

him are all the more precious – among them, surprisingly, Henry David Thoreau, the great opponent of violence: against the standard dismissal of Brown as bloodthirsty, foolish and insane, Thoreau painted a portrait of a peerless man whose embrace of a cause was unparalleled; he even goes so far as to liken Brown's execution to the death of Christ.[33] Thoreau vents at the scores of those who voiced their displeasure and scorn for Brown: they cannot relate to him because of their 'dead' existences; they are truly not living, for only a handful of men have lived.

It is, however, precisely this consistent egalitarianism which simultaneously marks the limitation of Jacobin politics. Recall Marx's fundamental insight regarding the 'bourgeois' limitation of the logic of equality: capitalist inequalities are not 'unprincipled violations of the principle of equality', but are absolutely inherent in the logic of equality, the paradoxical result of its consistent realisation. What we have in mind here is not only the tired motif of how market exchange presupposes formally equal subjects who meet and interact in the marketplace; the crucial point in Marx's critique of 'bourgeois' socialists is that capitalist exploitation does not involve any kind of 'unequal' exchange between the worker and the capitalist – the exchange is fully equal and 'just', since (in principle) the worker gets paid the full value of the commodity he is selling (his labour power). Of course, radical bourgeois revolutionaries are aware of this limitation, but they try to overcome it by way of a direct 'terroristic' imposition of more and more de facto equality (equal salaries, equal access to health services, etc.) which can only be imposed through new forms of formal inequality (i.e., preferential treatment of the underprivileged). In short, the axiom of 'equality' is either not enough (it remains the abstract form of actual inequality) or

---

33 See Henry David Thoreau, *Civil Disobedience and Other Essays*, New York: Dover, 1993.

too much (it requires the enforcing of 'terroristic' equality) – it is a formalist notion in a strict dialectical sense, i.e., its limitation is precisely that its form is not concrete enough, but a mere neutral container for some content that eludes this form.

The problem here is not terror as such – our task today is precisely to reinvent emancipatory terror. The problem lies elsewhere: egalitarian 'extremism' or 'excessive radicalism' should always be read as a phenomenon of ideologico-political *displacement*: as an index of its opposite, of a limitation, of a refusal effectively to 'go to the end'. What was the Jacobins' recourse to radical 'terror' if not a kind of hysterical acting-out bearing witness to their inability to disturb the fundamentals of the economic order (private property, etc.)? And could we not even say the same about the so-called 'excesses' of Political Correctness? Do they not also display a retreat from disturbing the effective (economic, etc.) causes of racism and sexism? Perhaps, then, the time has come to problematise the standard *topos* shared by practically all 'postmodern' leftists, according to which political 'totalitarianism' somehow results from the dominance of material production and technology over intersubjective communication and/or symbolic practice, as if the root of political terror lies in the fact that the 'principle' of instrumental reason, of the technological exploitation of nature, is also extended to society, so that people are treated as raw materials to be transformed into the New Man. What if it is the exact *opposite* which holds? What if political 'terror' signals precisely that the sphere of (material) production is *denied* in its autonomy and *subordinated* to political logic? Is it not that political 'terror', from the Jacobins to Mao's Cultural Revolution, presupposes the foreclosure of production proper, its reduction to the terrain of political battle? In other words, what it amounts to is nothing less than the abandonment of Marx's key insight into how political struggle is a spectacle which, in order to be deciphered, has to be referred to the sphere of economics: 'if Marxism had any analytical value for *political* theory, was it not in the insistence that the problem of freedom was contained in the social relations implicitly declared "unpolitical" – that is, naturalized – in liberal discourse'?[34]

In his last years, Lenin did indeed courageously confront this key point.

From Lenin to Stalin ... and Back

No doubt the early Bolsheviks would have been shocked at what the Soviet Union had turned into by the 1930s (as many of those still alive were, before being themselves ruthlessly liquidated in the great purges). Their tragedy, however, was that they were not able to perceive in the Stalinist terror the ultimate offspring of their own acts. What they needed was their own version of *ta twam atsi* ('thou art that'). This old saw – which, let me state clearly, cannot be dismissed as cheap anti-communism: it has its own logic, and it acknowledges a tragic grandeur in the Bolshevik old guard – is what one should nonetheless problematise. Here, the left should propose its own alternative to the rightist 'What If' histories: the answer to the eternal leftist query 'What would have happened had Lenin survived ten years longer with his health intact, and succeeded in deposing Stalin?' is not as clear as it may appear (basically, *nothing* – or nothing essentially different: the same Stalinism, just without its worst excesses), in spite of many good arguments on its behalf (did not Rosa Luxemburg herself, as early as 1918, predict the rise of bureaucratic Stalinism?).

But, although it is clear how Stalinism emerged from the initial conditions of the October Revolution and its immediate aftermath, one should not discount a priori the possibility

34 Wendy Brown, *States of Injury*, Princeton: Princeton University Press, 1995, p. 14.

that, had Lenin remained in good health and deposed Stalin, something different would have emerged – not, of course, the utopia of 'democratic socialism', but nonetheless something substantially different from the Stalinist 'socialism in one country', something resulting from a much more 'pragmatic' and improvisatory series of political and economic decisions, fully aware of its own limitations. Lenin's desperate last struggle against a reawakened Russian nationalism, his support of Georgian 'nationalists', his vision of a decentralised federation, etc., were not just tactical compromises: they implied a vision of state and society incompatible in their entirety with Stalin's. Two years before his death, when it became clear that there would be no immediate pan-European revolution, and given that the idea of building socialism in one country was nonsense, Lenin wrote: 'What if the complete hopelessness of the situation, by stimulating the efforts of the workers and peasants tenfold, offered us the opportunity to create the fundamental requisites of civilisation in a different way from that of the Western European countries?'[35]

Note here how Lenin uses a class-neutral term, 'the fundamental requisites of civilisation', and how, precisely when emphasising Russia's distance from the Western European countries, he clearly refers to them as the model. Communism is a European event, if ever there was one. When Marxists celebrate the power of capitalism to disintegrate old communal ties, when they detect in this disintegration an opening up of the space of radical emancipation, they speak on behalf of the emancipatory European legacy. Walter Mignolo and other postcolonial anti-Eurocentrists dismiss the idea of communism as being too European, and instead propose Asian, Latin American or African traditions as sources of resistance to global capitalism. There is a crucial choice to be made here: do we resist global capitalism on behalf of the local traditions

35   Lenin, *Collected Works*, Vol. 33, p. 479.

it undermines, or do we endorse this power of disintegration and oppose global capitalism on behalf of a universal emancipatory project? The reason anti-Eurocentrism is so popular today is precisely because global capitalism functions much better when its excesses are regulated by some ancient tradition: when global capitalism and local traditions are no longer opposites, but are on the same side.

To put it in Deleuzian terms, Lenin's moment is that of the 'dark precursor', the vanishing mediator, the displaced object never to be found at its own place, operating between the two series: the initial 'orthodox' Marxist series of revolution in the most developed countries, and the new 'orthodox' series of Stalinist 'socialism in one country' followed by the Maoist identification of Third World nations with the new world proletariat. The shift from Lenin to Stalinism here is clear and easy to determine: Lenin perceived the situation as desperate, unexpected, but for that reason as one that had to be creatively exploited for new political choices. With the notion of 'socialism in one country', Stalin re-normalised the situation, drafting it into a new narrative of linear development in 'stages'. In other words, while Lenin was fully aware that what had happened was an 'anomaly' (a revolution in a country lacking the preconditions for developing a socialist society), he rejected the vulgar evolutionist conclusion that the revolution had taken place 'prematurely', so that one had to take a step back and develop a modern democratic capitalist society, which would then slowly create the conditions for socialist revolution. It was precisely against this vulgar conclusion that Lenin insisted the 'complete hopelessness of the situation' offered 'the opportunity to create the fundamental requisites of civilisation in a different way from that of the Western European countries'. What he was proposing here was effectively an implicit theory of 'alternate history': under the 'premature' domination of the force of the future, the same 'necessary' historical process (that of modern civilisation) can be (re)run in a different way.

Even Badiou was perhaps too hasty here in ultimately locating the betrayal of the Event in the immediate aftermath of the October Revolution, indeed, in the revolutionary takeover of the state power itself – in that fateful moment when the Bolsheviks abandoned their focus on the revolutionary self-organisation of the proletarian masses. Badiou is fully justified in emphasising that only by reference to what happens *after* the revolution, to the 'morning after', to the hard work of fidelity to the Event, can we distinguish between pathetic libertarian outbursts and true revolutionary events: these upheavals lose their energy when one has to take up the prosaic work of social reconstruction – at this point, lethargy sets in. In contrast to this, recall the immense creativity of the Jacobins just prior to their fall: the numerous proposals for a new civic religion, for how to preserve the dignity of old people, and so on. Therein also resides the interest of reports about daily life in the Soviet Union in the early 1920s, with its enthusiastic urge to invent new rules for quotidian existence: how does one get married? What are the new rules of courting? How does one celebrate a birthday? How should one be buried?[36]

It was at this point that the Cultural Revolution miserably failed. It is difficult to miss the irony of the fact that Badiou, who adamantly opposes the notion of the act as negative, locates the historical significance of the Cultural Revolution in the negative gesture of signalling 'the end of the party-state as the central production of revolutionary political activity' – it

---

36 Was Che Guevara's withdrawal from official functions, even from Cuban citizenship, in 1965, in order to dedicate himself to world revolution – this suicidal gesture of cutting all links with the institutional universe – really an *act*? Or was it an escape from the impossible task of the positive construction of socialism, from remaining faithful to the *consequences* of the revolution – in other words, an implicit admission of failure?

1

is precisely here that, in order to be consistent, Badiou should have denied the eventual status of the Cultural Revolution: far from being an Event, it was rather a supreme display of what he likes to refer to as the 'morbid death drive'. The destruction of old monuments was not a true negation of the past, it was an impotent *passage à l'acte* bearing witness to a failure of that negation.

So, in a way, there is a kind of poetic justice in the fact that the final result of Mao's Cultural Revolution was the unprecedented explosion of capitalist dynamism in China. In other words, with the full deployment of capitalism, it is the predominant form of 'normal' life itself which, in a sense, becomes 'carnivalised', with its constant self-revolutionising, its reversals, crises and reinventions. There *is* thus, beyond all cheap jibes and superficial analogies, a profound structural homology between the Maoist permanent self-revolution- ising, its constant struggle against the ossification of state structures, and the inherent dynamic of capitalism. One is tempted here to paraphrase Brecht's 'What is the robbing of a bank compared to the founding of a bank?': what are the violent and destructive outbursts of a Red Guard caught up in the Cultural Revolution compared to the true Cultural Revolution, the permanent dissolution of all stable life-forms necessitated by capitalist reproduction? Today, the tragedy of the Great Leap Forward is repeating itself as the comedy of a rapid capitalist Great Leap Forward into modernisation, with the old slogan 'an iron foundry in every village' re-emerging as 'a skyscraper in every street'. This revolutionary aspect of the Cultural Revolution is sometimes admitted even by con- servative critics compelled to take note of the 'paradox' of the 'totalitarian' leader teaching people to 'think and act for them- selves', to rebel and destroy the very apparatus of 'totalitarian domination'. Take, for example, Gordon Chang's remarks in the conservative magazine *Commentary*:

Paradoxically, it was Mao himself, the great enslaver, who in his own way taught the Chinese people to think and act for themselves. In the Cultural Revolution, he urged tens of millions of radical youths ... to go to every corner of the country to tear down ancient temples, destroy cultural relics, and denounce their elders, including not only mothers and fathers but also government officials and Communist Party members ... The Cultural Revolution may have been Mao's idea of ruining his enemies, but it became a frenzy that destroyed the fabric of society. As government broke down, its functions taken over by revolutionary committees and 'people's communes', the strict restraints and repressive mechanisms of the state dissolved. People no longer had to wait for someone to instruct them what to do – Mao had told them they had 'the right to rebel'. For the radical young, this was a time of essentially unrestrained passion. In one magnificent stroke, the Great Helmsman had delegitimized almost all forms of authority.[37]

The Cultural Revolution can thus be read at two different levels. If we read it as a part of historical reality (Being), we can easily submit it to a 'dialectical' analysis which perceives the final outcome of a historical process as its 'truth': the ultimate failure of the Cultural Revolution bears witness to the inherent inconsistency of the very project (or 'notion') of Cultural Revolution, as the explication-deployment-actualisation of these inconsistencies (in the same way that, for Marx, the vulgar, non-heroic, daily reality of capitalist profit-seeking was the 'truth' of Jacobin revolutionary heroism). If, however, we analyse it as an Event, as an enactment of the eternal Idea of egalitarian Justice, then the ultimate factual result of the Cultural Revolution, its catastrophic failure and then reversal into the capitalist dynamic, does not exhaust the real of

_____

37 Gordon G. Chang, 'China in Revolt', *Commentary*, December 2006, available at commentarymagazine.com.

the Cultural Revolution: the eternal Idea of the Cultural Revolution survives its defeat in sociohistorical reality; it continues to lead a spectral life as the ghost of a failed utopia which returns to haunt future generations, patiently awaiting its next resurrection. This brings us back to Robespierre and his simple faith in the eternal Idea of freedom which persists through all defeats, and without which a revolution 'is just a noisy crime that destroys another crime', a faith most poignantly expressed in Robespierre's very last speech on 8 Thermidor 1794, the day before his arrest and execution:

> But there do exist, I can assure you, souls that are feeling and pure; it exists, that tender, imperious and irresistible passion, the torment and delight of magnanimous hearts; that deep horror of tyranny, that compassionate zeal for the oppressed, that sacred love for the homeland, that even more sublime and holy love for humanity, without which a great revolution is just a noisy crime that destroys another crime; it does exist, that generous ambition to establish here on earth the world's first Republic.[38]

Does not the same hold even more for the last big instalment in the life of this Idea, the Maoist Cultural Revolution – without this Idea which sustained revolutionary enthusiasm, the Cultural Revolution was to an even greater degree 'just a noisy crime that destroyed another crime'. We should recall here Hegel's sublime words on the French Revolution from his *Lectures on the Philosophy of World History*:

> It has been said that the French revolution resulted from philosophy, and it is not without reason that philosophy has been called *Weltweisheit* [world wisdom]; for it is not only truth

---

38 Robespierre, *Virtue and Terror*, p. 129.

in and for itself, as the pure essence of things, but also truth in its living form as exhibited in the affairs of the world. We should not, therefore, contradict the assertion that the revolution received its first impulse from philosophy ... Never since the sun had stood in the firmament and the planets revolved around him had it been perceived that man's existence centres in his head, i.e. in thought, inspired by which he builds up the world of reality ... not until now had man advanced to the recognition of the principle that thought ought to govern spiritual reality. This was accordingly a glorious mental dawn. All thinking being shared in the jubilation of this epoch. Emotions of a lofty character stirred men's minds at that time; a spiritual enthusiasm thrilled through the world, as if the reconciliation between the divine and the secular was now first accomplished.[39]

This, of course, did not prevent Hegel from coldly analysing the inner necessity of this explosion of abstract freedom turning into its opposite: self-destructive revolutionary terror. But we should never forget that Hegel's critique is immanent, accepting the basic principle of the French Revolution (and its key supplement, the Haiti Revolution). And one should do exactly the same apropos the October Revolution (and, later, the Chinese Revolution), which was, as Badiou has pointed out, the first case in the entire history of humanity of a successful revolt of the exploited poor – they were the zero-level members of the new society; they set the standards. The revolution stabilised itself into a new social order; a new world was created and miraculously survived for decades, amid unthinkable economic and military pressure and isolation. This was effectively 'a glorious mental dawn. All thinking beings shared in the jubilation of this epoch.' Against all hierarchical orders, egalitarian universality came directly to power.

---

39 G.W.F. Hegel, *Lectures on the Philosophy of World History*, Cambridge: Cambridge University Press, 1975, p. 263.

There is a basic philosophical dilemma underlying this alternative: it may seem that the only consistent Hegelian standpoint is one which measures the notion by the success or failure of its actualisation, so that, from the perspective of the total mediation of the essence by its appearance, any transcendence of the idea over its actualisation is discredited. The consequence of this is that, if we insist on the eternal Idea which survives its historical defeat, this necessarily entails – in Hegelese – a regression from the level of the Notion as the fully actualised unity of essence and appearance to the level of the Essence supposed to transcend its appearing. Is this true, however? One can also claim that the excess of the utopian Idea that survives its historical defeat does not contradict the total mediation of Idea and its appearing: the basic Hegelian insight, according to which the failure of reality to fully actualise an Idea is simultaneously the failure (limitation) of this Idea itself, continues to hold. What one should add is simply that the gap separating the Idea from its actualisation signals a gap within the Idea itself. This is why the spectral Idea that continues to haunt historical reality *signals the falsity of the new historical reality itself, its inadequacy in relation to its own Notion* – the failure of the Jacobin utopia, for example, its actualisation in utilitarian bourgeois reality, is simultaneously the limitation of this utilitarian reality itself. Its failure was precisely the failure to create a new form of everyday life: it remained a carnivalesque excess, with the state apparatus guaranteeing the continuation of daily life, of production.

The lesson of this failure is that we should shift the focus from the utopian goal of the full reign of productive expressivity that no longer needs representation, a state order, capital, and so on, to the problem of what kind of representation should replace the existing liberal-democratic representative state. This problem exploded soon after 1917 when the revolutionary state of exception gradually gave way to the task of organising everyday life. Trotsky pleaded for an interplay between class self-organisation and political leadership of the revolutionary vanguard party.[40] Lenin's solution was an almost Kantian one: freely debate at public meetings during the weekends, but obey and work while at work:

> Before the October Revolution [a worker] did *not* see a single instance of the propertied, exploiting classes making any real sacrifice for him, giving up anything for his benefit. He did *not* see them giving him the land and liberty that had been repeatedly promised him, giving him peace, sacrificing 'Great Power' interests and the interests of Great Power secret treaties, sacrificing capital and profits. He saw this only *after* October 25, 1917, when he took it himself by force, and had to defend by force what he had taken … Naturally, for a certain time, all his attention, all his thoughts, all his spiritual strength, were concentrated on taking a breath, on unbending his back, on straightening his shoulders, on taking the blessings of life that were there for the taking, and that had always been denied him by the now overthrown exploiters. Of course, a certain amount of time is required to enable the ordinary working man not only to see for himself, not only to become convinced, but also to feel that he cannot simply 'take', snatch, grab things, that this leads to increased disruption, to ruin, to the return of the Kornilovs. The corresponding change in the conditions of life (and consequently in the psychology) of the ordinary working men is only just beginning. And our whole task, the task of the Communist Party (Bolsheviks), which is the class-conscious spokesman for the strivings of the exploited for emancipation,

---

40 Especially interesting is one of Trotsky's arguments for the need for a vanguard party: self-organisation in councils cannot take over the role of the Party for a politico-psychological reason: people 'cannot live for years in an uninterrupted state of high tension and intense activity'. See Ernest Mandel, *Trotsky as Alternative*, London: Verso, 1995, p. 81.

is to appreciate this change, to understand that it is necessary, to stand at the head of the exhausted people who are wearily seeking a way out and lead them along the true path, along the path of labour discipline, along the path of co-ordinating the task of arguing at mass meetings *about* the conditions of work with the task of unquestioningly obeying the will of the Soviet leader, of the dictator, *during* the work ... We must learn to combine the 'public meeting' democracy of the working people – turbulent, surging, overflowing its banks like a spring flood – with *iron* discipline while at work, with *unquestioning obedience* to the will of a single person, the Soviet leader, while at work.[41]

It is easy to make fun of Lenin here (or to be horrified by what he is saying), easy to accuse him of being caught up in the industrialist paradigm, and so on – but the problem remains. The main form of direct democracy of the 'expressive' multitude in the twentieth century was the so-called workers' councils ('soviets') – (almost) everybody in the West loved them, including liberals like Hannah Arendt, who perceived in them an echo of the ancient Greek *polis*. Throughout the era of Really Existing Socialism, the secret hope of 'democratic socialists' lay in the direct democracy of the 'soviets', as the form of self-organisation of the people; it is deeply symptomatic how, with the decline of Really Existing Socialism, this emancipatory shadow which continually haunted it also disappeared. Is this not ultimate confirmation of the fact that the conciliar version of 'democratic socialism' was no more than a spectral double of the 'bureaucratic' Really Existing Socialism, its inherent transgression with no substantial positive content of its own, unable to serve as the permanent basic organising principle of a society? What both Really Existing Socialism

---

41 V.I. Lenin, 'The Immediate Tasks of the Soviet Government', *Collected Works*, Vol. 27, Moscow: Progress, 1972, p. 261.

and council democracy shared was a belief in the possibility of a self-transparent organisation of society that would preclude political 'alienation' (state apparatuses, institutionalised rules of political life, a legal order, police, etc.). Is not the basic experience of the end of Really Existing Socialism precisely the rejection of this *shared* feature, the resigned 'postmodern' acceptance of the fact that society is a complex network of 'sub-systems', which is why a certain level of 'alienation' is constitutive of social life, so that a totally self-transparent society is a utopia replete with totalitarian potential?[42] No wonder, then, that the same holds for contemporary practices of 'direct democracy', from the *favelas* to the 'postindustrial' digital culture (do not the descriptions of the new 'tribal' communities of computer hackers often evoke the logic of council democracy?): they all have to rely on a state apparatus since, for structural reasons, they cannot take over the entire field.

According to the ideologists of postmodern capitalism, Marxist theory (and practice) remains caught within the constraints of the hierarchical centralised state-control logic, and thus cannot cope with the social effects of the new information revolution. There are good empirical reasons for this claim: again, it is a supreme irony of history that the disintegration of communism is the most convincing example of the validity of the traditional Marxist dialectic of forces of production and relations of production, on which Marxism counted in its endeavour to overcome capitalism. What effectively ruined the communist regimes was their inability to adjust to the new social logic ushered in by the 'information revolution': they tried to steer this revolution into another large-scale centralised state-planning project. Today, however,

---

42 For a clear articulation of this stance, see Martin Jay, 'No Power to the Soviets', in *Cultural Semantics*, Amherst: University of Massachusetts Press, 1998.

there are increasingly signs that capitalism itself cannot cope with the informational revolution (problems with 'intellectual property' and the rise of 'cooperative commons', etc.).

What happened, then, when in his last years Lenin became fully aware of the limitations of Bolshevik power? It is here that once again we should oppose Lenin and Stalin: in Lenin's very last writings, long after he had renounced the utopia of *State and Revolution*, we can discern the contours of a modest 'realistic' project for what Bolshevik power should do. Because of the economic underdevelopment and cultural backwardness of the Russian masses, there was no way for the country to 'pass directly to socialism'; all the Soviet power could do was combine the moderate politics of 'state capitalism' with an intense cultural education of the inert peasant masses – *not* 'communist propaganda' brainwashing, but simply the patient, gradual imposition of developed standards of civilisation. Facts and figures revealed 'what a vast amount of urgent spadework we still have to do to reach the standard of an ordinary Western European civilised country ... We must bear in mind the semi-Asiatic ignorance from which we have not yet extricated ourselves.'[43] So Lenin repeatedly warns against any kind of direct 'implantation of communism': 'Under no circumstances must this be understood to mean that we should immediately propagate purely and strictly communist ideas in the countryside. As long as our countryside lacks the material basis for communism, it will be, I should say, harmful, in fact, I should say, fatal, for communism to do so.'[44] His recurrent motif is thus: 'The most harmful thing here would be haste.'[45] Against this stance of 'cultural revolution', Stalin opted for the thoroughly anti-Leninist notion of 'building socialism in one state'.

---

43 Lenin, *Collected Works*, Vol. 33, p. 463.
44 Ibid., p. 465.
45 Ibid., p. 488.

Does this mean that Lenin silently accepted the standard Menshevik criticism of Bolshevik utopianism, embracing their idea that revolution must follow necessary preordained stages? It is here that we can observe Lenin's refined dialectical sense at work: he was fully aware that, in the early 1920s, the main tasks for the Bolsheviks were those of a progressive bourgeois regime (general education of the population, etc.); however, the very fact that it was a *proletarian revolutionary* power undertaking these tasks changed the situation fundamentally – there was a unique chance that these 'civilising' measures could be implemented in such a way as to break with their limited bourgeois ideological framework (general education would be really in the service of the people, rather than an ideological mask for propagating narrow bourgeois class interests, etc.). The properly dialectical paradox is thus that it was the very *hopelessness* of the Russian situation (the backwardness compelling the proletarian power to initiate a bourgeois civilising process) that could be turned into a unique advantage.

We have here two models, two incompatible logics, of revolution: either to wait for the teleological moment of the final crisis when the revolution will explode 'at the proper time' by necessity of historical evolution; or to recognise that the revolution has no 'proper time', and see the revolutionary chance as something that emerges and has to be seized upon in the detours of 'normal' historical development. Lenin was not a voluntarist 'subjectivist' – what he insisted on was that the exception (an extraordinary set of circumstances, like those in Russia in 1917) offered a way to undermine the norm itself. And is not this line of argumentation, this fundamental stance, more relevant than ever today? Do we not also live in an era when the state and its apparatuses, inclusive of its political agents, are simply less and less able to articulate the key issues? The illusion of 1917 that the pressing problems facing Russia (peace, land distribution, etc.) could be solved through 'legal' parliamentary means is the same as the contemporary illusion that, say, the ecological threat can avoided by expanding the logic of the market to ecology (making the polluters pay the price for the damage they cause, etc.).

The Miracle of a New Master

This, however, is not all that we can learn from Lenin today. Towards the end of his life, he played with another idea which, marginal as it may appear, has tremendous consequences and opens up new horizons. It concerns the basic discursive status of the Soviet regime (we understand 'discourse' here in Lacan's sense of 'social link'). In terms of Lacan's formalisation of the four discourses, what type of discourse was Bolshevik power?[46] Let us begin with capitalism, which remains a master discourse but one in which the structure of domination is repressed, pushed beneath the bar (individuals are formally free and equal, domination is displaced onto relations between things/commodities). In other words, the underlying structure is that of a capitalist Master pushing his other (the worker) to produce surplus-value that he (the capitalist) appropriates. But since this structure of domination is repressed, its appearance cannot be a(nother) single discourse: it can only appear split into two discourses. Both university discourse and hysterical discourse are products of the failure of the Master's discourse: when the Master loses his authority and becomes hystericised (after his authority is questioned, experienced as fake), that authority reappears but is now displaced, de-subjectivised, in the guise of the authority

---

46 Lacan developed his matrix of four discourses in his *Seminar XVII: The Other Side of Psychoanalysis*, New York: Norton 2007, delivered in 1969–70. One should note that this seminar was Lacan's reaction to the events of May 1968.

of neutral expert-knowledge ('it's not *me* who exerts power, I just state objective facts and/or knowledge').

Now we come to an interesting conclusion: if capitalism is characterised by the parallax of hysterical and university discourses, is the resistance to capitalism, then, characterised by the opposite axis of master and analyst? The recourse to the Master does not designate the conservative attempt to counteract capitalist dynamism with a resuscitated figure of traditional authority; rather, it points towards the new type of communist master or leader emphasised by Badiou, who is not afraid to oppose the necessary role of the Master to our 'democratic' sensitivity: 'I am convinced that one has to reestablish the capital function of leaders in the communist process, whichever its stage.'[47] A true Master is not an agent of discipline and prohibition, his message is not 'You cannot!' or 'You have to …!', but a releasing 'You can!' – what? Do the impossible – in other words, what appears impossible within the coordinates of the existing constellation. And today, this means something very precise: you can think beyond capitalism and liberal democracy as the ultimate framework of our lives. A Master is a vanishing mediator who gives you back to yourself, who delivers you to the abyss of your freedom: when we listen to a true leader, we discover what we want (or, rather, what we always already wanted without knowing it). A Master is needed because we cannot accede to our freedom directly – to gain this access we have to be pushed from outside, since our 'natural state' is one of inert hedonism, of what Badiou calls the 'human animal'. The underlying paradox here is that the more we live as 'free individuals with no Master', the more we are effectively non-free, caught within the existing frame of possibilities – we have to be pushed or disturbed into freedom by a Master.

---

47 Personal communication, April 2013.

Lenin was fully aware of this urgent need for a new Master. In his extraordinary analysis of Lenin's much-maligned *What Is to Be Done?*, Lars T. Lih convincingly refuted the standard reading of this book as presenting an argument for a central-ised elitist professional revolutionary organisation. According to this reading, Lenin's main thesis was that the working class cannot achieve adequate class consciousness 'spontaneously', through its own 'organic' development; this truth has to be introduced into it from outside (by the Party intellectuals who provide 'objective' scientific knowledge).[48] Lih shifts the focus to the relationship between worker-followers and worker-leaders, and asks 'what happens when these two meet, when they interact. What happens can be summed up in one word: a miracle. This is Lenin's word, *chudo* in Russian, and, when you start looking, words like "miracle", "miraculous", are fairly common in Lenin's vocabulary.'[49] To exemplify this 'miracle', Lih explains, Lenin looked back to the Russian populist revolutionaries from the 1870s and asked:

Why are these people heroes? Why do we look up to them as model? Because they had a centralised, conspirational under-ground organisation? No, they are heroes because they were inspiring leaders. Here's what Lenin says about these earlier revolutionaries: 'their inspirational preaching met with an answering call from the masses awakening in elemental [*stikhi-inyi*] fashion, and the leaders' seething energy is taken up and supported by the energy of the revolutionary class.'[50]

---

48 For a more detailed reading of this topic, see Slavoj Žižek, *Revolution at the Gates*, London: Verso, 2011.

49 Quoted in Lars T. Lih: '"We Must Dream!" Echoes of "What Is to Be Done?" in Lenin's Later Career', available at links.org.au.

50 Ibid.

What Lenin expects from the Bolsheviks is something similar: not cold 'objective' (non-partisan) knowledge but a fully engaged subjective stance that can mobilise the followers – it is in this sense that even a single individual can trigger an avalanche: 'You brag about your practicability and you don't see (a fact known to any Russian *praktik*) what miracles for the revolutionary cause can be brought about not only by a circle but by a lone individual.'[51] Lih reads along the same lines the famous claim from *What Is to Be Done?*: 'Give me an organisation of revolutionaries and I will turn Russia around!' Again, rejecting the interpretation that 'a band of intelligentsia conspirators can somehow wave their hands and destroy tsarism', Lih provides his own paraphrase of Lenin:

> Comrades, look around you! Can't you see that the Russian workers are champing at the bit to receive the message of revolution and to act on it? Can't you see the potential for leadership that already exists among the activists, the *praktiki*? Can't you see how many more leaders would arise out of the workers if we set our minds to encouraging their rise? Given all this potential, what is holding things up? Why is the tsar still here? We, comrades – we're the bottleneck! If we could hone our underground skills and bring together what the tsarist regime wants so desperately to keep apart – worker leaders and worker followers, the message and the audience – then, by God, we could blow this joint apart![52]

Such a Master is needed especially in situations of deep crisis. The function of the Master here is to enact an authentic division – a division between those who want to hang on within the old parameters and those who recognise the necessity of

51 Lars T. Lih, *Lenin Rediscovered*, Chicago: Haymarket, 2008, p. 770.
52 Lih, 'We Must Dream!'.

change. Such a division, rather than opportunistic compromises, is the only path to true unity.

In the spirit of today's ideology which rejects traditional hierarchy, the pyramid-like subordination to a Master, in favour of pluralising rhizomatic networks, political analysts like to point out that the anti-neoliberal protests of recent years across Europe and the US, from Occupy Wall Street to Greece and Spain, had no central agency, no Central Committee, coordinating their activity – they were just multiple groups interacting, mostly through social media like Facebook or Twitter, and coordinating their actions spontaneously. But is this 'molecular' spontaneous self-organisation really the most effective new form of 'resistance'? Is it not that the opposite side, capital itself, already acts increasingly like what Deleuzian theory calls the post-Oedipal multitude? Power itself has to enter a dialogue at this level, answering tweet with tweet – the Pope and Trump are now both on Twitter.

Furthermore, as to the molecular self-organising multitude versus the hierarchical order sustained by a charismatic Leader, note the irony of the fact that Venezuela, a country praised by many for its attempts to develop modes of direct democracy (local councils, cooperatives, worker-run factories), was also a country led by Hugo Chávez, a strong charismatic leader if there ever was one. It is as if the Freudian rule of transference is at work here also: in order for individuals to 'reach beyond themselves', to break out of the passivity of representative politics and engage as direct political agents, the reference to a Leader is necessary, a Leader who allows them to pull themselves out of the swamp like Baron Munchhausen, a Leader who is 'supposed to know' what they want. The only path to liberation leads through transference: in order to really awaken individuals from their dogmatic 'democratic slumber', from their blind reliance on institutionalised forms of representative democracy, appeals to direct self-organisation are not enough – a new figure of the Master is needed. Recall the famous lines from Arthur Rimbaud's 'A une raison' ('To a Reason'):

> A tap of your finger on the drum releases all sounds
> and initiates the new harmony.
> A step of yours is the conscription of the new men
> and their marching orders.
> You look away: the new love!
> You look back, – the new love!

There is absolutely nothing inherently 'fascist' in these lines – the supreme paradox of the political dynamic is that a Master is needed to pull individuals out of the quagmire of their inertia and motivate them towards a self-transcending struggle for freedom.

Master and Analyst

No matter how emancipatory this new Master is, however, it has to be supplemented by another discursive form. As Moshe Lewin has noted, at the end of his life, Lenin himself intuited this necessity: while fully admitting the dictatorial nature of the Soviet regime, he proposed a new ruling body, the Central Control Commission (CCC). A series of features characterise Lenin's last struggle:

1) The insistence on full sovereignty for the national entities that composed the Soviet state: not phoney sovereignty, but full and real. No wonder that, as mentioned earlier, in a letter to the Politburo Stalin openly accused Lenin of 'national liberalism'.[53]

2) The insistence on the modesty of goals: *not* socialism, but culture (bourgeois), an efficient technocracy, in total opposition

---

53 Lewin, *Lenin's Last Struggle*, p. 52.

to 'socialism in one country'. This modesty is sometimes surprisingly open: Lenin mocks all attempts to 'build socialism', repeatedly varies the motif of 'we do not know what to do' and insists on the improvisational nature of Soviet policy.

3) The unexpected focus on politeness and civility – a strange thing coming from a hardened Bolshevik. Two things deeply upset Lenin: in a political debate, the Moscow representative in Georgia, Ordhonikidze, physically struck a member of the Georgian CC; and Stalin himself abused verbally Lenin's wife with threats and rude words (he acted in panic, after learning that she had transcribed and transmitted to Trotsky Lenin's letter in which he proposed a pact against Stalin). Lenin naively stated: 'If matters have come to such a pass … we can imagine what a mess we have got ourselves into.'[54] This incident prompted Lenin to write down his famous appeal to remove Stalin:

> Stalin is too rude and this defect, though quite tolerable in our midst and in dealings among us Communists, becomes intolerable in a secretary general. That is why I suggest that the comrades think about a way of removing Stalin from that post and appointing another man in his stead who in all other respects differs from Comrade Stalin in having only one advantage, namely, that of being more tolerant, more loyal, more polite and more considerate to the comrades, less capricious, etc.[55]

These proposals in no way indicate a liberal softening on Lenin's part – in a letter to Kamenev from this same period, he clearly states: 'It is a great mistake to think that NEP put an end to terror; we shall again have recourse to terror and to economic terror.'[56] However, this terror, which was meant

---

54 Quoted in ibid., p. 69.
55 Quoted in ibid., p. 84.
56 Ibid., p. 133.

to survive the planned reduction of the state apparatus and Cheka, was to be more of a threat than an actual programme: 'a means must be found whereby all those who would now [in the NEP] like to go beyond the limits assigned to businessmen by the state could be reminded "tactfully and politely" of the existence of this ultimate weapon'.[57] (Note how even here the motif of politeness reappears!) Lenin was right: 'dictatorship' refers to the constitutive excess of (state-)power, and at *this* level there is no neutrality, the crucial question is *whose is this 'excess'* – if it is not 'ours', it's 'theirs' …

4) Although Lenin's struggle against the rule of state bureaucracy is well known, what is less well known is that, as Lewin perspicuously notes, with his central proposal of the new ruling body, the Central Control Commission, Lenin was trying to square the circle of democracy and the dictatorship of the party-state. While admitting the dictatorial nature of the Soviet regime, he tried to

> establish at the summit of the dictatorship a balance between different elements, a system of reciprocal control that could serve the same function – the comparison is no more than approximate – as the separation of powers in a democratic regime. An important Central Committee, raised to the rank of Party Conference, would lay down the broad lines of policy and supervise the whole Party apparatus, while itself participating in the execution of more important tasks … Part of this Central Committee, the Central Control Commission, would, in addition to its work within the Central Committee, act as a control of the Central Committee and of its various offshoots – the Political Bureau, the Secretariat, the Orgburo. The Central Control Commission … would occupy a special position with relation to the other institutions; its independence would be

---

57 Ibid.

assured by its direct link to the Party Congress, without the mediation of the Politburo and its administrative organs or of the Central Committee.[58]

Checks and balances, the division of powers, mutual control – this was Lenin's desperate answer to the question: who controls the controllers? There is something dream-like, properly fantasmatic, in this idea of a CCC: an independent, educational and controlling body with an 'apolitical' edge, consisting of the best teachers and technocratic specialists monitoring the 'politicised' CC and its organs – in short, this was to be neutral expert knowledge keeping the Party executives in check. However, everything hinges here on the true independence of the Party congress, already undermined de facto by the prohibition of factions, which allowed the top Party apparatus to control it, dismissing its critics as 'factionalists'. The naivety of Lenin's trust in technocratic experts is all the more striking in that it came from a politician who was otherwise fully aware of the all-pervasiveness of a political struggle that allows for no neutral position. However, in 'dreaming' (his expression) about the kind of work to be done by the CCC, he describes how this body should resort

to some semi-humorous trick, cunning device, piece of trickery or something of that sort. I know that in the staid and earnest states of Western Europe such an idea would horrify people and that not a single decent official would even entertain it. I hope, however, that we have not yet become as bureaucratic as all that and that in our midst the discussion of this idea will give rise to nothing more than amusement. Indeed, why not combine pleasure with utility? Why not resort to some humorous or semi-humorous trick to expose something ridiculous,

---

58   Ibid., p. 132.

something harmful, something semi-ridiculous, semi-harmful, etc.?[59]

Is this not an almost obscene double of the 'serious' executive power concentrated in the Central Committee and Politburo, a kind of *non-organic intellectual* of the movement, an agent resorting to humour, tricks and the cunning of reason, keeping itself at a distance ... a kind of *analyst*? So why did Lenin's project miserably fail? (Stalin formally supported the idea, but the CCC was rendered totally impotent and subservient to the Politburo.) The problem was not that the Bolshevik Party was too dictatorial – in Lacanese: excessively functioning as the Master's discourse. Paradoxical as it may sound, the Party was *not functioning enough* as a Master, preferring to function more and more as the university discourse. But what does this mean, politically?

From his great text on ideological state apparatuses onwards, Louis Althusser focused on the material practice of ideology, on the state as a 'machine' with its own autonomous procedures that cannot be reduced to their role of representing struggles in civil society. Hegel was much more aware of this substantial weight of the state than was Marx, rejecting its reduction to an epiphenomenon of civil society. Marx ultimately reduced the state to an epiphenomenon of the productive process located in the 'economic base'; as such, the state is determined by the logic of representation – which class does the state represent? The paradox here is that it was this neglect of the question of state machinery that gave birth to the Stalinist state, to what one is quite justified in calling 'state socialism'. After the Civil War, which left Russia devastated and practically without a working class proper (since most workers had been absorbed into the Red Army and many died fighting the counter-revolution), Lenin himself was bothered

---

59 'Better Few, But Better', see below, p. 149.

by the problem of the state representation: what now was the 'class base' of the Soviet state? Whom does it represent in so far as it claims to be a workers' state, when the working class has been reduced to a minority? What Lenin forgot to include in the series of possible candidates for this role was the state (apparatus) itself, a powerful machine of millions that held all the economic–political power: as in the joke quoted by Lacan, 'I have three brothers, Paul, Ernest and myself', the Soviet state represented three classes: poor farmers, workers *and itself*. Or, to put it in Istvan Meszaros's terms: Lenin forgot to take into account the role of the state *within* the 'economic base', as its key factor. Far from preventing the growth of the tyrannical state released from any mechanism of social control, this neglect opened up the space for the state's unrestrained power: only if we admit that the state represents not only the social classes external to itself but also itself are we led to raise the question of who will contain its strength.

So how did we get from Lenin to Stalin? *Three* moments are in play: Lenin's politics before the Stalinist takeover, Stalinist politics, and the spectre of 'Leninism' retroactively generated by Stalinism (in its official version, but *also* in the version critical of Stalinism, as when the motto of a 'return to original Leninist principles' was invoked during the USSR's process of de-Stalinisation). One should therefore refuse the ridiculous game of opposing the Stalinist terror to the 'authentic' Leninist legacy betrayed by Stalinism: 'Leninism' is a thoroughly *Stalinist* notion. The gesture of projecting the emancipatory–utopian potential of Stalinism backwards to an earlier time signals the incapacity of thought to endure the 'absolute contradiction', the unbearable tension, inherent in the Stalinist project itself. It is therefore crucial to distinguish 'Leninism' (as the authentic core of Stalinism) from the actual political practice and ideology of Lenin's period: the real greatness of Lenin is *not* the same as the Stalinist myth of Leninism.

'The animal wrests the whip from its master and whips itself in order to become master, not knowing that it is only a fantasy produced by a new knot in the master's whiplash.' Is this remark by Kafka not the most succinct definition of what went wrong in the communist states of the twentieth century? Was the passage from Lenin to Stalin, then, necessary? The only appropriate answer is the Hegelian one, evoking a retroactive necessity: *once this passage happened*, once Stalin won, *it became necessary*. The task of a dialectical historian is to conceive this passage 'in becoming', bringing out all the contingency of the struggle which may have ended differently. Lenin's weakness was that he saw the problem of/ as 'bureaucracy', but understated its weight and true dimension: 'his social analysis', writes Lewin, 'was based on only three social classes – the workers, the peasants and the bourgeoisie – without taking any account of the state apparatus as a distinct social element in a country that has nationalized the main sectors of economy'.[60] In other words, the Bolsheviks quickly became aware that their political power lacked a distinct social basis: since most of the working class in whose name they ruled had vanished in the Civil War, they were in a sense ruling in a 'void' of social representation. But in imagining themselves as a 'pure' political power imposing its will on society, they overlooked how the state bureaucracy, since it de facto 'owned' the forces of production,

would become the true social basis of power. There is no such thing as 'pure' political power, devoid of any social foundation. A regime must find some other social basis than the apparatus of repression itself. The 'void' in which the Soviet regime had seemed to be suspended had soon been filled, even if the Bolsheviks had not seen it, or did not wish to see it.[61]

---

60 Lewin, *Lenin's Last Struggle*, p. 125.
61 Ibid., p. 124.

This base would have blocked Lenin's project for the CCC – why? In Badiou's terms of presence and representation: in an anti-economistic and anti-determinist manner, Lenin insisted on the autonomy of the political, but what he missed was not that every political force 'represents' some social force (class), but how this political force (of re-presentation) is directly *inscribed into the 'represented' level itself as a social force of its own.*

Working Through a Revolutionary Tragedy

Lenin's last struggle against Stalin thus has all the marks of a proper tragedy: it was not a melodrama in which the 'hero' fights a 'villain', but a story in which the hero becomes aware that he is fighting the progeny of his own politics, and that it is already too late to stop the fateful consequences of his own past mistakes. To understand properly the rise of Stalinism, one has to fully recognise the tragic dimension of the revolutionary process. This is the topic of Jeremy Glick's *The Black Radical Tragic*,[62] a book that goes much further than the standard notion of the revolutionary tragic deployed by Marx and Engels. The latter locate the tragedy of a revolution in the figure of a hero who arrives too early, ahead of his time, and is therefore destined to fail, even if, in the long view, he stands for historical progress (their exemplary figure is Thomas Muntzer). For Glick, by contrast, tragedy is immanent to a revolutionary process, it is inscribed in its very core and defined by a series of oppositions: leader(ship) versus the masses, radicality versus compromise, and so on. For example, with regard to the first opposition, there is no easy way out, the gap between leader(ship) and masses, their miscommunication, emerges necessarily. Glick quotes a touching passage

---

62   Jeremy Matthew Glick, *The Black Radical Tragic: Performance, Aesthetics, and the Unfinished Haitian Revolution*, New York: New York University Press, 2016.

from Edouard Glissant's play *Monsieur Toussaint* (Act IV, Scene V) where Toussaint, laughing in delirium, sadly reflects on how he 'can barely write': 'I write the word "Toussaint," Macaia spells out "traitor." I write the word "discipline" and Moyse without even a glance at the page shouts "tyranny." I write "prosperity"; Dessalines backs away, he thinks in his heart "weakness." No, I do not know how to write, Manuel.'[63] (Note the irony of how this passage refers to the racist cliché about the black who cannot write.) The background of the passage is the tension in the revolutionary process as reflected in personal relations: Toussaint's nephew Moyse advocates uncompromising fidelity to the masses and wants to break up the large estates. Toussaint, however, is possessed by a fear of the masses and sees his task as maintaining discipline and ensuring the smooth running of the production process, so he orders that Moyse be executed for sedition. Dessalines later triumphs and, after the establishment of a black state, proclaims himself emperor of Haiti, ordering the massacre of all the remaining white inhabitants, and introducing a new form of domination in the very triumph of the revolution. In order to grasp these tragic twists, it is crucial to count the crowd (which in the theatrical *dispositif* appears as a Chorus) as one of the active agents, not just as a passive commentator on the events – the title of Chapter 2 of Glick's book is, quite appropriately, 'Bringing in the Chorus'.[64] The principal antagonism underlying this tension is that between fidelity to the universal Cause and the necessity of compromise – and, at least from my standpoint, Glick's deployment of this antagonism is the theoretical and political climax of his book.

---

63 Ibid., p. 117.

64 On reading this, I realised with pleasure that I did the same in my version of *Antigone* where, at the end, the Chorus intervenes, arresting and executing both Antigone and Creon.

Glick's starting point is C.L.R. James, who clearly saw that the early Christian revolutionaries 'were not struggling to establish the medieval papacy. The medieval papacy was a mediation to which the ruling forces of society rallied in order to strangle the quest for universality of the Christian masses.'[65] Revolutions explode with radical millenarian demands for the actualisation of a new universality, and mediations are symptoms of its failure, of the thwarting of people's expectations. The masses' quest for universality 'forbids any mediation'[66] – was not the tragic turnaround of the Syriza government the last big case of such a mediation: the principled NO to European blackmail was followed immediately by a YES to the 'mediation'. Glick mentions here Georg Lukács, the great advocate of 'mediation', who in 1935 wrote 'Hölderlin's Hyperion', a weird but crucial short essay in which he praised Hegel's endorsement of the Napoleonic Thermidor against Hölderlin's intransigent fidelity to the heroic revolutionary utopia:

> Hegel comes to terms with the post-Thermidorian epoch and the close of the revolutionary period of bourgeois development, and he builds up his philosophy precisely on an understanding of this new turning-point in world history. Hölderlin makes no compromise with the post-Thermidorian reality; he remains faithful to the old revolutionary ideal of renovating 'polis' democracy and is broken by a reality which has no place for his ideals, not even on the level of poetry and thought.[67]

Lukács is here referring to Marx's notion that the heroic period of the French Revolution was the necessary enthusiastic breakthrough, followed by the unheroic phase of market relations:

---

65 Glick, *The Black Radical Tragic*, p. 138.
66 Ibid., p. 139.
67 Georg Lukács, 'Hölderlin's Hyperion', in *Goethe and His Age*, London: Allen & Unwin, 1968, p. 137.

the true social function of the Revolution was to establish the conditions for the prosaic reign of bourgeois economy, and true heroism lies not in blindly clinging to the early revolutionary enthusiasm but in recognising 'the rose in the cross of the present', as Hegel liked to paraphrase Luther; that is, in abandoning the position of the Beautiful Soul and fully accepting the present as the only possible domain of actual freedom. It was thus this 'compromise' with social reality that enabled Hegel's crucial philosophical advance, that of overcoming the proto-fascist notion of 'organic' community in his *System der Sittlichkeit* and engaging in a dialectical analysis of the antagonisms of bourgeois civil society. It is obvious that Lukács's analysis here is deeply allegorical: his essay was written a couple of months after Trotsky (another figure who appears in Glick's book) launched his characterisation of Stalinism as the Thermidor of the October Revolution. Lukács's text thus has to be read as an answer to Trotsky: he accepts the characterisation of Stalin's regime as 'Thermidorian', but gives it a positive twist – instead of bemoaning the loss of utopian energy, one should, in a heroically resigned way, accept its consequences as defining the only actual space of social progress. For Marx, of course, the sobering 'day after' that follows the revolutionary intoxication signals the original limitation of the 'bourgeois' revolutionary project, the falsity of its promise of universal freedom: the 'truth' of universal human rights is the rights of commerce and private property. If we read Lukács's endorsement of the Stalinist Thermidor, it implies (arguably against his intention) a pessimistic and utterly anti-Marxist perspective: the proletarian revolution itself is also characterised by the gap between its illusory assertion of universal freedom and the ensuing new relations of domination and exploitation, which means that the communist project of realising 'actual freedom' failed necessarily.

Or does it? There is a third way beyond the alternative of principled self-destruction or unheroic compromise: not by finding some kind of 'proper measure' between the two extremes but by focusing on what one might call the 'point of the impossible' of a certain field. The great art of politics is to detect such points locally, in a series of modest demands which appear as possible although they are de facto impossible. The situation is like that in science-fiction stories where the hero opens the wrong door (or presses the wrong button) and all of a sudden the entire reality around him disintegrates. In the United States, universal healthcare is obviously such a point of the impossible; in Europe, it seems to be the cancellation of the Greek debt, and so on. It is something you can, in principle, do, but de facto you cannot or should not do – you are free to choose it *on condition that you do not actually choose it.*

Today's political predicament provides a clear example of how *la vérité surgit de la méprise*, of how the wrong choice has to precede the right choice. In principle, the choice facing leftist politics is between social-democratic reformism and radical revolution, but the latter choice, although abstractly correct and true, is self-defeating and gets stuck in Beautiful Soul immobility: in the developed Western societies, calls for a radical revolution have no mobilising power. Only a modest 'wrong' choice can create the subjective conditions for an actual communist perspective: whether it fails or succeeds, it sets in motion a series of further demands ('in order to really have universal healthcare, we also need …') which will lead to the right choice. There is no shortcut here, the need for a radical universal change has to emerge by way of mediation with particular demands. To begin straightaway with the right choice is therefore even worse than making a wrong choice, as it amounts to saying 'I am right and the misery of the world which got it wrong just confirms how right I am.'

Such a stance relies on a faulty ('contemplative') notion of truth, totally neglecting the practical dimension.

The true art of politics is thus not to avoid mistakes and to make the right choices, but *to make the right mistakes*, to select the appropriate wrong choice. It is in this sense that Glick writes of 'the revolutionary leadership as vanishing mediator – the only responsible vanguard model. Political work in order to qualify as radical work should strive toward its redundancy.'[68] He combines here a sober and ruthless insight into the tragic twists of the revolutionary process with an unconditional fidelity to that process; he thus stands as far as possible from the standard 'anti-totalitarian' claim that, since every revolutionary process is destined to degenerate, it is better to abstain from such processes altogether. This readiness to take the risk and engage in the battle, although we know that we will probably be sacrificed in the course of the struggle, is the most precious insight for our new and dark times.

We should thus fully accept the fact that, since revolutionary activity is also not self-transparent but is caught up in conditions of alienation, it will necessarily include tragic reversals, acts whose final outcome is the opposite of what was intended. Here one should follow Badiou, who elaborates three distinct ways for a revolutionary movement to fail. First, there is, of course, a direct defeat: one is simply crushed by the enemy forces. Then there is a defeat in the victory itself: one wins (temporarily, at least) by taking over the main power-agenda of the enemy (the goal is to take state power, either in the parliamentary-democratic, social-democratic way or in a direct identification of the party with the state, as in Stalinism). Finally, there is perhaps the most authentic, but also the most terrifying, version: guided by the correct instinct that every solidification of the revolution into a new state power amounts

---

68   Glick, *The Black Radical Tragic*, p. 12.

to its betrayal, but unable to invent or impose on social reality a truly alternative social order, the revolutionary movement engages in the desperate strategy of protecting its purity with an 'ultra-leftist' resort to all-out terror. Badiou aptly calls this last version the 'sacrificial temptation of the void':

> One of the great Maoist slogans from the red years was 'Dare to fight, dare to win'. But we know that, if it is not easy to follow this slogan, if subjectivity is afraid not so much to fight but to win, it is because struggle exposes it to a simple failure (the attack didn't succeed), while victory exposes it to the most fearsome form of failure: the awareness that one won in vain, that victory prepares repetition, restoration. That a revolution is never more than a between-two-States. It is from here that the sacrificial temptation of the void comes. The most fearsome enemy of the politics of emancipation is not repression by the established order. It is the interiority of nihilism, and the cruelty without limits which can accompany its void.[69]

What Badiou is saying here is effectively the exact opposite of Mao's 'Dare to win!': one *should* be afraid to win (to take power, to establish a new sociopolitical reality), because the lesson of the twentieth century is that victory either ends in restoration (a return to the logic of state power) or gets caught up in an infernal cycle of self-destructive purification. This is why Badiou proposes to replace purification with subtraction: instead of 'winning' (taking power) one maintains a distance towards state power, one creates spaces subtracted from the state. But is this solution really adequate? What about heroic-ally accepting the risk of self-obliteration? A revolutionary process is not a well-planned strategic activity with no place for a full immersion in the Now without regard for the long-

---

69   Alain Badiou, *L'hypothèse communiste*, Paris: Lignes, 2009, p. 28.

term consequences. Quite the contrary: the suspension of all strategic considerations based upon the hope for a better future is a key part of any revolutionary process – or, as Lenin liked to quote Napoleon, *on s'engage et puis on le verra*.

One is tempted to repeat here a classic Soviet joke: in an official Moscow gallery there is a painting displayed with the title *Lenin in Warsaw*, depicting Nadezhda Krupskaya, Lenin's wife, in her Kremlin room, engaged in wild sex with a young Komsomol member. A surprised visitor asks the guide: 'But where is Lenin here?', to which the guide calmly replies: *Lenin is in Warsaw*. Let us imagine a similar exhibition in Moscow in 1980, displaying a picture with the same title but depicting a group of top Soviet *nomenklatura* debating the 'danger' the Polish Solidarity movement represents to the interests of the Soviet Union. A surprised visitor asks the guide: 'But where is Lenin?', and the guide replies: 'Lenin is in Warsaw.'[70] In spite of Western interventions coordinated by the Pope, Reagan, etc., Lenin *was* in Warsaw in the 1970s and 1980s, his spirit animating the workers' protests out of which Solidarity grew.

---

70 Along the same lines, we can imagine a painting depicting the French ruling elite enjoying a sumptuous feast to celebrate the overthrow of the Jacobin regime in 1794, with the title 'Robespierre in Haiti' – where Robespierre's spirit remained alive after the Thermidor.

Note on the Texts

This volume brings together essays, memos and letters from the last two years of Lenin's active life (titles in quotation marks originate with Lenin himself). The selection is intended to present Lenin's attempt to surmount the problems confronting the Soviet state at the end of the Civil War: the struggle to find new ways to organise daily life in the fledgling state; the difficulties of remaining faithful to the communist vision while avoiding the twin traps of unprincipled opportunism and dogmatic intransigence; the need to combine military discipline with proletarian democracy; the threat of Russian chauvinism; and so on. The concluding two short letters – his final message to Stalin announcing the break in contact between the two of them, following Stalin's rudeness to Lenin's wife, and Lenin's very last dictated message, a letter of support to the Georgian communists who were fighting Stalin's centralised 'anti-nationalist' vision of the Soviet state – render palpable not only Lenin's desperate effort to fight to the end but also the painful personal stakes of his last struggle.[1]

---

1 All notes are from the Fifth Edition of Lenin's *Collected Works*.

LENIN 2017

To M. F. Sokolov

16 May

Comrade *M. Sokolov*, Secretary of the Department for Management of Property Evacuated from Poland

Dear Comrade,

I have received and read your draft report for 18 May.[1] You write that I have 'slipped up'. On the one hand, you say, by leasing forests, land, etc., we are introducing *state capitalism*, and on the other hand, he (Lenin) 'talks' about 'expropriating the landowners'.

This seems to you a contradiction.

You are mistaken. Expropriation means *deprivation of property*. A lessee is *not* a property-owner. That means there is no contradiction.

The introduction of capitalism (*in moderation* and skilfully, as I say more than once in my pamphlet) is possible without restoring the landowners' property. A lease is a contract *for a period*. Both ownership and control remain *with us*, the workers' state.

'What fool of a lessee will spend money on model organisa-tion,' you write, 'if he is *pursued by the thought of possible expropriation …*'

---

1 Reference is to the co-report by Sokolov 'On the Tax in Kind and the Change in the Policy of Soviet Power' at the general meeting of the RCP(B) group at the People's Commissariat of Foreign Affairs, 18 May 1921. Sokolov sent it to Lenin, requesting him to read it and reply to a number of questions which it raised.

Expropriation is a *fact*, not a *possibility*. That makes a big difference. *Before* actual expropriation not a single capitalist would have entered our service as a lessee. Whereas now 'they', the capitalists, have fought three years, and wasted *hundreds of millions of rubles in gold* of their own (and those of the Anglo-French, the biggest *money-bags* in the world) on war with us. Now they are having a bad time abroad. What choice have they? Why should they not accept an agreement? For 10 years you get not a bad income, otherwise ... you die of hunger abroad. Many will hesitate. Even if only five out of 100 try the experiment, it won't be too bad.

You write:

'Independent mass activity is *possible* only when we *wipe off* the face of the earth that ulcer which is called the bureaucratic chief administrations and central boards.'

Although I have not been out in the provinces, I know this bureaucracy and all the harm it does. Your mistake is to think that it can be destroyed all at once, like an ulcer, that it can be 'wiped off the face of the earth'.

This is a mistake. You can throw out the tsar, throw out the landowners, throw out the capitalists. We have done this. But you cannot 'throw out' bureaucracy in a peasant country, you cannot 'wipe it off the face of the earth'. You can only *reduce* it by slow and stubborn effort.

To 'throw off' the 'bureaucratic ulcer', as you put it in another place, is wrong in its very formulation. It means you don't understand the question. To 'throw off' an ulcer of this kind is *impossible*. It can only be *healed*. Surgery in *this* case is an absurdity, an *impossibility*; only a *slow* care – all the rest is charlatanry or naivety.

You are naive, that's just what it is, excuse my frankness. But you yourself write about your youth.

It's naive to wave aside a healing process by referring to the fact that you have 2–3 times tried to fight the bureaucrats and suffered defeat. First of all, I reply to this, your unsuccessful experiment, you have to try, not 2–3 times, but 20–30 times – repeat your attempts, start over again.

Second, where is the evidence that you fought correctly, skilfully? Bureaucrats are smart fellows, many scoundrels among them are extremely cunning. You won't catch them with your bare hands. Did you fight correctly? Did you *encircle* the 'enemy' according to all the rules of the art of war? I don't know.

It's no use your quoting Engels.[2] Was it not some 'intellectual' who suggested that quotation to you? A futile quotation, if not something worse. It smells of the doctrinaire. It resembles despair. But for us to despair is either ridiculous or disgraceful.

The struggle against bureaucracy in a peasant and absolutely exhausted country is a long job, and this struggle must be carried on persistently, without losing heart at the first reverse.

'*Throw off*' the 'chief administrations'? Nonsense. What will you set up *instead*? You don't know. You must not *throw them off*, but cleanse them, heal them, heal and cleanse them ten times and a hundred times. And not lose heart.

If you give your lecture (I have absolutely no objection to this), read out my letter to you as well, please.

I shake your hand, and beg you not to tolerate the 'spirit of dejection' in yourself.

2　In the draft of his co-report Sokolov quoted the following passage from Engels: 'The worst thing that can befall a leader of an extreme party is to be compelled to take over a government at a time when society is not yet ripe for the domination of the class he represents and for the measures which that domination implies' (Friedrich Engels, *The Peasant War in Germany*, Moscow: Progress Publishers, 1965, p. 112).

To G. Myasnikov

5 August 1921

Comrade Myasnikov,

I have only just managed to read both your articles.[1] I am unaware of the nature of the speeches you made in the Perm (I think it was Perm) organisation and of your conflict with it. I can say nothing about that; it will be dealt with by the Organisation Bureau, which, I hear, has appointed a special commission.

My object is a different one: it is to appraise your articles as literary and political documents.

They are interesting documents.

Your main mistake is, I think, most clearly revealed in the article 'Vexed Questions'. And I consider it my duty to do all I can to try to convince you.

At the beginning of the article you make a correct application of dialectics. Indeed, whoever fails to understand the

---

1 Lenin wrote the letter in connection with Myasnikov's article 'Vexed Questions', his memo to the Central Committee of the RCP(B) and his speeches in the Petrograd and Perm Party organisations. Myasnikov had set up an anti-Party group in the Motovilikha District of Perm Gubernia which fought against Party policy. A Central Committee commission investigated his activity and proposed his expulsion from the Party for repeated breaches of discipline and organisation of an anti-Party group contrary to the resolution 'On Party Unity' of the Party's Tenth Congress. His expulsion was approved by the Political Bureau of the Central Committee of the RCP(B) on 20 February 1922.

substitution of the slogan 'civil peace' for the slogan 'civil war' lays himself open to ridicule, if nothing worse. In this, you are right.

But precisely because you are right on this point, I am surprised that in drawing your conclusions, you should have forgotten the dialectics which you yourself had properly applied.

'Freedom of the press, from the monarchists to the anarchists, inclusively' ... Very good! But just a minute: every Marxist and every worker who ponders over the four years' experience of our revolution will say, 'Let's look into this – what sort of freedom of the press? What for? For which class?'

We do not believe in 'absolutes'. We laugh at 'pure democracy'.

The 'freedom of the press' slogan became a great world slogan at the close of the Middle Ages and remained so up to the nineteenth century. Why? Because it expressed the ideas of the progressive bourgeoisie, i.e., its struggle against kings and priests, feudal lords and landowners.

No country in the world has done as much to liberate the masses from the influence of priests and landowners as the RSFSR has done, and is doing. We have been performing this function of 'freedom of the press' better than anyone else in the world.

All over the world, wherever there are capitalists, freedom of the press means freedom to buy up newspapers, to buy writers, to bribe, buy and fake 'public opinion' for the benefit of the bourgeoisie.

This is a fact.

No one will ever be able to refute it.

And what about us?

Can anyone deny that the bourgeoisie in this country has been defeated, but not destroyed? That it has gone into hiding? Nobody can deny it.

Freedom of the press in the RSFSR, which is surrounded by the bourgeois enemies of the whole world, means freedom of political organisation for the bourgeoisie and its most loyal servants, the Mensheviks and Socialist-Revolutionaries.

This is an irrefutable fact.

The bourgeoisie (all over the world) is still very much stronger than we are. To place in its hands yet another weapon like freedom of political organisation (= freedom of the press, for the press is the core and foundation of political organisation) means facilitating the enemy's task, means helping the class enemy.

We have no wish to commit suicide, and therefore, we will not do this.

We clearly see this fact: 'freedom of the press' means in practice that the international bourgeoisie will immediately buy up hundreds and thousands of Cadet, Socialist-Revolutionary and Menshevik writers, and will organise their propaganda and fight against us.

That is a fact. 'They' are richer than we are and will buy a 'force' ten times larger than we have, to fight us.

No, we will not do it; we will not help the international bourgeoisie.

How could you descend from a class appraisal–from the appraisal of the relations between all classes–to the sentimental, philistine appraisal? This is a mystery to me.

On the question: 'civil peace or civil war', on the question of how we have won over, and will continue to 'win over', the peasantry (to the side of the proletariat), on these two key world questions (= questions that affect the very substance of world politics), on these questions (which are dealt with in both your articles), you were able to take the Marxist standpoint, instead of the philistine, sentimental standpoint. You did take account of the relationships of all classes in a practical, sober way.

And suddenly you slide down into the abyss of sentimentalism!

'Outrage and abuses are rife in this country: freedom of the press will expose them.'

That, as far as I can judge from your two articles, is where you slipped up. You have allowed yourself to be depressed by certain sad and deplorable facts, and lost the ability soberly to appraise the forces.

Freedom of the press will help the force of the world bourgeoisie. That is a fact; 'Freedom of the press' will not help to purge the Communist Party in Russia of a number of its weaknesses, mistakes, misfortunes and maladies (it cannot be denied that there is a spate of these maladies), because this is not what the world bourgeoisie wants. But freedom of the press will be a weapon in the hands of this world bourgeoisie. It is not dead; it is alive. It is lurking nearby and watching. It has already hired Milyukov, to whom Chernov and Martov (partly because of their stupidity, and partly because of factional spleen against us; but mainly because of the objective logic of their petty-bourgeois democratic position) are giving 'faithful and loyal' service.

You took the wrong fork in the road.

You wanted to cure the Communist Party of its maladies and have snatched at a drug that will cause certain death not at your hands, of course, but at the hands of the world bourgeoisie (+Milyukov+Chernov-J--Martov).

You forgot a minor point, a very tiny point, namely the world bourgeoisie and its 'freedom' to buy up for itself newspapers, and centres of political organisation.

No, we will not take this course. Nine hundred out of every thousand politically conscious workers will refuse to take this course.

We have many maladies. Mistakes (our common mistakes, all of us have made mistakes, the Council of Labour and

Defence, the Council of People's Commissars and the Central Committee) like those we made in distributing fuel and food in the autumn and winter of 1920 (those were enormous mistakes!) have greatly aggravated the maladies springing from our situation.

Want and calamity abound.

They have been terribly intensified by the famine of 1921.

It will cost us a supreme effort to extricate ourselves, but we will get out, and have already begun to do so.

We will extricate ourselves, for, in the main, our policy is a correct one, and takes into account all the class forces on an international scale. We will extricate ourselves because we do not try to make our position look better than it is. We realise all the difficulties. We see all the maladies, and are taking measures to cure them methodically, with perseverance, and without giving way to panic.

You have allowed panic to get the better of you; panic is a slope–once you step on it you slide down into a position that looks very much as if you are forming a new party, or are about to commit suicide.

You must not give way to panic.

Is there any isolation of the Communist Party cells from the Party? There is. It is an evil, a misfortune, a malaise.

It is there. It is a severe ailment.

We can see it.

It must be cured by proletarian and Party measures and not by means of 'freedom' (for the bourgeoisie).

Much of what you say about reviving the country's economy, about mechanical ploughs, etc., about fighting for 'influence' over the peasantry, etc., is true and useful.

Why not bring this out separately? We shall get together and work harmoniously in one party. The benefits will be great; they will not come all at once, but very slowly.

Revive the Soviets; secure the cooperation of non-Party

people; let non-Party people verify the work of Party members: this is absolutely right. No end of work there, and it has hardly been started.

Why not amplify this in a practical way? In a pamphlet for the congress?

Why not take that up?

Why be afraid of spadework (denounce abuses through the Central Control Commission, or the Party press, *Pravda*)? Misgivings about slow, difficult and arduous spadework cause people to give way to panic and to seek an 'easy' way out: 'freedom of the press' (for the bourgeoisie).

Why should you persist in your mistake – an obvious mistake – in your non-Party, anti-proletarian slogan of 'freedom of the press'? Why not take up the less 'brilliant' (scintillating with bourgeois brilliance) spadework of driving out abuses, combating them, and helping non-Party people in a practical and businesslike way?

Have you ever brought any particular abuse to the notice of the CC, and suggested a definite means of eradicating it?

No, you have not.

Not a single time.

You saw a spate of misfortunes and maladies, gave way to despair and rushed into the arms of the enemy, the bourgeoisie ('freedom of the press' for the bourgeoisie). My advice is: do not give way to despair and panic.

We, and those who sympathise with us, the workers and peasants, still have an immense reservoir of strength. We still have plenty of health and vigour.

We are not doing enough to cure our ailments.

We are not doing a good job of practising the slogan: promote non-Party people, let non-Party people verify the work of Party members.

But we can, and will, do a hundred times more in this field than we are doing.

I hope that after thinking this over carefully you will not, out of false pride, persist in an obvious political mistake ('freedom of the press'), but, pulling yourself together and overcoming the panic, will get down to practical work: help to establish ties with non-Party people, and help non-Party people to verify the work of Party members.

There is no end to work in this field. Doing this work you can (and should) help to cure the disease, slowly but surely, instead of chasing after will-o'-the-wisps like 'freedom of the press'.

With communist greetings,

New Times and Old Mistakes in a New Guise

Every specific turn in history causes some change in the form of petty-bourgeois wavering, which always occurs alongside the proletariat, and which, to one degree or an other, always penetrates its midst.

This wavering flows in two 'streams': petty-bourgeois reformism, i.e., servility to the bourgeoisie covered by a cloak of sentimental democratic and 'Social'-Democratic phrases and fatuous wishes; and petty-bourgeois revolutionism – menacing, blustering and boastful in words, but a mere bubble of disunity, disruption and brainlessness in deeds. This wavering will inevitably occur until the taproot of capitalism is cut. Its form is now changing owing to the change taking place in the economic policy of the Soviet government.

The leitmotif of the Mensheviks is this: 'The Bolsheviks have reverted to capitalism; that is where they will meet their end. The revolution, including the October Revolution, has turned out to be a bourgeois revolution after all! Long live democracy! Long live reformism!'[1] Whether this is said in

---

1 The Mensheviks were adherents to a right-wing trend in the Russian Social-Democratic movement. They received their name at the close of the Second R.S.D.L.P. Congress in August 1905, when at the elections to the Party's central organs they found themselves in the minority (*menshinstvo*), and the revolutionary Social-Democrats headed by Lenin won the majority (*bolshinstvo*); hence the names Bolsheviks and Mensheviks. The Mensheviks sought to secure agreement between the proletariat and the bourgeoisie. In the period of dual power after the bourgeois-democratic revolution of February 1917, when the dictatorship of the bourgeoisie as represented by the Provisional Government intertwined with the

the purely Menshevik spirit or in the spirit of the Socialist-Revolutionaries,[2] in the spirit of the Second International or in the spirit of the Two-and-a-Half International,[3] it amounts to the same thing.

---

dictatorship of the proletariat and peasants as represented by the Soviets, the Mensheviks and the Socialist-Revolutionaries accepted posts in the Provisional Government, supported its imperialist policy and opposed the mounting proletarian revolution. In the Soviets the Mensheviks pursued the same policy of supporting the Provisional Government and diverting the masses from the revolutionary movement.

After the October Revolution, they became an openly counter-revolutionary party, organising and participating in conspiracies and revolts against Soviet power.

2   The Socialist-Revolutionaries were members of a peasant-orientated party in Russia, which emerged at the end of 1901 and the beginning of 1902.

After the February bourgeois-democratic revolution in 1917 they were, together with the Mensheviks, the mainstay of the counter-revolutionary Provisional Government of the bourgeoisie and landowners, while their leaders held posts in that government. Far from supporting the peasants' demand for the abolition of landlordism, the Socialist-Revolutionary Party pressed for its preservation. The Socialist-Revolutionary ministers of the Provisional Government sent punitive detachments against peasants who seized landed estates.

At the close of November 1917, the Left Socialist-Revolutionaries formed an independent party.

During the years of foreign military intervention and the Civil War the Socialist-Revolutionaries carried on counter-revolutionary subversive activities, supported the interventionists and whiteguards, took part in counter-revolutionary plots and organised terrorist acts against leaders of the Soviet government and the Communist Party. After the Civil War they continued their hostile activities within the country and among whiteguard émigrés.

3   The Two-and-a-Half International (whose official name was the International Association of Socialist Parties) was an international organisation of centrist socialist parties and groups that had been forced out of the Second International by the revolutionary masses. It was formed at a conference in Vienna in February 1921. While criticising the Second International, the leaders of the Two-and-a-Half International pursued an opportunist, splitting policy on all key issues of the proletarian movement and sought to utilise their association to offset the growing influence of the Communists among the working-class masses.

In May 1925, the Second and Two-and-a-Half Internationals merged into the so-called Socialist Labour International.

The leitmotif of semi-anarchists like the German 'Communist Workers' Party',[4] or of that section of our former Workers' Opposition[5] which has left or is becoming estranged from the Party, is: 'The Bolsheviks have lost faith in the working class.' The slogans they deduce from this are more or less akin to the 'Kronstadt' slogans of the spring of 1921.[6]

---

4 The Communist Workers Party of Germany was formed in April 1920 by 'Left' Communists, who had been expelled from the Communist Party of Germany at the Heidelberg Congress in 1919. In November 1920, in order to facilitate the unification of all communist forces in Germany and satisfy the wishes of the best proletarian elements within it, the C.W.P.G. was temporarily admitted to the Comintern with the rights of a sympathising member on the condition that it merged with the United Communist Party of Germany and supported its actions. The C.W.P.G. leadership did not fulfil the instructions of the Comintern Executive Committee. For the sake of the workers still supporting the C.W.P.G., the Third Comintern Congress decided to give it two or three months in which to convene a congress and settle the question of unification. The C.W.P.G. leadership failed to fulfil the decision of the Third Congress and continued their splitting tactics with the result that the Comintern Executive Committee was compelled to break off relations with the party. The C.W.P.G. found itself outside the Comintern and subsequently degenerated into an insignificant sectarian group that had no proletarian support whatever and was hostile to the working class of Germany.

5 The Workers' Opposition was an anti-Party faction formed in the Russian Communist Party in 1920 by Shlyapnikov, Medvedyev, Kollontai and others. It took final shape during the debates on the role of the trade unions in 1920–1. Actually there was nothing of the working class about this opposition, which expressed the mood and aspirations of the petty bourgeoisie. It counterposed the trade unions to the Soviet Government and the Communist Party, considering them the highest form of working-class organisation.

After the Tenth Party Congress, which found the propagation of the ideas of the Workers' Opposition incompatible with membership in the Communist Party, a large number of rank-and-file members of that opposition broke away from it.

6 This is a reference to the counter-revolutionary mutiny which broke out in Kronstadt on 28 February 1921. Organised by Socialist-Revolutionaries, Mensheviks and whiteguards, it involved a considerable number of sailors, most of whom were raw recruits from the villages, who had little or no knowledge of politics and voiced the peasants' dissatisfaction

In contrast to the whining and panic of the philistines from among reformists and of the philistines from among revolutionaries, the Marxists must weigh the alignment of actual class forces and the incontrovertible facts as soberly and as accurately as possible.

Let us recall the main stages of our revolution. The first stage: the purely political stage, so to speak, from 25 October to 5 January, when the Constituent Assembly was dissolved.[7]

---

with the requisitioning of surplus food. The economic difficulties in the country and the weakening of the Bolshevik organisation at Kronstadt facilitated the mutiny.

Hesitating to oppose the Soviet system openly, the counter-revolutionary bourgeoisie adopted new tactics. With the purpose of deceiving the masses, the leaders of the revolt put forward the slogan 'Soviets without Communists', hoping to remove the Communists from the leadership of the Soviets, destroy the Soviet system and restore the capitalist regime in Russia.

On 2 March, the mutineers arrested the fleet command. They contacted foreign imperialists, who promised them financial and military aid. The seizure of Kronstadt by the mutineers created a direct threat to Petrograd.

Regular Red Army units commanded by Mikhail Tukhachevsky were sent by the Soviet Government to crush the mutiny. The Communist Party reinforced these units with more than 500 delegates of the Tenth Party Congress; all these men, with Kliment Voroshilov at their head, had had fighting experience. The mutiny was snuffed out on 18 March.

7 The elections to the Constituent Assembly were held on 12 (25) November 1917 according to lists drawn up before the October Revolution. Most of the seats were held by Right Socialist-Revolutionaries and other counter-revolutionary elements. Though it did not mirror the new alignment of forces that took shape in the country as a result of the revolution, the Communist Party and the Soviet Government felt the necessity of convening it because backward sections of the working population still believed in bourgeois parliamentarianism. The assembly opened in Petrograd on 5 (18) January 1918, but was dissolved on the next day by a decree of the All-Russia Central Executive Committee when the counter-revolutionary majority in it rejected the Declaration of Rights of the Working and Exploited People submitted by the All-Russia Central Executive Committee and refused to endorse the decrees of the Second Congress of Soviets on peace, land and the transfer of power to the Soviets. The decision to dissolve the assembly

In a matter of ten weeks we did a hundred times more to actually and completely destroy the survivals of feudalism in Russia than the Mensheviks and Socialist-Revolutionaries did during the eight months *they* were in power – from February to October 1917. At that time, the Mensheviks and Socialist-Revolutionaries in Russia, and all the heroes of the Two-and-a-Half International abroad, acted as miserable accomplices of reaction. As for the anarchists, some stood aloof in perplexity, while others helped us. Was the revolution a bourgeois revolution at that time? Of course it was, insofar as our function was to complete the bourgeois democratic revolution, insofar as there was as yet no class struggle among the 'peasantry'. But, at the same time, we accomplished a great deal *over and above* the bourgeois revolution *for* the socialist, proletarian revolution: 1) we developed the forces of the working class for *its* utilisation of state power to an extent never achieved before; 2) we struck a blow that was felt all over the world against the fetishes of petty-bourgeois democracy, the Constituent Assembly and bourgeois 'liberties' such as freedom of the press for the rich; 3) we created the Soviet *type* of state, which was a gigantic step in advance of 1795 and 1871.

The second stage: the Brest-Litovsk peace.[8] There was a riot

---

was wholeheartedly approved by broad masses of workers, soldiers and peasants.

8   This peace treaty was signed between Soviet Russia and the Quadruple Alliance (Germany, Austria–Hungary, Bulgaria and Turkey) on 5 March 1918. It was ratified on 15 March by the Extraordinary Fourth All-Russia Congress of Soviets. The terms were extremely onerous for Soviet Russia. They gave Germany and Austria–Hungary control over Poland, almost the whole Baltic area and part of Byelorussia; Ukraine was separated from Soviet Russia and became dependent upon Germany. Turkey received the towns of Kars, Batum and Ardagan.

The signing of the Brest Treaty was preceded by a vehement struggle against Trotsky and the anti-Party group of 'Left Communists'. The treaty was signed thanks to a huge effort on Lenin's part. It was a wise political of revolutionary phrase-mongering against peace – the semi-jingoist phrase-mongering of the Socialist-Revolutionaries and Mensheviks, and the 'Left' phrase-mongering of a certain section of the Bolsheviks. 'Since you have made peace with imperialism you are doomed,' argued the philistines, some in panic and some with malicious glee. But the Socialist-Revolutionaries and the Mensheviks made peace with imperialism as participants in the bourgeois robbery of the workers. We 'made peace', surrendering to the robbers part of our property, only in order to save the workers' rule, and in order to be able to strike heavier blows at the robbers later on. At that time we heard no end of talk about our having 'lost faith in the forces of the working class'; but we did not allow ourselves to be deceived by this phrase-mongering.

The third stage: the Civil War, beginning with the Czechoslovaks[9] and the Constituent Assembly crowd and

---

compromise, for it gave Soviet Russia a peaceful respite and enabled her to demobilise the old disintegrating army and create the new Red Army, start socialist construction and muster her forces for the coming struggle against internal counter-revolution and foreign intervention. This policy promoted the further intensification of the struggle for peace and the growth of revolutionary sentiments among the troops and the masses of all belligerent countries. After the monarchy in Germany was overthrown by the revolution of November 1918, the All-Russia Central Executive Committee abrogated the predatory Brest Treaty.

9   Lenin refers to the counter-revolutionary mutiny of the Czechoslovak Corps inspired by the Entente with the connivance of the Mensheviks and Socialist-Revolutionaries. The corps, consisting of Czech and Slovak war prisoners, was formed in Russia before the Great October Socialist Revolution. In the summer of 1918 it had more than 60,000 men (altogether in Russia there were about 200,000 Czech and Slovak prisoners of war). After Soviet rule was established, the financing of the corps was undertaken by the Entente powers, who decided to use it against the Soviet Republic. Tomas Masaryk, president of the Czechoslovak National Council, proclaimed the corps part of the French Army, and Entente representatives raised the question of evacuating it to France. The Soviet Government agreed to its evacuation on condition that the Russian soldiers in France were allowed to return home. Under an agreement signed

ending with Wrangel, from 1918 to 1920.[10] At the beginning of the war our Red Army was non-existent. Judged as a material force, this army is even now insignificant compared with the army of any of the Entente powers. Nevertheless, we emerged victorious from the struggle against the mighty Entente. The alliance between the peasants and the workers led by proletarian rule – this achievement of epoch-making importance – was raised to an unprecedented level. The Mensheviks and Socialist-Revolutionaries acted as the accomplices of the monarchy overtly (as ministers, organisers and propagandists) and covertly (the more 'subtle' and despicable method adopted by the Chernovs and Martovs, who pretended to wash their hands of the affair but actually used

---

on 26 March 1918, the corps was given the possibility of leaving Russia via Vladivostok, provided it surrendered its weapons and removed the counter-revolutionary Russian officers from its command. But the counter-revolutionary command of the corps perfidiously violated the agreement with the Soviet Government on the surrender of weapons and, acting on orders from the Entente imperialists, provoked an armed mutiny at the close of May. Operating in close contact with the whiteguards and kulaks, the White Czechs occupied considerable territory in the Urals, the Volga country and Siberia, everywhere restoring bourgeois rule.

On 11 June soon after the mutiny broke out, the Central Executive Committee of the Czechoslovak communist groups in Russia appealed to the soldiers of the corps, exposing the counter-revolutionary objectives of the mutiny and calling upon the Czech and Slovak workers and peasants to end the mutiny and join the Czechoslovak units of the Red Army. Most of the Czech and Slovak war prisoners were favourably disposed to Soviet power and did not succumb to the anti-Soviet propaganda of the corps's reactionary command. Many of the soldiers refused to fight Soviet Russia after they realised that they were being deceived. Nearly 12,000 Czechs and Slovaks joined the Red Army.

The Volga country was liberated by the Red Army in the autumn of 1918. The White Czechs were finally routed early in 1920.

10 *Wrangel* – baron, tsarist general and rabid monarchist. During the foreign military intervention and Civil War he was a puppet of the British, French and US imperialists. In April–November 1920 he was commander-in-chief of the whiteguard armed forces in South Russia. He fled abroad after his forces were defeated by Trotsky's Red Army.

their pens against us). The anarchists too vacillated helplessly, one section of them helping us, another hindering us by their clamour against military discipline or by their scepticism.

The fourth stage: the Entente is compelled to cease (for how long?) its intervention and blockade. Our unprecedentedly dislocated country is just barely beginning to recover, is only just realising the full depth of its ruin, is suffering the most terrible hardships – stoppage of industry, crop failures, famine, epidemics.

We have risen to the highest and at the same time the most difficult stage of our historic struggle. Our enemy at the present moment and in the present period is not the same one that faced us yesterday. He is not the hordes of white-guards commanded by the landowners and supported by all the Mensheviks and Socialist-Revolutionaries, by the whole international bourgeoisie. He is everyday economics in a small-peasant country with a ruined large-scale industry. He is the petty-bourgeois element which surrounds us like the air, and penetrates deep into the ranks of the proletariat. And the proletariat is declassed, i.e., dislodged from its class groove. The factories and mills are idle – the proletariat is weak, scattered, enfeebled. On the other hand, the petty-bourgeois element within the country is backed by the whole international bourgeoisie, which still retains its power throughout the world.

Is this not enough to make people quail, especially heroes like the Mensheviks and Socialist-Revolutionaries, the knights of the Two-and-a-Half International, the helpless anarchists and the lovers of 'Left' phrases? 'The Bolsheviks are reverting to capitalism; the Bolsheviks are done for. Their revolution, too, has not gone beyond the confines of a bourgeois revolution.' We hear plenty of wails of this sort.

But we have grown accustomed to them.

We do not belittle the danger. We look it straight in the face.

We say to the workers and peasants: the danger is great; more solidarity, more staunchness, more coolness; turn the pro-Menshevik and pro-Socialist-Revolutionary panic-mongers and tub-thumpers out with contempt.

The danger is great. The enemy is far stronger than we are economically, just as yesterday he was far stronger than we were militarily. We know that; and in that knowledge lies our strength. We have already done so tremendously much to purge Russia of feudalism, to develop all the forces of the workers and peasants, to promote the worldwide struggle against imperialism and to advance the international proletarian movement, which is freed from the banalities and baseness of the Second and Two-and-a-Half Internationals, that panicky cries no longer affect us. We have more than fully 'justified' our revolutionary activity; we have shown the whole world by our deeds what proletarian revolutionism is capable of in contrast to Menshevik–Socialist Revolutionary 'democracy' and cowardly reformism decked with pompous phrases.

Anyone who fears defeat on the eve of a great struggle can call himself a socialist only out of sheer mockery of the workers.

It is precisely because we are not afraid to look danger in the face that we make the best use of our forces for the struggle – we weigh the chances more dispassionately, cautiously and prudently – we make every concession that will strengthen us and break up the forces of the enemy (now even the biggest fool can see that the 'Brest peace' was a concession that strengthened us and dismembered the forces of international imperialism).

The Mensheviks are shouting that the tax in kind, the freedom to trade, the granting of concessions and state capitalism signify the collapse of communism. Abroad, the ex-Communist Levi has added his voice to that of the Mensheviks. This same Levi had to be defended as long as the mistakes he had made could be explained by his reaction to some of the mistakes of the 'Left' Communists, particularly in March 1921 in Germany;[11] but this same Levi cannot be defended when, instead of admitting that he is wrong, he slips into Menshevism all along the line.

To the Menshevik shouters we shall simply point out that as early as the spring of 1918 the Communists proclaimed and advocated the idea of a bloc, an alliance with state capitalism against the petty-bourgeois element. That was three years ago! In the first months of the Bolshevik victory! Even then the Bolsheviks took a sober view of things. And since then nobody has been able to challenge the correctness of our sober calculation of the available forces.

Levi, who has slipped into Menshevism, advises the Bolsheviks (whose defeat by capitalism he 'forecasts' in the same way as all the philistines, democrats, Social-Democrats and others had forecast our doom if we dissolved the Constituent Assembly!) to appeal for aid to the whole working class! Because, if you please, up to now only part of the working class has been helping us!

What Levi says here remarkably coincides with what is said by those semi-anarchists and tub-thumpers, and also by certain members of the former 'Workers' Opposition', who are so fond of talking large about the Bolsheviks now having 'lost faith in the forces of the working class'. Both the Mensheviks

---

11 The 'mistakes of the "Lefts" in the Communist Party of Germany' were that they incited the working class to premature actions. The German bourgeoisie utilised these mistakes to provoke the workers into armed action at an unpropitious time. A workers' revolt broke out in central Germany in March 1921. That revolt was not supported by the workers of other industrial regions, with the result that despite a heroic struggle it was quickly crushed. For Lenin's assessment of this revolt and criticism of the mistakes of the 'Lefts' see his 'Speech in Defence of the Tactics of the Communist International' at the Third Comintern Congress and his 'A Letter to the German Communists' (see *Collected Works*, Vol. 52, pp. 468–77 and 512–25).

and those with anarchist leanings make a fetish of the concept 'forces of the working class'; they are incapable of grasping its actual, concrete meaning. Instead of studying and analysing its meaning, they declaim.

The gentlemen of the Two-and-a-Half International pose as revolutionaries; but in every serious situation they prove to be counter-revolutionaries because they shrink from the violent destruction of the old state machine; they have no faith in the forces of the working class. It was not a mere catchphrase we uttered when we said this about the Socialist-Revolutionaries and Co. Everybody knows that the October Revolution actually brought new forces, a new class, to the forefront, that the best representatives of the proletariat are now governing Russia, built up an army, led that army, set up local government, etc., are running industry, and so on. If there are some bureaucratic distortions in this administration, we do not conceal this evil; we expose it, combat it. Those who allow the struggle against the distortions of the new system to obscure its content and to cause them to forget that the working class has created and is guiding a state of the Soviet type are incapable of thinking, and are merely throwing words to the wind.

But the 'forces of the working class' are not unlimited. If the flow of fresh forces from the working class is now feeble, sometimes very feeble, if, notwithstanding all our decrees, appeals and agitation, notwithstanding all our orders for 'the promotion of non-Party people', the flow of forces is still feeble, then resorting to mere declamations about having 'lost faith in the forces of the working class' means descending to vapid phrase-mongering.

Without a certain 'respite' these new forces will not be forthcoming; they can only grow slowly; and they can grow only on the basis of restored large-scale industry (i.e., to be more precise and concrete, on the basis of electrification). They can be obtained from *no other* source.

After an enormous, unparalleled exertion of effort, the working class in a small-peasant, ruined country, the working class which has very largely become declassed, needs an interval of time in which to allow new forces to grow and be brought to the fore, and in which the old and worn-out forces can 'recuperate'. The creation of a military and state machine capable of successfully withstanding the trials of 1917–21 was a great effort, which engaged, absorbed and exhausted real 'forces of the working class' (and not such as exist merely in the declamations of the tub-thumpers). One must understand this and reckon with the necessary, or rather inevitable, *slackening* of the rate of growth of *new* forces of the working class.

When the Mensheviks shout about the 'Bonapartism' of the Bolsheviks (who, they claim, rely on troops and on the machinery of state against the will of 'democracy'), they magnificently express the tactics of the bourgeoisie; and Milyukov, from his own standpoint, is right when he supports them, supports the 'Kronstadt' (spring of 1921) slogans. The bourgeoisie quite correctly takes into consideration the fact that the *real* 'forces of the working class' now consist of the mighty vanguard of that class (the Russian Communist Party, which – not at one stroke, but in the course of twenty-five years – won for itself by deeds the role, the name and the power of the 'vanguard' of the only revolutionary class) plus the elements which have been most weakened by being declassed, and which are most susceptible to Menshevik and anarchist vacillations.

The slogan 'more faith in the forces of the working class' is now being used, *in fact*, to increase the influence of the Mensheviks and anarchists, as was vividly proved and demonstrated by Kronstadt in the spring of 1921. Every class-conscious worker should expose and send packing those who shout about our having 'lost faith in the forces of the working class', because these tub-thumpers are actually the accomplices of the bourgeoisie and the landowners, who seek to weaken the proletariat for their benefit by helping to spread the influence of the Mensheviks and the anarchists.

That is the crux of the matter if we dispassionately examine what the concept 'forces of the working class' really means.

Gentlemen, what are you really doing to promote non-Party people to what is the main 'front' today, the economic front, for the work of economic development? That is the question that class-conscious workers should put to the tub-thumpers. That is how the tub-thumpers always can and should be exposed. That is how it can always be proved that, actually, they are not assisting but hindering economic development; that they are not assisting but hindering the proletarian revolution; that they are pursuing not proletarian, but petty-bourgeois aims; and that they are serving an alien class.

Our slogans are: down with the tub-thumpers! Down with the unwitting accomplices of the whiteguards who are repeating the mistakes of the hapless Kronstadt mutineers of the spring of 1921! Get down to businesslike, practical work that will take into account the specific features of the present situation and its tasks. We need not phrases but deeds.

A sober estimation of these specific features and of the real, not imaginary, class forces tells us:

The period of unprecedented proletarian achievements in the military, administrative and political fields has given way to a period in which the growth of new forces will be much slower; and that period did not set in by accident, it was inevitable; it was due to the operation not of persons or parties, but of objective causes. In the economic field, development is inevitably more difficult, slower, and more gradual; that arises from the very nature of the activities in this field compared with military, administrative and political activities. It follows from the specific difficulties of this work, from its being more deep-rooted, if one may so express it.

That is why we shall strive to formulate our tasks in this new, higher stage of the struggle with the greatest, with treble caution. We shall formulate them as moderately as possible. We shall make as many concessions as possible within the limits, of course, of what the proletariat *can* concede and yet remain the ruling class. We shall collect the moderate tax in kind as quickly as possible and allow the greatest possible scope for the development, strengthening and revival of peasant farming. We shall lease the enterprises that are not absolutely essential for us to lessees, including private capitalists and foreign concessionaires. We need a bloc, or alliance, between the proletarian state and state capitalism against the petty-bourgeois element. We must achieve this alliance skilfully, following the rule: 'Measure your cloth seven times before you cut.' We shall leave ourselves a smaller field of work, only what is absolutely necessary. We shall concentrate the enfeebled forces of the working class on something *less*, but we shall consolidate ourselves all the more and put ourselves to the test of practical experience not once or twice, but over and over again. Step by step, inch by inch – for at present the 'troops' we have at our command *cannot* advance any other way on the difficult road we have to travel, in the stern conditions under which we are living, and amidst the dangers we have to face. Those who find this work 'dull', 'uninteresting' and 'unintelligible', those who turn up their noses or become panic-stricken, or who become intoxicated with their own declamations about the absence of the 'previous elation', the 'previous enthusiasm', etc., had better be 'relieved of their jobs' and given a back seat, so as to prevent them from causing harm; for they will not or cannot understand the specific features of the present stage, the present phase of the struggle.

Amidst the colossal ruin of the country and the exhaustion of the forces of the proletariat, by a series of almost super-human efforts, we are tackling the most difficult job: laying the foundation for a really socialist economy, for the regular exchange of commodities (or, more correctly, exchange of products) between industry and agriculture. The enemy is still far stronger than we are; anarchic, profiteering, individual commodity exchange is undermining our efforts at every step. We clearly see the difficulties and will systematically and perseveringly overcome them. More scope for independent local enterprise; more forces to the localities; more attention to their practical experience. The working class can heal its wounds, its proletarian 'class forces' can recuperate, and the confidence of the peasantry in proletarian leadership can be strengthened *only* as real success is achieved in restoring industry and in bringing about a regular exchange of products through the medium of the state that benefits both the peasant and the worker. And as we achieve this we shall get an influx of new forces, not as quickly as every one of us would like, perhaps, but we shall get it nevertheless.

Let us get down to work, to slower, more cautious, more persevering and persistent work!

20 August 1921

Notes of a Publicist

On Ascending a High Mountain; the Harm of Despondency; the Utility of Trade; Attitude towards the Mensheviks, Etc.

I. *By Way of Example*

Let us picture to ourselves a man ascending a very high, steep and hitherto unexplored mountain. Let us assume that he has overcome unprecedented difficulties and dangers and has succeeded in reaching a much higher point than any of his predecessors, but still has not reached the summit. He finds himself in a position where it is not only difficult and dangerous to proceed in the direction and along the path he has chosen, but positively impossible. He is forced to turn back, descend, seek another path, longer, perhaps, but one that will enable him to reach the summit. The descent from the height that no one before him has reached proves, perhaps, to be more dangerous and difficult for our imaginary traveller than the ascent – it is easier to slip; it is not so easy to choose a foothold; there is not that exhilaration that one feels in going upwards, straight to the goal, etc. One has to tie a rope round oneself, spend hours with all alpenstock to cut footholds or a projection to which the rope could be tied firmly; one has to move at a snail's pace, and move downwards, descend, away from the goal; and one does not know where this extremely dangerous and painful descent will end, or whether there is a fairly safe detour by which one can ascend more boldly, more quickly and more directly to the summit.

It would hardly be natural to suppose that a man who had climbed to such an unprecedented height but found himself in such a position did not have his moments of despondency. In all probability these moments would be more numerous, more frequent and harder to bear if he heard the voices of those below, who, through a telescope and from a safe distance, are watching his dangerous descent, which cannot even be described as what the *Smena Vekh* people call 'ascending with the brakes on';[1] brakes presuppose a well-designed and tested vehicle, a well-prepared road and previously tested appliances. In this case, however, there is no vehicle, no road, absolutely nothing that had been tested beforehand.

The voices from below ring with malicious joy. They do not conceal it; they chuckle gleefully and shout: 'He'll fall in a minute! Serves him right, the lunatic!' Others try to conceal their malicious glee and behave mostly like Judas Golovlyov.[2] They moan and raise their eyes to heaven in sorrow, as if to say: 'It grieves us sorely to see our fears justified! But did not we, who have spent all our lives working out a judicious plan for scaling this mountain, demand that the ascent be postponed until our plan was complete? And if we so vehemently protested against taking this path, which this lunatic is now

---

1   A certain revival of capitalist elements in Soviet Russia following the implementation of the New Economic Policy served as the social foundation for this trend. When its adherents saw that foreign military intervention could not overthrow Soviet rule they began advocating cooperation with the Soviet government, hoping for a bourgeois regeneration of the Soviet state. They regarded the New Economic Policy as an evolution of Soviet rule towards the restoration of capitalism. Some of them were prepared loyally to cooperate with the Soviet government and promote the country's economic rejuvenation. Subsequently, most of them openly sided with the counter-revolution.

2   *Judas Golovlyov* – a landowner and main personage of M. Y. Saltykov-Shchedrin's *The Golovlyov Family*. He was called Judas for his bigotry, hypocrisy and callousness. The name Judas Golovlyov has become a synonym for these negative traits.

abandoning (look, look, he has turned back! He is descending! A single step is taking him hours of preparation! And yet we were roundly abused when time and again we demanded moderation and caution!), if we so fervently censured this lunatic and warned everybody against imitating and helping him, we did so entirely because of our devotion to the great plan to scale this mountain, and in order to prevent this great plan from being generally discredited!'

Happily, in the circumstances we have described, our imaginary traveller cannot hear the voices of these people who are 'true friends' of the idea of ascent; if he did, they would probably nauseate him. And nausea, it is said, does not help one to keep a clear head and a firm step, particularly at high altitudes.

II. Without Metaphors

An analogy is not proof. Every analogy is lame. These are incontrovertible and common truths; but it would do no harm to recall them in order to see the limits of every analogy more clearly.

Russia's proletariat rose to a gigantic height in its revolution, not only when it is compared with 1789 and 1793, but also when compared with 1871. We must take stock of what we have done and what we have not as dispassionately, as clearly and as concretely as possible. If we do that we shall be able to keep clear heads. We shall not suffer from nausea, illusions or despondency.

We wound up the bourgeois-democratic revolution more thoroughly than had ever been done before anywhere in the world. That is a great gain, and no power on earth can deprive us of it.

We accomplished the task of getting out of the most reactionary imperialist war in a revolutionary way. That, too, is a gain no power on earth can deprive us of; it is a gain which is all the more valuable for the reason that reactionary imperialist massacres are inevitable in the not distant future if capitalism continues to exist; and the people of the twentieth century will not be so easily satisfied with a second edition of the 'Basle Manifesto', with which the renegades, the heroes of the Second and the Two-and-a-Half Internationals, fooled themselves and the workers in 1912 and 1914–18.

We have created a Soviet type of state and by that we have ushered in a new era in world history, the era of the political rule of the proletariat, which is to supersede the era of bourgeois rule. Nobody can deprive us of this, either, although the Soviet type of state will have the finishing touches put to it only with the aid of the practical experience of the working class of several countries.

But we have not finished building even the foundations of socialist economy and the hostile powers of moribund capitalism can still deprive us of that. We must clearly appreciate this and frankly admit it; for there is nothing more dangerous than illusions (and vertigo, particularly at high altitudes). And there is absolutely nothing terrible, nothing that should give legitimate grounds for the slightest despondency, in admitting this bitter truth; for we have always urged and reiterated the elementary truth of Marxism – that the joint efforts of the workers of several advanced countries are needed for the victory of socialism. We are still alone and in a backward country, a country that was ruined more than others, but we have accomplished a great deal. More than that – we have preserved intact the army of the revolutionary proletarian forces; we have preserved its manoeuvring ability; we have kept clear heads and can soberly calculate where, when and how far to retreat (in order to leap further forward); where, when and how to set to work to alter what has remained unfinished. Those Communists are doomed who imagine that it is possible to finish such an epoch-making undertaking as completing the foundations of socialist economy (particularly in a small-peasant country) without making mistakes, without retreats, without numerous alterations to what is unfinished or wrongly done. Communists who have no illusions, who do not give way to despondency, and who preserve their strength and flexibility 'to begin from the beginning' over and over again in approaching an extremely difficult task, are not doomed (and in all probability will not perish).

And still less permissible is it for us to give way to the slightest degree of despondency; we have still less grounds for doing so because, notwithstanding the ruin, poverty, backwardness and starvation prevailing in our country, in the *economics* that prepare the way for socialism we have *begun to make progress*, while side by side with us, all over the world, countries which are more advanced, and a thousand times wealthier and militarily stronger than we are, *are still retrogressing* in *their* own vaunted, familiar, capitalist economic field, in which they have worked for centuries.

III. *Catching Foxes; Levi and Serrati*

The following is said to be the most reliable method of catching foxes. The fox that is being tracked is surrounded at a certain distance with a rope which is set at a little height from the snow-covered ground and to which are attached little red flags. Fearing this obviously artificial human device, the fox will emerge only if and where an opening is allowed in this fence of flags; and the hunter waits for it at this opening. One would think that caution would be the most marked trait of an animal that is hunted by everybody. But it turns out that in this case, too, 'virtue unduly prolonged' is a fault. The fox is caught precisely because it is over-cautious.

I must confess to a mistake I made at the Third Congress of the Communist International also as a result of over-caution. At that Congress, I was on the extreme right flank. I am convinced that it was the only correct stand to take, for a very large (and influential) group of delegates, headed by many German, Hungarian and Italian comrades, occupied an inordinately 'left' and incorrectly left position, and far too often, instead of soberly weighing up the situation that was not very favourable for immediate and direct revolutionary action, they vigorously indulged in the waving of little red flags. Out of caution and a desire to prevent this undoubtedly wrong deviation towards leftism from giving a false direction to the whole tactics of the Communist International, I did all I could to defend Levi. I suggested that perhaps he had lost his head (I did not deny that he had lost his head) because he had been very frightened by the mistakes of the lefts; and I argued that there had been cases of Communists who had lost their heads 'finding' them again afterwards. Even while admitting, under pressure of the lefts, that Levi was a Menshevik, I said that such an admission did not settle the question. For example, the whole history of the fifteen years of struggle between the Mensheviks and the Bolsheviks in Russia (1903–17) proves, as the three Russian revolutions also prove, that, in general, the Mensheviks were absolutely wrong and that they were, in fact, agents of the bourgeoisie in the working-class movement. This fact is incontrovertible. But this incontrovertible fact does not eliminate the other fact that in *individual* cases the Mensheviks were right and the Bolsheviks wrong, as, for example, on the question of boycotting the Stolypin Duma in 1907.

Eight months have elapsed since the Third Congress of the Communist International. Obviously, our controversy with the Lefts is now outdated; events have settled it. It has been proved that I was wrong about Levi, because he has definitely shown that he took the Menshevik path not accidentally, not temporarily, not by 'going too far' in combating the very dangerous mistakes of the lefts, but deliberately and permanently, because of his very nature. Instead of honestly admitting that it was necessary for him to appeal for readmission to the party after the Third Congress of the Communist International, as every person who had temporarily lost his head when irritated by some mistakes committed by the lefts should have done, Levi began to play sly tricks on the party, to try to put a spoke in its wheel, i.e., actually he began to serve those agents of the bourgeoisie, the Second and the Two-and-a-Half Internationals. Of course, the German Communists were quite right when they retaliated to this recently by expelling several more gentlemen from their party, those who were found to be secretly helping Paul Levi in this noble occupation.

The development of the German and Italian Communist Parties since the Third Congress of the Comintern has shown that the mistakes committed by the lefts at that Congress have been noted and are being rectified – little by little, slowly, but steadily; the decisions of the Third Congress of the Communist International are being loyally carried out. The process of transforming the old type of European parliamentary party – which in fact is reformist and only slightly tinted with revolutionary colours – into a *new type* of party, into a genuinely revolutionary, genuinely communist, party, is an extremely arduous one. This is demonstrated most clearly, perhaps, by the example of France. The process of changing the *type* of Party work in everyday life, of getting it out of the humdrum channel; the process of converting the Party into the vanguard of the revolutionary proletariat without permitting it to become divorced from the masses, but, on the contrary, by linking it more and more closely with them, imbuing them with revolutionary consciousness and rousing them for the revolutionary struggle, is a very difficult, but most important, one. If the European Communists do not take advantage of the intervals (probably very short) between the periods of particularly acute revolutionary battles – such as took place in many capitalist countries of Europe and America in 1921 and the beginning of 1922 – for the purpose of bringing about this fundamental, internal, profound reorganisation of the whole structure of their parties and of their work, they will be committing the gravest of crimes. Fortunately, there is no reason to fear this. The quiet, steady, calm, not very rapid, but profound, work of creating genuine communist parties, genuine revolutionary vanguards of the proletariat, has begun and is proceeding in Europe and America.

Political lessons taken even from the observation of such a trivial thing as catching foxes prove to be useful. On the one hand, excessive caution leads to mistakes. On the other hand, it must not be forgotten that if we give way to mere 'sentiment' or indulge in the waving of little red flags instead of soberly weighing up the situation, we may commit irreparable mistakes; we may perish where there is absolutely no need to, although the difficulties are great.

Paul Levi now wants to get into the good graces of the bourgeoisie – and, *consequently*, of its agents, the Second and the Two-and-a-Half Internationals – by republishing precisely those writings of Rosa Luxemburg in which she was wrong. We shall reply to this by quoting two lines from a good old Russian fable:[3] 'Eagles may at times fly lower than hens, but hens can never rise to the height of eagles.' Rosa Luxemburg was mistaken on the question of the independence of Poland; she was mistaken in 1903 in her appraisal of Menshevism; she was mistaken on the theory of the accumulation of capital; she was mistaken in July 1914, when, together with Plekhanov, Vandervelde, Kautsky and others, she advocated unity between the Bolsheviks and Mensheviks; she was mistaken in what she wrote in prison in 1918 (she corrected most of these mistakes at the end of 1918 and the beginning of 1919 after she was released). But in spite of her

---

3 This is a reference to the fable *The Eagle and the Hens* by Ivan Krylov.

mistakes she was – and remains for us – an eagle. And not only will communists all over the world cherish her memory, but her biography and her *complete* works (the publication of which the German communists are inordinately delaying, which can only be partly excused by the tremendous losses they are suffering in their severe struggle) will serve as useful manuals for training many generations of communists all over the world. 'Since 4 August 1914, German social democracy has been a stinking corpse' – this statement will make Rosa Luxemburg's name famous in the history of the international working-class movement.[4] And, of course, in the backyard of the working-class movement, among the dung heaps, hens like Paul Levi, Scheidemann, Kautsky and all that fraternity will cackle over the mistakes committed by the great communist. To every man his own.

As for Serrati, he is like a bad egg, which bursts with a loud noise and with an exceptionally pungent smell. Is it not too rich to get carried at 'his' congress a resolution that declares readiness to submit to the decision of the Congress of the Communist International, then to send old Lazzari to the congress, and finally, to cheat the workers as brazenly as a horse-coper? The Italian communists who are training a real party of the revolutionary proletariat in Italy will now be able to give the working masses an object lesson in political chicanery and Menshevism. The useful, repelling effect of this will not be felt immediately, not without many repeated object lessons, but it will be felt. The victory of the Italian communists is assured if they do not isolate themselves from the masses, if they do not lose patience in the hard work of exposing all of Serrati's chicanery to rank-and-file workers in

---

4   In the Reichstag on 4 August 1914, the social democratic faction voted with the bourgeois representatives in favour of granting the imperial government war credits amounting to 5,000 million marks, thereby approving Wilhelm II's imperialist policy.

a practical way, if they do not yield to the very easy and very dangerous temptation to say 'minus *a*' whenever Serrati says '*a*', if they steadily train the masses to adopt a revolutionary world outlook and prepare them for revolutionary action, if they also take practical advantage of the practical and magnificent (although costly) object lessons of fascism.

Levi and Serrati are not characteristic in themselves; they are characteristic of the modern type of the extreme left wing of petty-bourgeois democracy, of the camp of the 'other side', the camp of the international capitalists, the camp that is against us. The whole of 'their' camp, from Gompers to Serrati, are gloating, exulting or else shedding crocodile tears over our retreat, our 'descent', our New Economic Policy. Let them gloat, let them perform their clownish antics. To every man his own. But we shall not harbour any illusions or give way to despondency. If we are not afraid of admitting our mistakes, not afraid of making repeated efforts to rectify them – we shall reach the very summit. The cause of the international bloc from Gompers to Serrati is doomed.[5]

Late February 1922

---

5 The article was never completed.

Eleventh Congress of the RCP(B)

*Political Report of the Central Committee
of the RCP(B) 27 March*
...

Hence ... I shall now proceed to deal with the issues which, in my opinion, have been the major political questions of the past year and which will be such in the ensuing year.[1] It seems to me that the political report of the Central Committee should not merely deal with the events of the year under review, but also point out (that, at any rate, is what I usually do) the main, fundamental political lessons of the events of that year, so that we may learn something for the ensuing year and be in a position to correctly determine our policy for that year.

---

1 The Eleventh Congress of the RCP(B) was held in Moscow on 27 March–2 April 1922. It was convened a year after the Civil War ended and the country went over to peaceful economic development. Its purpose was to sum up the results of the first year of the New Economic Policy and map out the further plan of socialist construction.

This was the last Party congress in which Lenin participated. It was attended by 522 delegates with a casting vote and 165 delegates with a consultative voice. It discussed 1) the political report of the Central Committee, 2) the organisation report of the Central Committee, 3) the report of the Auditing Commission, 4) the report of the Central Control Commission, 5) the report of the Communist International, 6) the trade unions, 7) the Red Army, 8) the financial policy, 9) the results of the Party purge and the accompanying strengthening of the Party ranks, and the co-reports on work with young people and on the press and propaganda, and 10) elections to the Central Committee and the Central Control Commission.

Lenin opened the congress, and delivered the political report of the RCP(B), a closing speech on the report and a speech closing the congress.

The New Economic Policy is, of course, the major question. This has been the dominant question throughout the year under review. If we have any important, serious and irrevocable gain to record for this year (and I am not so very sure that we have), it is that we have learnt something from the launching of this New Economic Policy. If we have learnt even a little, then, during the past year, we have learnt a great deal in this field. And the test of whether we have really learnt anything, and to what extent, will probably be made by subsequent events of a kind which we ourselves can do little to determine, as for example the impending financial crisis. It seems to me that in connection with the New Economic Policy, the most important things to keep in mind as a basis for all our arguments, as a means of testing our experience during the past year, and of learning practical lessons for the ensuing year, are contained in the following three points.

First, the New Economic Policy is important for us primarily as a means of testing whether we are really establishing a link with the peasant economy. In the preceding period of development of our revolution, when all our attention and all our efforts were concentrated mainly on, or almost entirely absorbed by, the task of repelling invasion, we could not devote the necessary attention to this link; we had other things to think about. To some extent we could and had to ignore this bond when we were confronted by the absolutely urgent and overshadowing task of warding off the danger of being immediately crushed by the gigantic forces of world imperialism.

The turn towards the New Economic Policy was decided on at the last congress with exceptional unanimity, with even greater unanimity than other questions have been decided by our Party (which, it must be admitted, is generally distinguished for its unanimity). This unanimity showed that the need for a new approach to socialist economy had fully matured. People who differed on many questions, and who assessed the situation from different angles, unanimously and very quickly and unhesitatingly agreed that we lacked a real approach to socialist economy, to the task of building its foundation; that the only means of finding this approach was the New Economic Policy. Owing to the course taken by the development of war events, by the development of political events, by the development of capitalism in the old, civilised West, and owing also to the social and political conditions that developed in the colonies, we were the first to make a breach in the old bourgeois world at a time when our country was economically, if not the most backward, at any rate one of the most backward countries in the world. The vast majority of the peasants in our country are engaged in small individual farming. The items of our programme of building a communist society, that we could apply immediately, were to some extent outside the sphere of activity of the broad mass of the peasantry, upon whom we imposed very heavy obligations, which we justified on the grounds that war permitted no wavering in this matter. Taken as a whole, this was accepted as justification by the peasantry, notwithstanding the mistakes we could not avoid. On the whole, the mass of the peasantry realised and understood that the enormous burdens imposed upon them were necessary in order to save the workers' and peasants' rule from the landowners and prevent it from being strangled by capitalist invasion, which threatened to wrest away all the gains of the revolution. But there was no link between the peasant economy and the economy that was being built up in the nationalised, socialised factories and on state farms.

We saw this clearly at the last Party congress. We saw it so clearly that there was no hesitation whatever in the Party on the question whether the New Economic Policy was inevitable or not.

It is amusing to read what is said about our decision in the numerous publications of the various Russian parties abroad.

There are only trifling differences in the opinions they express. Living with memories of the past, they still continue to reiterate that to this day the Left Communists are opposed to the New Economic Policy. In 1921 they remembered what had occurred in 1918 and what our Left Communists themselves have forgotten; and they go on chewing this over and over again, assuring the world that these Bolsheviks are a sly and false lot, and that they are concealing from Europe that they have disagreements in their ranks. Reading this, one says to oneself, 'Let them go on fooling themselves.' If this is what they imagine is going on in this country, we can judge the degree of intelligence of these allegedly highly educated old fogies who have fled abroad. We know that there have been no disagreements in our ranks, and the reason for this is that the practical necessity of a different approach to the task of building the foundation of socialist economy was clear to all.

There was no link between the peasant economy and the new economy we tried to create. Does it exist now? Not yet. We are only approaching it. The whole significance of the New Economic Policy – which our press still often searches for everywhere except where it should search – the whole purpose of this policy is to find a way of establishing a link between the new economy, which we are creating with such enormous effort, and the peasant economy. That is what stands to our credit; without it we would not be communist revolutionaries.

We began to develop the new economy in an entirely new way, brushing aside everything old. Had we not begun to develop it we would have been utterly defeated in the very first months, in the very first years. But the fact that we began to develop this new economy with such splendid audacity does not mean that we must necessarily continue in the same way. Why should we? There is no reason.

From the very beginning we said that we had to undertake an entirely new task, and that unless we received speedy assistance from our comrades, the workers in the capitalistically more developed countries, we should encounter incredible difficulties and certainly make a number of mistakes. The main thing is to be able dispassionately to examine where such mistakes have been made and to start again from the beginning. If we begin from the beginning, not twice, but many times, it will show that we are not bound by prejudice, and that we are approaching our task, which is the greatest the world has ever seen, with a sober outlook.

Today, as far as the New Economic Policy is concerned the main thing is to assimilate the experience of the past year correctly. That must be done, and we want to do it. And if we want to do it, come what may (and we do want to do it, and shall do it!), we must know that the problem of the New Economic Policy, the fundamental, decisive and overriding problem, is to establish a link between the new economy that we have begun to create (very badly, very clumsily, but have nevertheless begun to create, on the basis of an entirely new, socialist economy, of a new system of production and distribution) and the peasant economy, by which millions and millions of peasants obtain their livelihood.

This link has been lacking, and we must create it before anything else. Everything else must be subordinated to this. We have still to ascertain the extent to which the New Economic Policy has succeeded in creating this link without destroying what we have begun so clumsily to build.

We are developing our economy together with the peasantry. We shall have to alter it many times and organise it in such a way that it will provide a link between our socialist work on large-scale industry and agriculture and the work every peasant is doing as best he can, struggling out of poverty, without philosophising (for how can philosophising help him to extricate himself from his position and save him from the very real danger of a painful death from starvation?).

We must reveal this link so that we may see it clearly, so that all the people may see it, and so that the whole mass of the peasantry may see that there is a connection between their present severe, incredibly ruined, incredibly impoverished and painful existence and the work which is being done for the sake of remote socialist ideals. We must bring about a situation where the ordinary rank-and-file working man realises that he has obtained some improvement, and that he has obtained it not in the way a few peasants obtained improvements under the rule of landowners and capitalists, when every improvement (undoubtedly there were improvements and very big ones) was accompanied by insult, derision and humiliation for the *muzhik*, by violence against the masses, which not a single peasant has forgotten, and which will not be forgotten in Russia for decades. Our aim is to restore the link, to prove to the peasant by deeds that we are beginning with what is intelligible, familiar and immediately accessible to him, in spite of his poverty, and not with something remote and fantastic from the peasant's point of view. We must prove that we can help him and that in this period, when the small peasant is in a state of appalling ruin, impoverishment and starvation, the Communists are really helping him. Either we prove that, or he will send us to the devil. That is absolutely inevitable.

Such is the significance of the New Economic Policy; it is the basis of our entire policy; it is the major lesson taught by the whole of the past year's experience in applying the New Economic Policy, and, so to speak, our main political rule for the coming year. The peasant is allowing us credit, and, of course, after what he has lived through, he cannot do otherwise. Taken in the mass, the peasants go on saying: 'Well, if you are not able to do it yet, we shall wait; perhaps you will learn.' But this credit cannot go on for ever.

This we must know; and having obtained credit we must hurry. We must know that the time is approaching when this peasant country will no longer give us credit, when it will demand cash, to use a commercial term. It will say: 'You have postponed payment for so many months, so many years. But by this time, dear rulers, you must have learnt the most sound and reliable method of helping us free ourselves from poverty, want, starvation and ruin. You can do it, you have proved it.' This is the test that we shall inevitably have to face; and, in the last analysis, this test will decide everything: the fate of the NEP and the fate of Communist rule in Russia.

Shall we accomplish our immediate task or not? Is this NEP fit for anything or not? If the retreat turns out to be correct tactics, we must link up with the peasant masses while we are in retreat, and subsequently march forward with them a hundred times more slowly, but firmly and unswervingly, in a way that will always make it apparent to them that we really are marching forward. Then our cause will be absolutely invincible, and no power on earth can vanquish us. We did not accomplish this in the first year. We must say this frankly. And I am profoundly convinced (and our New Economic Policy enables us to draw this conclusion quite definitely and firmly) that if we appreciate the enormous danger harboured by the NEP and concentrate all our forces on its weak points, we shall solve this problem.

Link up with the peasant masses, with the rank-and-file working peasants, and begin to move forward immeasurably, infinitely more slowly than we expected, but in such a way that the entire mass will actually move forward with us. If we do that we shall in time progress much more quickly than we even dream of today. This, in my opinion, is the first fundamental political lesson of the New Economic Policy.

The second, more specific lesson is the test through competition between state and capitalist enterprises. We are now forming mixed companies – I shall have something to say about these later on – which, like our state trade and our New Economic Policy as a whole, mean that we Communists are resorting to commercial, capitalist methods. These mixed companies are also important because through them practical competition is created between capitalist methods and our methods. Consider it practically. Up to now we have been writing a programme and making promises. In its time this was absolutely necessary. It is impossible to launch a world revolution without a programme and without promises. If the whiteguards, including the Mensheviks, jeer at us for this, it only shows that the Mensheviks and the socialists of the Second and Two-and-a-Half Internationals have no idea, in general, of the way a revolution develops. We could proceed in no other way.

Now, however, the position is that we must put our work to a serious test, and not the sort of test that is made by control institutions set up by the Communists themselves, even though these control institutions are magnificent, even though they are almost the ideal control institutions in the Soviet system and the Party; such a test may be mockery from the point of view of the actual requirements of the peasant economy, but it is certainly no mockery from the standpoint of our construction. We are now setting up these control institutions but I am referring not to this test but to the test from the point of view of the entire economy.

The capitalist was able to supply things. He did it inefficiently, charged exorbitant prices, and insulted and robbed us. The ordinary workers and peasants, who do not argue about communism because they do not know what it is, are well aware of this.

'But the capitalists were, after all, able to supply things – are you? You are not able to do it.' That is what we heard last spring; though not always clearly audible, it was the undertone of the whole of last spring's crisis. 'As people you are splendid, but you cannot cope with the economic task you have undertaken.' This is the simple and withering criticism which the peasantry – and through the peasantry, some sections of workers – levelled at the Communist Party last year. That is why in the NEP question, this old point acquires such significance.

We need a real test. The capitalists are operating alongside us. They are operating like robbers; they make profit; but they know how to do things. But you – you are trying to do it in a new way: you make no profit, your principles are communist, your ideals are splendid; they are written out so beautifully that you seem to be saints, that you should go to heaven while you are still alive. But can you get things done? We need a test, a real test, not the kind the Central Control Commission makes when it censures somebody and the All-Russia Central Executive Committee imposes some penalty. Yes, we want a real test from the viewpoint of the national economy.

We Communists have received numerous deferments, and more credit has been allowed us than any other government has ever been given. Of course, we Communists helped to get rid of the capitalists and landowners. The peasants appreciate this and have given us an extension of time, longer credit, but only for a certain period. After that comes the test: can you run the economy as well as the others? The old capitalist can; you cannot.

That is the first lesson, the first main part of the political report of the Central Committee. We cannot run the economy. This has been proved in the past year. I would like very much to quote the example of several Gos-trests (if I may express myself in the beautiful Russian language that Turgenev praised so highly)[2] to show how we run the economy.

Unfortunately, for a number of reasons, and largely owing to ill health, I have been unable to elaborate this part of my

---

2   An ironical reference to the habit, then emerging, of abbreviating the names of various institutions. Here the abbreviation stands for state trusts. *Translator's note.*

report and so I must confine myself to expressing my conviction, which is based on my observations of what is going on. During the past year we showed quite clearly that we cannot run the economy. That is the fundamental lesson. Either we prove the opposite in the coming year, or Soviet power will not be able to exist. And the greatest danger is that not everybody realises this. If all of us Communists, the responsible officials, clearly realise that we lack the ability to run the economy, that we must learn from the very beginning, then we shall win – that, in my opinion, is the fundamental conclusion that should be drawn. But many of us do not appreciate this and believe that if there are people who do think that way, it can only be the ignorant, who have not studied communism; perhaps they will someday learn and understand. No, excuse me, the point is not that the peasant or the non-Party worker has not studied communism, but that the time has passed when the job was to draft a programme and call upon the people to carry out this great programme. That time has passed. Today you must prove that you can give practical economic assistance to the workers and to the peasants under the present difficult conditions, and thus demonstrate to them that you have stood the test of competition.

The mixed companies that we have begun to form, in which private capitalists, Russian and foreign, and Communists participate, provide one of the means by which we can learn to organise competition properly and show that we are no less able to establish a link with the peasant economy than the capitalists; that we can meet its requirements; that we can help the peasant make progress even at his present level, in spite of his backwardness, for it is impossible to change him in a brief span of time.

That is the sort of competition confronting us as an absolutely urgent task. It is the pivot of the New Economic Policy and, in my opinion, the quintessence of the Party's policy.

We are faced with any number of purely political problems and difficulties. You know what they are: Genoa, the danger of intervention. The difficulties are enormous but they are nothing compared with this economic difficulty. We know how things are done in the political field; we have gained considerable experience; we have learned a lot about bourgeois diplomacy. It is the sort of thing the Mensheviks taught us for fifteen years, and we got something useful out of it. This is not new.

But here is something we must do now in the economic field. We must win the competition against the ordinary shop assistant, the ordinary capitalist, the merchant, who will go to the peasant without arguing about communism. Just imagine, he will not begin to argue about communism, but will argue in this way – if you want to obtain something, or carry on trade properly, or if you want to build, I will do the building at a high price; the Communists will, perhaps, build at a higher price, perhaps even ten times higher. It is this kind of agitation that is now the crux of the matter; herein lies the root of economics.

I repeat, thanks to our correct policy, the people allowed us a deferment of payment and credit, and this, to put it in terms of the NEP, is a promissory note. But this promissory note is undated, and you cannot learn from the wording when it will be presented for redemption. Therein lies the danger; this is the specific feature that distinguishes these political promissory notes from ordinary, commercial promissory notes. We must concentrate all our attention on this, and not rest content with the fact that there are responsible and good Communists in all the state trusts and mixed companies. That is of no use, because these Communists do not know how to run the economy and, in that respect, are inferior to the ordinary capitalist salesmen, who have received their training in big factories and big firms. But we refuse to admit this; in this field communist conceit –

komchvanstvo,[3] to use the great Russian language again – still persists. The whole point is that the responsible Communists, even the best of them, who are unquestionably honest and loyal, who in the old days suffered penal servitude and did not fear death, do not know how to trade, because they are not businessmen, they have not learnt to trade, do not want to learn and do not understand that they must start learning from the beginning. Communists, revolutionaries who have accomplished the greatest revolution in the world, on whom the eyes of, if not forty pyramids, then, at all events, forty European countries are turned in the hope of emancipation from capitalism, must learn from ordinary salesmen. But these ordinary salesmen have had ten years' warehouse experience and know the business, whereas the responsible Communists and devoted revolutionaries do not know the business, and do not even realise that they do not know it.

And so, comrades, if we do away with at least this elementary ignorance we shall achieve a tremendous victory. We must leave this congress with the conviction that we are ignorant of this business and with the resolve to start learning it from the bottom. After all, we have not ceased to be revolutionaries (although many say, and not altogether without foundation, that we have become bureaucrats) and can understand this simple thing, that in a new and unusually difficult undertaking we must be prepared to start from the beginning over and over again. If after starting you find yourselves at a dead end, start again, and go on doing it ten times if necessary, until you attain your object. Do not put on airs; do not be conceited because you are a Communist while there is some non-Party salesman, perhaps a whiteguard – and very likely he is a whiteguard – who can do things which economically must be done at all costs, but which you cannot do. If you, responsible Communists, who have hundreds of ranks and titles and wear

3   Literally, 'comconceit'. *Translator's note.*

communist and Soviet orders, realise this, you will attain your object, because this is something that can be learned.

We have some successes, even if only very tiny ones, to record for the past year, but they are insignificant. The main thing is that there is no realisation nor widespread conviction among all Communists that at the present time the responsible and most devoted Russian Communist is less able to perform these functions than any salesman of the old school. I repeat, we must start learning from the very beginning. If we realise this, we shall pass our test; and the test is a serious one which the impending financial crisis will set – the test set by the Russian and international market to which we are subordinated, with which we are connected, and from which we cannot isolate ourselves. The test is a crucial one, for here we may be beaten economically and politically.

That is how the question stands and it cannot be otherwise, for the competition will be very severe, and it will be decisive. We had many outlets and loopholes that enabled us to escape from our political and economic difficulties. We can proudly say that up to now we have been able to utilise these outlets and loopholes in various combinations corresponding to the varying circumstances. But now we have no other outlets. Permit me to say this to you without exaggeration, because in this respect it is really 'the last and decisive battle', not against international capitalism – against that we shall yet have many 'last and decisive battles' – but against Russian capitalism, against the capitalism that is growing out of the small peasant economy, the capitalism that is fostered by the latter. Here we shall have a fight on our hands in the immediate future, and the date of it cannot be fixed exactly. Here the 'last and decisive battle' is impending; here there are no political or any other flanking movements that we can undertake, because this is a test in competition with private capital. Either we pass this test in competition with private capital, or we fail completely. To help us pass it we have political power and a host of economic and other resources; we have everything you want except ability. We lack ability. And if we learn this simple lesson from the experience of last year and take it as our guiding line for the whole of 1922, we shall conquer this difficulty, too, in spite of the fact that it is much greater than the previous difficulty, for it rests upon ourselves. It is not like some external enemy. The difficulty is that we ourselves refuse to admit the unpleasant truth forced upon us; we refuse to undertake the unpleasant duty that the situation demands of us, namely to start learning from the beginning. That, in my opinion, is the second lesson that we must learn from the New Economic Policy.

The third, supplementary lesson is on the question of state capitalism. It is a pity Comrade Bukharin is not present at the congress. I should have liked to argue with him a little, but that had better be postponed to the next congress. On the question of state capitalism, I think that generally our press and our Party make the mistake of dropping into intellectualism, into liberalism; we philosophise about how state capitalism is to be interpreted, and look into old books. But in those old books you will not find what we are discussing; they deal with the state capitalism that exists under capitalism. Not a single book has been written about state capitalism under communism. It did not occur even to Marx to write a word on this subject; and he died without leaving a single precise statement or definite instruction on it. That is why we must overcome the difficulty entirely by ourselves. And if we make a general mental survey of our press and see what has been written about state capitalism, as I tried to do when I was preparing this report, we shall be convinced that it is missing the target, that it is looking in an entirely wrong direction.

The state capitalism discussed in all books on economics is that which exists under the capitalist system, where the state brings under its direct control certain capitalist enterprises. But ours is a proletarian state: it rests on the proletariat, it gives the proletariat all political privileges, and through the medium of the proletariat it attracts to itself the lower ranks of the peasantry (you remember that we began this work through the Poor Peasants' Committees). That is why very many people are misled by the term 'state capitalism'. To avoid this we must remember the fundamental thing that state capitalism in the form we have here is not dealt with in any theory, or in any books, for the simple reason that all the usual concepts connected with this term are associated with bourgeois rule in capitalist society. Our society is one which has left the rails of capitalism, but has not yet got on to new rails. The state in this society is not ruled by the bourgeoisie, but by the proletariat. We refuse to understand that when we say 'state' we mean ourselves, the proletariat, the vanguard of the working class. State capitalism is capitalism which we shall be able to restrain, and the limits of which we shall be able to fix. This state capitalism is connected with the state, and the state is the workers, the advanced section of the workers, the vanguard. We are the state.

State capitalism is capitalism that we must confine within certain bounds; but we have not yet learned to confine it within those bounds. That is the whole point. And it rests with us to determine what this state capitalism is to be. We have sufficient, quite sufficient, political power; we also have sufficient economic resources at our command, but the vanguard of the working class which has been brought to the forefront to directly supervise, to determine the boundaries, to demarcate, to subordinate and not be subordinated itself, lacks sufficient ability for it. All that is needed here is ability, and that is what we do not have.

Never before in history has there been a situation in which the proletariat, the revolutionary vanguard, possessed sufficient political power and had state capitalism existing alongside it. The whole question turns on our understanding that this is the capitalism that we can and must permit, that we can and must confine within certain bounds; for this capitalism is essential for the broad masses of the peasantry and for private capital, which must trade in such a way as to satisfy the needs of the peasantry. We must organise things in such a way as to make possible the customary operation of capitalist economy and capitalist exchange, because this is essential for the people. Without it, existence is impossible. All the rest is not an absolutely vital matter to this camp. They can resign themselves to all that. You Communists, you workers, you, the politically enlightened section of the proletariat, which undertook to administer the state, must be able to arrange it so that the state, which you have taken into your hands, shall function the way you want it to. Well, we have lived through a year; the state is in our hands; but has it operated the New Economic Policy in the way we wanted in this past year? No. But we refuse to admit that it did not operate in the way we wanted. How did it operate? The machine refused to obey the hand that guided it. It was like a car that was going not in the direction the driver desired, but in the direction someone else desired; as if it were being driven by some mysterious, lawless hand, God knows whose, perhaps of a profiteer, or of a private capitalist, or of both. Be that as it may, the car is not going quite in the direction the man at the wheel imagines, and often it goes in an altogether different direction. This is the main thing that must be remembered with regard to state capitalism. In this main field we must start learning from the very beginning, and only when we have thoroughly understood and appreciated this can we be sure that we shall learn.

Now I come to the question of halting the retreat, a question I dealt with in my speech at the Congress of Metalworkers. Since then I have not heard any objection, either in the Party press, or in private letters from comrades, or in the Central Committee. The Central Committee approved my plan, which was, that in the report of the Central Committee to the present congress strong emphasis should be laid on calling a halt to this retreat and that the congress should give binding instructions on behalf of the whole Party accordingly. For a year we have been retreating. On behalf of the Party we must now call a halt. The purpose pursued by the retreat has been achieved. This period is drawing, or has drawn, to a close. We now have a different objective, that of regrouping our forces. We have reached a new line; on the whole, we have conducted the retreat in fairly good order. True, not a few voices were heard from various sides which tried to convert this retreat into a stampede. Some – for example, several members of the group which bore the name Workers' Opposition (I don't think they had any right to that name) – argued that we were not retreating properly in some sector or other. Owing to their excessive zeal they found themselves at the wrong door, and now they realise it. At that time they did not see that their activities did not help us to correct our movement, but merely had the effect of spreading panic and hindering our effort to beat a disciplined retreat.

Retreat is a difficult matter, especially for revolutionaries who are accustomed to advance; especially when they have been accustomed to advance with enormous success for several years; especially if they are surrounded by revolutionaries in other countries who are longing for the time when they can launch an offensive. Seeing that we were retreating, several of them burst into tears in a disgraceful and childish manner, as was the case at the last extended Plenary Meeting of the Executive Committee of the Communist International. Moved by the best communist sentiments and communist aspirations, several of the comrades burst into tears because – oh horror! – the good Russian Communists were retreating.

Perhaps it is now difficult for me to understand this Western European mentality, although I lived for quite a number of years in those marvellous democratic countries as an exile. Perhaps from their point of view this is such a difficult matter to understand that it is enough to make one weep. We, at any rate, have no time for sentiment. It was clear to us that because we had advanced so successfully for many years and had achieved so many extraordinary victories (and all this in a country that was in an appalling state of ruin and lacked the material resources!), to consolidate that advance, since we had gained so much, it was absolutely essential for us to retreat. We could not hold all the positions we had captured in the first onslaught. On the other hand, it was because we had captured so much in the first onslaught, on the crest of the wave of enthusiasm displayed by the workers and peasants, that we had room enough to retreat a long distance, and can retreat still further now, without losing our main and fundamental positions. On the whole, the retreat was fairly orderly, although certain panic-stricken voices, among them that of the Workers' Opposition (this was the tremendous harm it did!), caused losses in our ranks, caused a relaxation of discipline, and disturbed the proper order of retreat. The most dangerous thing during a retreat is panic. When a whole army (I speak in the figurative sense) is in retreat, it cannot have the same morale as when it is advancing. At every step you find a certain mood of depression. We even had poets who wrote that people were cold and starving in Moscow, that 'everything before was bright and beautiful, but now trade and profiteering abound'. We have had quite a number of poetic effusions of this sort.

Of course, retreat breeds all this. That is where the serious danger lies; it is terribly difficult to retreat after a great victorious advance, for the relations are entirely different. During a victorious advance, even if discipline is relaxed, everybody presses forward of his own accord. During a retreat, however, discipline must be more conscious and is a hundred times more necessary, because, when the entire army is in retreat, it does not know or see where it should halt. It sees only retreat; under such circumstances a few panic-stricken voices are, at times, enough to cause a stampede. The danger here is enormous. When a real army is in retreat, machine guns are kept ready, and when an orderly retreat degenerates into a disorderly one, the command to fire is given, and quite rightly, too.

If, during an incredibly difficult retreat, when everything depends on preserving proper order, anyone spreads panic – even from the best of motives – the slightest breach of discipline must be punished severely, sternly, ruthlessly; and this applies not only to certain of our internal Party affairs, but also, and to a greater extent, to such gentry as the Mensheviks, and to all the gentry of the Two-and-a-Half International.

The other day I read an article by Comrade Rakosi in No 20 of the *Communist International* on a new book by Otto Bauer, from whom at one time we all learned, but who, like Kautsky, became a miserable petty bourgeois after the war.[4] Bauer now writes: 'There, they are now retreating to capitalism! We have always said that it was a bourgeois revolution.'

And the Mensheviks and Socialist-Revolutionaries, all of whom preach this sort of thing, are astonished when we declare that we shall shoot people for such things. They are

---

4 Here Lenin refers to Matyas Rakosi's article 'The New Economic Policy in Soviet Russia', which analyses Otto Bauer's pamphlet '*Der neue Kurs' in Sowjetrussland* ('The New Policy' in Soviet Russia), published in Vienna in 1921. Rakosi's article appeared on 22 March in the magazine *Communist International*, No 20. *Communist International*, organ of the Executive Committee of the Communist International, was published in Russian, German, French, English, Spanish and Chinese. The first issue was put out on 1 May 1919. Publication was stopped in June 1943 following the decision of the Presidium of the Comintern Executive Committee of 15 May 1943 to dissolve the Communist International.

amazed; but surely it is clear. When an army is in retreat a hundred times more discipline is required than when it is advancing, because during an advance everybody presses forward. If everybody started rushing back now, it would spell immediate and inevitable disaster.

The most important thing at such a moment is to retreat in good order, to fix the precise limits of the retreat, and not to give way to panic. And when a Menshevik says, 'You are now retreating; I have been advocating retreat all the time, I agree with you, I am your man, let us retreat together,' we say in reply, 'For the public manifestations of Menshevism our revolutionary courts must pass the death sentence, otherwise they are not our courts, but God knows what.'

They cannot understand this and exclaim: 'What dictatorial manners these people have!' They still think we are persecuting the Mensheviks because they fought us in Geneva.[5] But had we done that we should have been unable to hold power even for two months. Indeed, the sermons which Otto Bauer, the leaders of the Second and Two-and-a Half Internationals, the Mensheviks and Socialist-Revolutionaries preach express their true nature – 'The revolution has gone too far. What you are saying now we have been saying all the time, permit us to say it again.' But we say in reply: 'Permit us to put you before a firing squad for saying that. Either you refrain from expressing your views, or, if you insist on expressing your political views publicly in the present circumstances, when our position is far more difficult than it was when the whiteguards were directly attacking us, then you will have only yourselves to blame if we treat you as the worst and most pernicious whiteguard elements.' We must never forget this.

When I speak about halting the retreat I do not mean that we have learned to trade. On the contrary, I am of the oppo-

---

5 Lenin has in mind the struggle waged abroad between the Bolsheviks and the Mensheviks.

site opinion; and if my speech were to create that impression it would show that I had been misunderstood and that I am unable to express my thoughts properly.

The point, however, is that we must put a stop to the nervousness and fuss that have arisen with the introduction of the NEP – the desire to do everything in a new way and to adapt everything. We now have a number of mixed companies. True, we have only very few. There are nine companies formed in conjunction with foreign capitalists and sanctioned by the Commissariat of Foreign Trade. The Sokolnikov Commission.[6] has sanctioned six and the Northern Timber Trust[7] has sanctioned two. Thus we now have seventeen companies with an aggregate capital amounting to many millions, sanctioned by several government departments (of course, there is plenty of confusion with all these departments, so that some slip here is also possible). At any rate we have formed companies jointly with Russian and foreign capitalists. There are only a few of them. But this small but practical start shows that the Communists have been judged by what they do. They have not been judged by such high institutions as the Central Control Commission and the All-Russia Central Executive Committee. The Central Control Commission is a splendid institution, of course, and we shall now give it more power. For all that, the judgement these institutions pass on Communists is not – just imagine – recognised on the international market. [*Laughter.*] But now that ordinary Russian and foreign capitalists are joining the Communists in forming mixed companies, we say, 'We can do things after all; bad as

6 The Commission for Mixed Companies under the Council of Labour and Defence. This commission was set up by a decision of the Council of Labour and Defence on 15 February 1922. Its chairman was Sokolnikov.

7 The Northern Timber Trust was a special administrative body of the timber industry of the North White Sea area. It was established in 1921.

it is, meagre as it is, we have got something for a start.' True, it is not very much. Just think of it: a year has passed since we declared that we would devote all our energy (and it is said that we have a great deal of energy) to this matter, and in this year we have managed to form only seventeen companies.

This shows how devilishly clumsy and inept we are; how much Oblomovism still remains, for which we shall inevitably get a good thrashing. For all that, I repeat, a start, a reconnaissance has been made. The capitalists would not agree to have dealings with us if the elementary conditions for their operations did not exist. Even if only a very small section of them has agreed to this, it shows that we have scored a partial victory.

Of course, they will cheat us in these companies, cheat us so that it will take several years before matters are straightened out. But that does not matter. I do not say that that is a victory; it is a reconnaissance, which shows that we have an arena, we have a terrain, and can now stop the retreat.

The reconnaissance has revealed that we have concluded an insignificant number of agreements with capitalists; but we have concluded them for all that. We must learn from that and continue our operations. In this sense we must put a stop to nervousness, screaming and fuss. We received notes and telephone messages, one after another asking, 'Now that we have the NEP, may we be reorganised too?' Everybody is bustling, and we get utter confusion, nobody is doing any practical work; everybody is continuously arguing about how to adapt oneself to the NEP, but no practical results are forthcoming.

The merchants are laughing at us Communists, and in all probability are saying, 'Formerly there were Persuaders-in-Chief, now we have Talkers-in-Chief.'[8] That the capitalists

---

8 Persuader-in-Chief was the nickname given by the soldiers to A.F. Kerensky, then the war and navy minister of the Provisional Government, for trying to persuade the soldiers to start an offensive when he toured the

gloated over the fact that we started late, that we were not sharp enough – of that there need not be the slightest doubt. In this sense, I say, these instructions must be endorsed in the name of the congress.

The retreat is at an end. The principal methods of operation, of how we are to work with the capitalists, are outlined. We have examples, even if an insignificant number.

Stop philosophising and arguing about the NEP. Let the poets write verses; that is what they are poets for. But you economists, you stop arguing about the NEP and get more companies formed; check up on how many Communists we have who can organise successful competition with the capitalists.

The retreat has come to an end; it is now a matter of regrouping our forces. These are the instructions that the congress must pass so as to put an end to fuss and bustle. Calm down, do not philosophise; if you do, it will be counted as a black mark against you. Show by your practical efforts that you can work no less efficiently than the capitalists. The capitalists create an economic link with the peasants in order to amass wealth; you must create a link with peasant economy in order to strengthen the economic power of our proletarian state. You have the advantage over the capitalists in that political power is in your hands; you have a number of economic weapons at your command; the only trouble is that you cannot make proper use of them. Look at things more soberly. Cast off the tinsel, the festive communist garments, learn a simple thing simply, and we shall beat the private capitalist. We possess political power; we possess a host of economic weapons. If we beat capitalism and create a link with peasant farming we shall become an absolutely invincible power. Then the building of socialism will not be the task of that drop in

---

front in the summer of 1917. This attempt was made on orders from the Anglo-French imperialists and the Russian bourgeoisie.

the ocean, called the Communist Party, but the task of the entire mass of the working people. Then the rank-and-file peasants will see that we are helping them and they will follow our lead. Consequently, even if the pace is a hundred times slower, it will be a million times more certain and more sure.

It is in this sense that we must speak of halting the retreat; and the proper thing to do is, in one way or another, to make this slogan a congress decision.

In this connection, I should like to deal with the question: what is the Bolsheviks' New Economic Policy – evolution or tactics? This question has been raised by the *Smena Vekh* people, who, as you know, are a trend which has arisen among Russian émigrés; it is a sociopolitical trend led by some of the most prominent Constitutional Democrats, several ministers of the former Kolchak government, people who have come to the conclusion that the Soviet government is building up the Russian state and therefore should be supported. They argue as follows: 'What sort of state is the Soviet government building? The Communists say they are building a communist state and assure us that the new policy is a matter of tactics: the Bolsheviks are making use of the private capitalists in a difficult situation, but later they will get the upper hand. The Bolsheviks can say what they like; as a matter of fact it is not tactics but evolution, internal regeneration; they will arrive at the ordinary bourgeois state, and we must support them. History proceeds in devious ways.'

Some of them pretend to be Communists; but there are others who are more straightforward, one of these is Ustryalov. I think he was a minister in Kolchak's government. He does not agree with his colleagues and says: 'You can think what you like about communism, but I maintain that it is not a matter of tactics, but of evolution.' I think that by being straightforward like this, Ustryalov is rendering us a great service. We, and I particularly, because of my position, hear a lot of sentimental communist lies; 'communist fibbing', every day, and sometimes we get sick to death of them. But now instead of these 'communist fibs' I get a copy of *Smena Vekh*, which says quite plainly: 'Things are by no means what you imagine them to be. As a matter of fact, you are slipping into the ordinary bourgeois morass with communist flags inscribed with catchwords stuck all over the place.' This is very useful. It is not a repetition of what we are constantly hearing around us, but the plain class truth uttered by the class enemy. It is very useful to read this sort of thing; and it was written not because the communist state allows you to write some things and not others, but because it really is the class truth, bluntly and frankly uttered by the class enemy. 'I am in favour of supporting the Soviet government,' says Ustryalov, although he was a Constitutional Democrat, a bourgeois, and supported intervention. 'I am in favour of supporting Soviet power because it has taken the road that will lead it to the ordinary bourgeois state.'

This is very useful, and I think that we must keep it in mind. It is much better for us if the *Smena Vekh* people write in that strain than if some of them pretend to be almost communists, so that from a distance one cannot tell whether they believe in God or in the communist revolution. We must say frankly that such candid enemies are useful. We must say frankly that the things Ustryalov speaks about are possible. History knows all sorts of metamorphoses. Relying on firmness of convictions, loyalty, and other splendid moral qualities is anything but a serious attitude in politics. A few people may be endowed with splendid moral qualities, but historical issues are decided by vast masses, which, if the few do not suit them, may at times treat them none too politely.

There have been many cases of this kind; that is why we must welcome this frank utterance of the *Smena Vekh* people. The enemy is speaking the class truth and is pointing to the danger that confronts us, and which the enemy is striving to make inevitable. *Smena Vekh* adherents express the sentiments of thousands and tens of thousands of bourgeois, or of Soviet employees whose function it is to operate our New Economic Policy. This is the real and main danger. And that is why attention must be concentrated mainly on the question: 'Who will win?' I have spoken about competition. No direct onslaught is being made on us now; nobody is clutching us by the throat. True, we have yet to see what will happen tomorrow; but today we are not being subjected to armed attack. Nevertheless, the fight against capitalist society has become a hundred times more fierce and perilous, because we are not always able to tell enemies from friends.

When I spoke about communist competition, what I had in mind were not communist sympathies but the development of economic forms and social systems. This is not competition but, if not the last, then nearly the last, desperate, furious, life-and-death struggle between capitalism and communism.

And here we must squarely put the question: wherein lies our strength and what do we lack? We have quite enough political power. I hardly think there is anyone here who will assert that on such-and-such a practical question, in-such and-such a business institution, the Communists, the Communist Party, lack sufficient power. There are people who think only of this, but these people are hopelessly looking backward and cannot understand that one must look ahead. The main economic power is in our hands. All the vital large enterprises, the railways, etc., are in our hands. The number of leased enterprises, although considerable in places, is on the whole insignificant; altogether it is infinitesimal compared with the rest. The economic power in the hands of the proletarian state of Russia is quite adequate to ensure the transition to communism. What, then, is lacking? Obviously, what is lacking is culture among the stratum of the Communists who perform administrative functions. If we take Moscow with its 4,700 Communists in responsible positions, and if we take that huge bureaucratic machine, that gigantic heap, we must ask: who is directing whom? I doubt very much whether it can truthfully be said that the Communists are directing that heap. To tell the truth they are not directing, they are being directed. Something analogous happened here to what we were told in our history lessons when we were children: sometimes one nation conquers another, the nation that conquers is the conqueror and the nation that is vanquished is the conquered nation. This is simple and intelligible to all. But what happens to the culture of these nations? Here things are not so simple. If the conquering nation is more cultured than the vanquished nation, the former imposes its culture upon the latter; but if the opposite is the case, the vanquished nation imposes its culture upon the conqueror. Has not something like this happened in the capital of the RSFSR? Have the 4,700 Communists (nearly a whole army division, and all of them the very best) come under the influence of an alien culture? True, there may be the impression that the vanquished have a high level of culture. But that is not the case at all. Their culture is miserable, insignificant, but it is still at a higher level than ours. Miserable and low as it is, it is higher than that of our responsible Communist administrators, for the latter lack administrative ability. Communists who are put at the head of departments – and sometimes artful saboteurs deliberately put them in these positions in order to use them as a shield – are often fooled. This is a very unpleasant admission to make, or, at any rate, not a very pleasant one; but I think we must admit it, for at present this is the salient problem. I think that this is the political lesson of the past year; and it is around this that the struggle will rage in 1922.

Will the responsible Communists of the RSFSR and of the Russian Communist Party realise that they cannot administer;

that they only imagine they are directing, but are, actually, being directed? If they realise this they will learn, of course; for this business can be learnt. But one must study hard to learn it, and our people are not doing this. They scatter orders and decrees right and left, but the result is quite different from what they want.

The competition and rivalry that we have placed on the order of the day by proclaiming the NEP is a serious business. It appears to be going on in all government offices; but as a matter of fact it is one more form of the struggle between two irreconcilably hostile classes. It is another form of the struggle between the bourgeoisie and the proletariat. It is a struggle that has not yet been brought to a head, and culturally it has not yet been resolved even in the central government departments in Moscow. Very often the bourgeois officials know the business better than our best Communists, who are invested with authority and have every opportunity, but who cannot make the slightest use of their rights and authority.

I should like to quote a passage from a pamphlet by Alexander Todorsky.[9] It was published in Vesyegonsk (there is an *uyezd* town of that name in Tver Gubernia) on the first anniversary of the Soviet revolution in Russia, on 7 November 1918, a long, long time ago. Evidently this Vesyegonsk comrade is a member of the Party – I read the pamphlet a long time ago and cannot say for certain. He describes how he set to work to equip two Soviet factories, and for this purpose enlisted the services of two bourgeois. He did this in the way these things were done at that time – threatened to imprison them and to confiscate all their property. They were enlisted for the task of restoring the factories. We know how the

9　Alexander Todorsky's book *A Year with a Rifle and a Plough* was published in 1918 by the Vesyegonsk Uyezd Executive Committee of Soviets, Tver Gubernia. Lenin speaks of this book in his article 'A Little Picture in Illustration of Big Problems'.

services of the bourgeoisie were enlisted in 1918 [*laughter*]; so there is no need for me to go into details. The methods we are now using to enlist the bourgeoisie are different. But here is the conclusion he arrived at: 'This is only half the job. It is not enough to defeat the bourgeoisie, to overpower them; they must be compelled to work for us.'

Now these are remarkable words. They are remarkable for they show that even in the town of Vesyegonsk, even in 1918, there were people who had a correct understanding of the relationship between the victorious proletariat and the vanquished bourgeoisie.

When we rap the exploiters' knuckles, render them innocuous, overpower them, it is only half the job. In Moscow, however, ninety out of a hundred responsible officials imagine that all we have to do is to overpower, render innocuous and rap knuckles. What I have said about the Mensheviks, Socialist-Revolutionaries and whiteguards is very often interpreted solely as rendering innocuous, rapping knuckles (and, perhaps, not only the knuckles, but some other place) and overpowering. But that is only half the job. It was only half the job even in 1918, when this was written by the Vesyegonsk comrade; now it is even less than one-fourth. We must make these hands work for us, and not have responsible Communists at the head of departments, enjoying rank and title, but actually swimming with the stream together with the bourgeoisie. That is the whole point.

The idea of building communist society exclusively with the hands of the Communists is childish, absolutely childish. We Communists are but a drop in the ocean, a drop in the ocean of the people. We shall be able to lead the people along the road we have chosen only if we correctly determine it not only from the standpoint of its direction in world history. From that point of view we have determined the road quite correctly, and this is corroborated by the situation in every country. We must also determine it correctly for our own native land, for our country. But the direction in world history is not the only factor. Other factors are whether there will be intervention or not, and whether we shall be able to supply the peasants with goods in exchange for their grain. The peasants will say: 'You are splendid fellows; you defended our country. That is why we obeyed you. But if you cannot run the show, get out!' Yes, that is what the peasants will say.

We Communists shall be able to direct our economy if we succeed in utilising the hands of the bourgeoisie in building up this economy of ours and in the meantime learn from these bourgeoisie and guide them along the road we want them to travel. But when a Communist imagines that he knows everything, when he says: 'I am a responsible Communist, I have beaten enemies far more formidable than any salesman. We have fought at the front and have beaten far more formidable enemies' – it is this prevailing mood that is doing us great harm.

Rendering the exploiters innocuous, rapping them over the knuckles, clipping their wings is the least important part of the job. That must be done; and our State Political Administration and our courts must do it more vigorously than they have up to now. They must remember that they are proletarian courts surrounded by enemies the world over. This is not difficult; and in the main we have learned to do it. Here a certain amount of pressure must be exercised; but that is easy.

To win the second part of the victory, i.e., to build communism with the hands of non-Communists, to acquire the practical ability to do what is economically necessary, we must establish a link with peasant farming; we must satisfy the peasant, so that he will say: 'Hard, bitter and painful as starvation is, I see a government that is an unusual one, is no ordinary one, but is doing something practically useful, something tangible.' We must see to it that the numerous elements with whom we are cooperating, and who far exceed us in number, work in such a way as to enable us to supervise them; we must learn to understand this work, and direct their hands so that they do something useful for communism. This is the key point of the present situation; for although individual Communists have understood and realised that it is necessary to enlist the non-Party people for this work, the rank-and-file of our Party have not. Many circulars have been written, much has been said about this, but has anything been accomplished during the past year? Nothing. Not five Party committees out of a hundred can show practical results. This shows how much we lag behind the requirements of the present time; how much we are still living in the traditions of 1918 and 1919. Those were great years; a great historical task was then accomplished. But if we only look back on those years and do not see the task that now confronts us, we shall be doomed, certainly and absolutely. And the whole point is that we refuse to admit it.

I should now like to give two practical examples to illustrate how we administer. I have said already that it would be more correct to take one of the state trusts as an example, but I must ask you to excuse me for not being able to apply this proper method, for to do so it would have been necessary to study the concrete material concerning at least one state trust. Unfortunately, I have been unable to do that, and so I will take two small examples. One example is the accusation of bureaucracy levelled at the People's Commissariat of Foreign Trade by the Moscow Consumers' Cooperative Society. The other example I will take from the Donets basin.

The first example is not quite relevant – I am unable to find a better – but it will serve to illustrate my main point. As you know from the newspapers, I have been unable to deal with affairs directly during these past few months. I have not been attending the Council of People's Commissars, or the

Central Committee. During the short and rare visits I made to Moscow I was struck by the desperate and terrible complaints levelled at the People's Commissariat of Foreign Trade. I have never doubted for a moment that the People's Commissariat of Foreign Trade functions badly and that it is tied up with red tape. But when the complaints became particularly bitter I tried to investigate the matter, to take a concrete example and for once get to the bottom of it; to ascertain the cause, to ascertain why the machine was not working properly.

The MCCS wanted to purchase a quantity of canned goods. A French citizen appeared and offered some. I do not know whether he did it in the interests of the international policy and with the knowledge of the leadership of the Entente countries, or with the approval of Poincaré and the other enemies of the Soviet government (I think our historians will investigate and make this clear after the Genoa Conference), but the fact is that the French bourgeoisie took not only a theoretical, but also a practical interest in this business, as a French bourgeois turned up in Moscow with an offer of canned goods. Moscow is starving; in the summer the situation will be worse; no meat has been delivered, and knowing the merits of our People's Commissariat of Railways, probably none will be delivered.

An offer is made to sell canned meat for Soviet currency (whether the meat is entirely bad or not will be established by a future investigation). What could be simpler? But if the matter is approached in the Soviet way, it turns out to be not so simple after all. I was unable to go into the matter personally, but I ordered an investigation and I have before me the report which shows how this celebrated case developed. It started with the decision adopted on 11 February by the Political Bureau of the Central Committee of the Russian Communist Party on the report of Comrade Kamenev concerning the desirability of purchasing food abroad. Of course, how could a Russian citizen decide such a question without the consent of the Political Bureau of the Central Committee of the Russian Communist Party! Think of it! How could 4,700 responsible officials (and this is only according to the census) decide a matter like purchasing food abroad without the consent of the Political Bureau of the Central Committee? This would be something supernatural, of course. Evidently, Comrade Kamenev understands our policy and the realities of our position perfectly well, and therefore, he did not place too much reliance on the numerous responsible officials. He started by taking the bull by the horns – if not the bull, at all events the Political Bureau – and without any difficulty (I did not hear that there was any discussion over the matter) obtained a resolution stating: 'To call the attention of the People's Commissariat of Foreign Trade to the desirability of importing food from abroad; the import duties ...', etc. The attention of the People's Commissariat of Foreign Trade was drawn to this. Things started moving. This was on 11 February. I remember that I had occasion to be in Moscow at the very end of February, or about that time, and what did I find? The complaints, the despairing complaints of the Moscow comrades. 'What's the matter?' I ask. 'There is no way we can buy these provisions.' 'Why?' 'Because of the red tape of the People's Commissariat of Foreign Trade.' I had not been taking part in affairs for a long time and I did not know that the Political Bureau had adopted a decision on the matter. I merely ordered the Executive Secretary of our Council to investigate, procure the relevant documents and show them to me. The matter was settled when Krasin arrived. Kamenev discussed the matter with him, the transaction was arranged, and the canned meat was purchased. All's well that ends well.

I have not the least doubt that Kamenev and Krasin can come to an understanding and correctly determine the political line desired by the Political Bureau of the Central Committee of the Russian Communist Party. If the political line on commercial matters were decided by Kamenev and Krasin, ours would be the best Soviet Republic in the world. But Kamenev, a member of the Political Bureau, and Krasin – the latter is busy with diplomatic affairs connected with Genoa, affairs which have entailed an enormous, an excessive, amount of labour – cannot be dragged into every transaction, dragged into the business of buying canned goods from a French citizen. That is not the way to work. This is not new, not economic, and not a policy, but sheer mockery. Now I have the report of the investigation into this matter. In fact, I have two reports: one, the report of the investigation made by Gorbunov, the executive secretary of the Council of People's Commissars, and his assistant, Miroshnikov; and the other, the report of the investigation made by the State Political Administration. I do not know why the latter interested itself in the matter, and I am not quite sure whether it was proper for it to do so; but I will not go into that now, because I am afraid this might entail another investigation. The important thing is that material on the matter has been collected and I now have it before me.

On arriving in Moscow at the end of February I heard bitter complaints, 'We cannot buy the canned goods,' although in Libau there was a ship with a cargo of canned goods, and the owners were prepared to take Soviet currency for real canned goods! [*Laughter*.] If these canned goods are not entirely bad (and I now emphasise the 'if', because I am not sure that I shall not call for another investigation, the results of which, however, we shall have to report at the next Congress), if, I say, these goods are not entirely bad and they have been purchased, I ask: why could not this matter have been settled without Kamenev and Krasin? From the report I have before me I gather that one responsible Communist sent another responsible Communist to the devil. I also gather from this report that one responsible Communist said to another responsible Communist: 'From now on I shall not talk to you except in the presence of a lawyer.' Reading this report I recalled the time when I was in exile in Siberia, twenty-five years ago, and had occasion to act in the capacity of a lawyer. I was not a certified lawyer, because, being summarily exiled, I was not allowed to practise; but as there was no other lawyer in the region, people came and confided their troubles to me. But sometimes I had the greatest difficulty in understanding what the trouble was. A woman would come and, of course, start telling me a long story about her relatives, and it was incredibly difficult to get from her what she really wanted. I said to her: 'Bring me a copy.' She went on with her endless and pointless story. When I repeated, 'Bring me a copy,' she left, complaining: 'He won't hear what I have to say unless I bring a copy.' In our colony we had a hearty laugh over this copy. I was able, however, to make some progress. People came to me, brought copies of the necessary documents, and I was able to gather what their trouble was, what they complained of, what ailed them. This was twenty-five years ago, in Siberia, in a place many hundreds of *versts* from the nearest railway station.

But why was it necessary, three years after the revolution, in the capital of the Soviet Republic, to have two investigations, the intervention of Kamenev and Krasin and the instructions of the Political Bureau to purchase canned goods? What was lacking? Political power? No. The money was forthcoming, so they had economic as well as political power. All the necessary institutions were available. What was lacking, then? Culture. Ninety-nine out of every hundred officials of the MCCS – against whom I have no complaint to make whatever, and whom I regard as excellent Communists – and of the Commissariat of Foreign Trade lack culture. They were unable to approach the matter in a cultured manner.

When I first heard of the matter I sent the following written proposal to the Central Committee: 'All the officials concerned of the Moscow government departments – except the members of the All-Russia Central Executive Committee, who, as you know, enjoy immunity – should be put in the worst prison in Moscow for six hours, and those of the People's Commissariat of Foreign Trade for thirty-six hours.' And then it turned out that no one could say who the culprits were [*laughter*], and from what I have told you it is evident that the culprits will never be discovered. It is simply the usual inability of the Russian intellectuals to get things done – inefficiency and slovenliness. First they rush at a job, do a little bit, and then think about it, and when nothing comes of it, they run to complain to Kamenev and want the matter to be brought before the Political Bureau. Of course, all difficult state problems should be brought before the Political Bureau – I shall have to say something about that later on – but one should think first and then act. If you want to bring up a case, submit the appropriate documents. First send a telegram, and in Moscow we also have telephones; send a telephone message to the competent department and a copy to Tsyurupa saying: 'I regard the transaction as urgent and will take proceedings against anyone guilty of red tape.' One must think of this elementary culture; one must approach things in a thoughtful manner. If the business is not settled in the course of a few minutes, by telephone, collect the documents and say: 'If you start any of your red tape I shall have you clapped in gaol.' But not a moment's thought is given to the matter; there is no preparation, the usual bustle, several commissions; everybody is tired out, exhausted, run down; and things begin to move only when Kamenev is put in touch with Krasin. All this is typical of what goes on not only in the capital, Moscow, but also in the other capitals, in the capitals of all independent republics and regions. And the same thing, even a hundred times worse, constantly goes on in the provincial towns.

In our struggle we must remember that Communists must be able to reason. They may be perfectly familiar with the

revolutionary struggle and with the state of the revolutionary movement all over the world; but if we are to extricate
ourselves from desperate poverty and want, we need culture,
integrity and an ability to reason. Many lack these qualities.
It would be unfair to say that the responsible Communists
do not fulfil their functions conscientiously. The overwhelming majority of them, ninety-nine out of a hundred, are not
only conscientious – they proved their devotion to the revolution under the most difficult conditions before the fall of
tsarism and after the revolution; they were ready to lay down
their lives. Therefore, it would be radically wrong to attribute
the trouble to lack of conscientiousness. We need a cultured
approach to the simplest affairs of state. We must all understand that this is a matter of state, a business matter; and if
obstacles arise we must be able to overcome them and take
proceedings against those who are guilty of red tape. We have
proletarian courts in Moscow; they must bring to account the
persons who are to blame for the failure to effect the purchase of several tens of thousands of *poods* of canned food. I
think the proletarian courts will be able to punish the guilty;
but in order to punish, the culprits must be found. I assure
you that in this case no culprits will be found. I want you
all to look into this business: no one is guilty; all we see is a
lot of fuss and bustle and nonsense. Nobody has the ability
to approach the business properly; nobody understands that
affairs of state must not be tackled in this way. And all the
whiteguards and saboteurs take advantage of this. At one time
we waged a fierce struggle against the saboteurs; that struggle
confronts us even now. There are saboteurs today, of course,
and they must be fought. But can we fight them when the
position is as I have just described it? This is worse than any
sabotage. The saboteur could wish for nothing better than
that two Communists should argue over the question of when
to appeal to the Political Bureau for instructions on principles

in buying food; and of course he would soon slip in between them and egg them on. If any intelligent saboteur were to stand behind these Communists, or behind each of them in turn, and encourage them, that would be the end. The matter would be doomed for ever. Who is to blame? Nobody, because two responsible Communists, devoted revolutionaries, are arguing over last year's snow; are arguing over the question of when to appeal to the Political Bureau for instructions on principles in buying food.

That is how the matter stands and that is the difficulty that confronts us. Any salesman trained in a large capitalist enterprise knows how to settle a matter like that; but ninety-nine responsible Communists out of a hundred do not. And they refuse to understand that they do not know how and that they must learn the ABC of this business. Unless we realise this, unless we sit down in the preparatory class again, we shall never be able to solve the economic problem that now lies at the basis of our entire policy.

The other example I wanted to give you is that of the Donets basin. You know that this is the centre, the real basis of our entire economy. It will be utterly impossible to restore large-scale industry in Russia, to really build socialism – for it can only be built on the basis of large scale industry – unless we restore the Donets basin and bring it up to the proper level. The Central Committee is closely watching developments there.

As regards this region there was no unjustified, ridiculous or absurd raising of minor questions in the Political Bureau; real, absolutely urgent business was discussed.

The Central Committee ought to see to it that in such real centres, bases and foundations of our entire economy, work is carried on in a real businesslike manner. At the head of the Central Coal Industry Board we had not only undoubtedly devoted, but really educated and very capable, people.

I should not be wrong even if I said talented people. That is why the Central Committee has concentrated its attention on it. Ukraine is an independent republic. That is quite all right. But in Party matters it sometimes – what is the politest way of saying it? – takes a roundabout course, and we shall have to get at them. For the people in charge there are sly, and their Central Committee I shall not say deceives us, but somehow edges away from us. To obtain a general view of the whole business, we discussed it in the Central Committee here and discovered that friction and disagreement exist. There is a Commission for the Utilisation of Small Mines there and, of course, severe friction between it and the Central Coal Industry Board. Still we, the Central Committee, have a certain amount of experience and we unanimously decided not to remove the leading people, but if there was any friction it was to be reported to us, down to the smallest detail. For since we have not only devoted but capable people in the region, we must back them up, and enable them to complete their training, assuming that they have not done so. In the end, a Party congress was held in Ukraine – I do not know what happened there; all sorts of things happened. I asked for information from the Ukrainian comrades, and I asked Comrade Orjonikidze particularly – and the Central Committee did the same – to go down there and ascertain what had happened. Evidently, there was some intrigue and an awful mess, which the Commission on Party History would not be able to clear up in ten years should it undertake to do so. But the upshot of it all was that contrary to the unanimous instructions of the Central Committee, this group was superseded by another group. What was the matter? In the main, notwithstanding all its good qualities, a section of the group made a mistake. They were overzealous in their methods of administration. There we have to deal with workers. Very often the word 'workers' is taken to mean the factory proletariat. But it does not mean

that at all. During the war people who were by no means proletarians went into the factories; they went into the factories to
dodge the war. Are the social and economic conditions in our
country today such as to induce real proletarians to go into the
factories? No. It would be true according to Marx; but Marx
did not write about Russia; he wrote about capitalism as a
whole, beginning with the fifteenth century. It held true over a
period of six hundred years, but it is not true for present-day
Russia. Very often those who go into the factories are not proletarians; they are casual elements of every description.

The task is to learn to organise the work properly, not
to lag behind; to remove friction in time, not to separate
administration from politics. For our administration and our
politics rest on the ability of the entire vanguard to maintain
contact with the entire mass of the proletariat and with the
entire mass of the peasantry. If anybody forgets these cogs
and becomes wholly absorbed in administration, the result
will be a disastrous one. The mistake the Donets basin officials made is insignificant compared with other mistakes of
ours, but this example is a typical one. The Central Committee
unanimously ordered: 'Allow this group to remain; bring all
conflicts, even minor ones, before the Central Committee, for
the Donets basin is not an ordinary district, but a vital one,
without which socialist construction would simply remain a
pious wish.' But all our political power, all the authority of the
Central Committee proved of no avail.

This time there was a mistake in administration, of course;
in addition, a host of other mistakes were made.

This instance shows that it is not a matter of possessing political power, but of administrative ability, the ability to put the
right man in the right place, the ability to avoid petty conflicts,
so that state economic work may be carried on without inter-
ruption. This is what we lack; this is the root of the mistake.

I think that in discussing our revolution and weighing

up its prospects, we must carefully single out the problems which the revolution has solved completely and which have irrevocably gone down in history as an epoch-making departure from capitalism. Our revolution has such solutions to its credit. Let the Mensheviks and Otto Bauer of the Two-and-a-Half International shout: 'Theirs is a bourgeois revolution.' We say that our task was to consummate the bourgeois revolution. As a certain whiteguard newspaper expressed it: dung had accumulated in our state institutions for four hundred years; but we cleaned it all out in four years. This is the great service we rendered. What have the Mensheviks and Socialist-Revolutionaries done? Nothing. The dung of medievalism has not been cleared out either in our country, or even in advanced, enlightened Germany. Yet they reproach us for doing what stands very much to our credit. The fact that we have consummated the revolution is an achievement that can never be expunged from our record.

War is now in the air. The trade unions, for example, the reformist trade unions, are passing resolutions against war and are threatening to call strikes in opposition to war. Recently, if I am not mistaken, I read a report in the newspapers to the effect that a certain very good communist delivered an anti-war speech in the French Chamber of Deputies in the course of which he stated that the workers would prefer to rise in revolt rather than go to war. This question cannot be formulated in the way we formulated it in 1912, when the Basle Manifesto was issued. The Russian revolution alone has shown how it is possible to emerge from war, and what effort this entails. It showed what emerging from a reactionary war by revolutionary methods means. Reactionary imperialist wars are inevitable in all parts of the world; and in solving problems of this sort mankind cannot and will not forget that tens of millions were slaughtered then, and will be slaughtered again if war breaks out. We are living in the twentieth century, and the only nation that emerged from a reactionary war by revolutionary methods not for the benefit of a particular government, but by overthrowing it, was the Russian nation, and it was the Russian revolution that extricated it. What has been won by the Russian revolution is irrevocable. No power on earth can erase that; nor can any power on earth erase the fact that the Soviet state has been created. This is a historic victory. For hundreds of years states have been built according to the bourgeois model, and for the first time a non-bourgeois form of state has been discovered. Our machinery of government may be faulty, but it is said that the first steam engine that was invented was also faulty. No one even knows whether it worked or not, but that is not the important point; the important point is that it was invented. Even assuming that the first steam engine was of no use, the fact is that we now have steam engines. Even if our machinery of government is very faulty, the fact remains that it has been created; the greatest invention in history has been made; a proletarian type of state has been created. Therefore, let all Europe, let thousands of bourgeois newspapers, broadcast news about the horrors and poverty that prevail in our country, about suffering being the sole lot of the working people in our country; the workers all over the world are still drawn towards the Soviet state. These are the great and irrevocable gains that we have achieved. But for us, members of the Communist Party, this meant only opening the door. We are now confronted with the task of laying the foundations of socialist economy. Has this been done? No, it has not. We still lack the socialist foundation. Those Communists who imagine that we have it are greatly mistaken. The whole point is to distinguish firmly, clearly and dispassionately what constitutes the historic service rendered by the Russian revolution from what we do very badly, from what has not yet been created, and what we shall have to redo many times yet.

Political events are always very confused and complicated.

They can be compared with a chain. To hold the whole chain you must grasp the main link. Not a link chosen at random. What was the central event in 1917? Withdrawal from the war. The entire nation demanded this, and it overshadowed everything. Revolutionary Russia accomplished this withdrawal from the war. It cost tremendous effort; but the major demand of the people was satisfied, and that brought us victory for many years. The people realised, the peasants saw, every soldier returning from the front understood perfectly well that the Soviet government was a more democratic government, one that stood closer to the working people. No matter how many outrageous and absurd things we may have done in other spheres, the fact that we realised what the main task was proved that everything was right.

What was the key feature of 1919 and 1920? Military resistance. The all-powerful Entente was marching against us, was at our throats. No propaganda was required there. Every non-Party peasant understood what was going on. The landowners were coming back. The Communists knew how to fight them. That is why, taken in the mass, the peasants followed the lead of the Communists; that is why we were victorious.

In 1921, the key feature was an orderly retreat. This required stern discipline. The Workers' Opposition said: 'You are underrating the workers; the workers should display greater initiative.' But initiative had to be displayed then by retreating in good order and by maintaining strict discipline. Anyone who introduced an undertone of panic or insubordination would have doomed the revolution to defeat; for there is nothing more difficult than retreating with people who have been accustomed to victory, who are imbued with revolutionary views and ideals, and who, in their hearts, regard every retreat as a disgraceful matter. The greatest danger was the violation of good order, and the greatest task was to maintain good order.

And what is the key feature now? The key feature now – and I would like to sum up my report with this – is not that we have changed our line of policy. An incredible lot of nonsense is being talked about this in connection with the NEP. It is all hot air, pernicious twaddle. In connection with the NEP some people are beginning to fuss around, proposing to reorganise our government departments and to form new ones. All this is pernicious twaddle. In the present situation the key feature is people, the proper choice of people. A revolutionary who is accustomed to struggle against petty reformists and uplift educators finds it hard to understand this. Soberly weighed up, the political conclusion to be drawn from the present situation is that we have advanced so far that we cannot hold all the positions; and we need not hold them all.

Internationally our position has improved vastly these last few years. The Soviet type of state is our achievement; it is a step forward in human progress; and the information the Communist International receives from every country every day corroborates this. Nobody has the slightest doubt about that. From the point of view of practical work, however, the position is that unless the Communists render the masses of the peasants practical assistance they will lose their support. Passing laws, passing better decrees, etc., is not now the main object of our attention. There was a time when the passing of decrees was a form of propaganda. People used to laugh at us and say that the Bolsheviks do not realise that their decrees are not being carried out; the entire whiteguard press was full of jeers on that score. But at that period this passing of decrees was quite justified. We Bolsheviks had just taken power, and we said to the peasant, to the worker: 'Here is a decree; this is how we would like to have the state administered. Try it!' From the very outset we gave the ordinary workers and peasants an idea of our policy in the form of decrees. The result was the enormous confidence we enjoyed and now enjoy among the masses of the people. This was an essential period at the beginning of the revolution; without it we should not have risen on the crest of the revolutionary wave; we should have wallowed in its trough. Without it we should not have won the confidence of all the workers and peasants who wanted to build their lives on new lines. But this period has passed, and we refuse to understand this. Now the peasants and workers will laugh at us if we order this or that government department to be formed or reorganised. The ordinary workers and peasants will display no interest in this now, and they will be right, because this is not the central task today. This is not the sort of thing with which we Communists should now go to the people. Although we who are engaged in government departments are always overwhelmed with so many petty affairs, this is not the link that we must grasp, this is not the key feature. The key feature is that we have not got the right men in the right places; that responsible Communists who acquitted themselves magnificently during the revolution have been given commercial and industrial functions about which they know nothing; and they prevent us from seeing the truth, for rogues and rascals hide magnificently behind their backs. The trouble is that we have no such thing as practical control of how things have been done. This is a prosaic job, a small job; these are petty affairs. But after the greatest political change in history, bearing in mind that for a time we shall have to live in the midst of the capitalist system, the key feature now is not politics in the narrow sense of the word (what we read in the newspapers is just political fireworks; there is nothing socialist in it at all), the key feature is not resolutions, not departments and not reorganisation. As long as these things are necessary we shall do them, but don't go to the people with them. Choose the proper men and introduce practical control. That is what the people will appreciate.

In the sea of people we are, after all, but a drop in the ocean, and we can administer only when we express correctly what the people are conscious of. Unless we do this the Communist Party will not lead the proletariat, the proletariat will not lead the masses, and the whole machine will collapse. The chief thing the people, all the working people, want today is nothing but help in their desperate hunger and need; they want to be shown that the improvement needed by the peasants is really taking place in the form they are accustomed to. The peasant knows and is accustomed to the market and trade. We were unable to introduce direct communist distribution. We lacked the factories and their equipment for this. That being the case, we must provide the peasants with what they need through the medium of trade, and provide it as well as the capitalist did, otherwise the people will not tolerate such an administration. This is the key to the situation; and unless something unexpected arises, this, given three conditions, should be the central feature of our activities in 1922.

The first condition is that there shall be no intervention. We are doing all we can in the diplomatic field to avoid it; nevertheless, it may occur any day. We must really be on the alert, and we must agree to make certain big sacrifices for the sake of the Red Army, within definite limits, of course. We are confronted by the entire bourgeois world, which is only seeking a way in which to strangle us. Our Mensheviks and Socialist-Revolutionaries are nothing more nor less than the agents of this bourgeoisie. Such is their political status.

The second condition is that the financial crisis shall not be too severe. The crisis is approaching. You will hear about that when we discuss financial policy. If it is too severe and rigorous we shall have to revise many things again and concentrate all efforts on one thing. If it is not too severe it may even be useful; it will give the Communists in all the state trusts a good shaking; only we must not forget to do it. The financial crisis will shake up government departments and industrial enterprises, and those that are not equal to their task will be the first to burst; only we must take care that all the blame for this is not thrown on the specialists while the responsible Communists are praised for being very good fellows who have fought at the fronts and have always worked well. Thus, if the financial crisis is not too severe we can derive some benefit from it and comb the ranks of the responsible Communists engaged in the business departments not in the way the Central Control Commission and the Central Verification Commission comb them, but very thoroughly.[10]

The third condition is that we shall make no political mistakes in this period. Of course, if we do make political mistakes all our work of economic construction will be disrupted and we shall land ourselves in controversies about how to rectify them and what direction to pursue. But if we make no sad mistakes, the key feature in the near future will be not decrees and politics in the narrow sense of the word, not departments and their organisation – the responsible Communists and the Soviet institutions will deal with these things whenever necessary – the main thing in all our activities will be choosing the right people and making sure that decisions are carried out. If, in this respect, we learn something practical, if we do something practically useful, we shall again overcome all difficulties.

In conclusion I must mention the practical side of the question of our Soviet institutions, the higher government bodies and the Party's relation to them. The relations between the Party and the Soviet government bodies are not what they ought to be. On this point we are quite unanimous. I have given one example of how minor matters are dragged before

10   The Central Verification Commission was set up on 25 June 1921 by the CC, RCP(B) to direct the work of local verification commissions during the period of the Party purge. It consisted of five men.

the Political Bureau. It is extremely difficult to get out of this by formal means, for there is only one governing party in our country; and a member of the Party cannot be prohibited from lodging complaints. That is why everything that comes up on the Council of People's Commissars is dragged before the Political Bureau. I, too, am greatly to blame for this, for to a large extent contact between the Council of People's Commissars and the Political Bureau was maintained through me. When I was obliged to retire from work it was found that the two wheels were not working in unison and Kamenev had to bear a treble load to maintain this contact. Inasmuch as it is barely probable that I shall return to work in the near future, all hope devolves on the fact that there are two other deputies – Comrade Tsyurupa, who has been cleansed by the Germans, and Comrade Rykov, whom they have splendidly cleansed. It seems that even Wilhelm, the German emperor, has stood us in good stead – I never expected it. He had a surgeon, who happened to be the doctor treating Comrade Rykov, and he removed his worst part, keeping it in Germany, and left the best part intact, sending that part of Comrade Rykov thoroughly cleansed to us. If that method continues to be used it will be a really good thing.

Joking aside, a word or two about the main instructions. On this point there is complete unanimity on the Central Committee, and I hope that the congress will pay the closest attention to it and endorse the instructions that the Political Bureau and the Central Committee be relieved of minor matters, and that more should be shifted to the responsible officials. The people's commissars must be responsible for their work and should not bring these matters up first on the Council of People's Commissars and then on the Political Bureau. Formally, we cannot abolish the right to lodge complaints with the Central Committee, for our Party is the only governing party in the country. But we must put a stop to the habit of bringing every petty matter before the Central Committee; we must raise the prestige of the Council of People's Commissars. The commissars and not the deputy commissars must mainly attend the meetings of the council. The functions of the council must be changed in the direction in which I have not succeeded in changing them during the past year; that is, it must pay much more attention to executive control. We shall have two more deputies – Rykov and Tsyurupa. When Rykov was in the Extraordinary Authorised Council of Workers' and Peasants' Defence for the Supply of the Red Army and Navy he tightened things up and the work went well. Tsyurupa organised one of the most efficient people's commissariats. If together they make the maximum effort to improve the People's Commissariats in the sense of efficiency and responsibility, we shall make some, even if a little, progress here. We have eighteen people's commissariats, of which not less than fifteen are of no use at all – efficient people's commissars cannot be found everywhere, and I certainly hope that people give this more of their attention. Comrade Rykov must be a member, of the Central Committee Bureau and of the Presidium of the All-Russia Central Executive Committee because there must be a tie-up between these two bodies, for without this tie-up the main wheels some times spin in the air.

In this connection, we must see to it that the number of commissions of the Council of People's Commissars and of the Council of Labour and Defence is reduced. These bodies must know and settle their own affairs and not split up into an infinite number of commissions. A few days ago the commissions were overhauled. It was found that there were one hundred and twenty of them. How many were necessary? Sixteen. And this is not the first cut. Instead of accepting responsibility for their work, preparing a decision for the Council of People's Commissars and knowing that they bear responsibility for this decision, there is a tendency to take shelter behind commissions. The devil himself would lose his way in this maze of commissions. Nobody knows what is going on, who is responsible; everything is mixed up, and finally a decision is passed for which everybody is held responsible.

In this connection, reference must be made to the need for extending and developing the autonomy and activities of the regional economic conferences. The administrative division of Russia has now been drawn up on scientific lines; the economic and climatic conditions, the way of life, the conditions of obtaining fuel, of local industry, etc., have all been taken into account. On the basis of this division, district and regional economic conferences have been instituted. Changes may be made here and there, of course, but the prestige of these economic conferences must be enhanced.

Then we must see to it that the All-Russia Central Executive Committee works more energetically, meets in session more regularly, and for longer periods. The sessions of the All-Russia Central Executive Committee should discuss bills which sometimes are hastily brought before the Council of People's Commissars when there is no need to do so. It would be better to postpone such bills and give the local workers an opportunity to study them carefully. Stricter demands should be made upon those who draft the bills. This is not done.

If the sessions of the All-Russia Central Executive Committee last longer, they can split up into sections and sub-commissions, and thus will be able to verify the work more strictly and strive to achieve what in my opinion is the key, the quintessence of the present political situation: to concentrate attention on choosing the right people and on verifying how decisions are carried out.

It must be admitted, and we must not be afraid to admit, that in ninety-nine cases out of a hundred the responsible Communists are not in the jobs they are now fit for; that they are unable to perform their duties, and that they must sit down to learn. If this is admitted, and since we have the opportunity to learn – judging by the general international situation we shall have time to do so – we must do it, come what may. [*Tumultuous applause.*]

Closing Speech on the Political Report of the Central Committee of the RCP(B), 28 March

[*Applause.*] First of all I shall have to devote a little time to criticising the remarks made here by Comrades Preobrazhensky and Osinsky. I think that on the most important and fundamental question Comrades Preobrazhensky and Osinsky were wide of the mark, and their own statements have proved their line of policy to be wrong.

Comrade Preobrazhensky spoke about capitalism and said that we ought to open a general discussion on our programme. I think that this would be the most unproductive and unjustified waste of time.

First of all about state capitalism.

'State capitalism is capitalism,' said Preobrazhensky, 'and that is the only way it can and should be interpreted.' I say that that is pure scholasticism. Up to now nobody could have written a book about this sort of capitalism, because this is the first time in human history that we see anything like it. All the more or less intelligible books about state capitalism that have appeared up to now were written under conditions and in a situation where state capitalism was capitalism. Now things are different; and neither Marx nor the Marxists could foresee this. We must not look to the past. When you write history, you will write it magnificently; but when you write a textbook, you will say: state capitalism is the most unexpected and absolutely unforeseen form of capitalism – for nobody could foresee that the proletariat would achieve power in one of the least developed countries, and would first try to organise large-scale production and distribution for the peasantry and then, finding that it could not cope with the task owing to the low standard of culture, would enlist the services of capitalism. Nobody ever foresaw this; but it is an incontrovertible fact.

Comrade Larin, in his speech, revealed that he has a very vague conception of the New Economic Policy and of how it should be handled.

Not a single serious objection has been raised to our adoption of the New Economic Policy. The proletariat is not afraid to admit that certain things in the revolution went off magnificently, and that others went awry. All the revolutionary parties that have perished so far, perished because they became conceited, because they failed to see the source of their strength and feared to discuss their weaknesses. We, however, shall not perish, because we are not afraid to discuss our weaknesses and will learn to overcome them. [*Applause.*] The capitalism that we have permitted is essential. If it is ugly and bad, we shall be able to rectify it, because power is in our hands and we have nothing to fear. Everybody admits this, and so it is ridiculous to confuse this with panic-mongering. If we were afraid to admit this our doom would be sealed. But the fact that we will learn and want to learn this is proved by the experience of the past three, four, five years, during which we learnt more complicated matters in a shorter period. True, then we were driven by necessity. During the war we were driven very hard; I think there was neither a front nor a campaign in which we were not hard pressed. The enemy came within a hundred *versts* of Moscow, was approaching Orel, was within five *versts* of Petrograd. That was the time we really woke up and began to learn and to put the lessons we had learnt into practice, and we drove out the enemy.

The position now is that we have to deal with an enemy in mundane economics, and this is a thousand times more difficult. The controversies over state capitalism that have been raging in our literature up to now could at best be included in textbooks on history. I do not in the least deny that textbooks are useful, and recently I wrote that it would be far better if our authors devoted less attention to newspapers and political twaddle and wrote textbooks, as many of them, including Comrade Larin, could do splendidly. His talent would prove most useful on work of this kind and we would solve the problem that Comrade Trotsky emphasised so well when he said that the main task at the present time is to train the younger generation, but we have nothing to train them with. Indeed, from what can the younger generation learn the social sciences? From the old bourgeois junk. This is disgraceful! And this is at a time when we have hundreds of Marxist authors who could write textbooks on all social problems, but do not do so because their minds are taken up with other things.

As regards state capitalism, we ought to know what should be the slogan for agitation and propaganda, what must be explained, what we must get everyone to understand practically. And that is that the state capitalism that we have now is not the state capitalism that the Germans wrote about. It is capitalism that we ourselves have permitted. Is that true or not? Everybody knows that it is true!

At a congress of Communists we passed a decision that state capitalism would be permitted by the proletarian state, and we are the state. If we did wrong we are to blame and it is no use shifting the blame to somebody else! We must learn, we must see to it that in a proletarian country state capitalism cannot and does not go beyond the framework and conditions delineated for it by the proletariat, beyond conditions that benefit the proletariat. It was quite rightly pointed out here that we had to give consideration to the peasants as a mass, and enable them to trade freely. Every intelligent worker appreciates that this is necessary for the proletarian dictatorship, and only Comrade Shlyapnikov can joke about it and mock it. This is appreciated by everybody and has been chewed over a thousand times, but you simply refuse to understand it. If under present conditions the peasant must have freedom to trade within certain limits, we must give it to him, but this does not mean that we are permitting trade in raw brandy. We shall punish people for that sort of trade. It does not mean that we are permitting the sale of political literature called Menshevik and Socialist-Revolutionary and financed by the capitalists of the whole world.

That is what I meant when I mentioned machine guns, and Comrade Shlyapnikov should have understood it. What he says is nonsensical!

You will not frighten anybody and you will not win any sympathy! [*Applause. Laughter.*]

Poor Shlyapnikov! Lenin had planned to use machine guns against him!

What I had in mind was Party disciplinary measures, and not machine guns as such. When we talk about machine guns we have in mind the people in this country whom we call Mensheviks and Socialist-Revolutionaries and who argue as follows: 'You say you are retreating towards capitalism, and we say the same thing; we agree with you!' We are constantly hearing this sort of thing; and abroad a gigantic propaganda campaign is being conducted to prove that while we Bolsheviks are keeping the Mensheviks and Socialist-Revolutionaries in prison, we ourselves are permitting capitalism. True, we are permitting capitalism, but within the limits that the peasants need. This is essential! Without it the peasants could not exist and continue with their husbandry. But we maintain that the Russian peasants can do very well without Socialist-Revolutionary and Menshevik propaganda. To those who assert the contrary we say: we would rather perish to the last man than yield to you! And our courts must understand all this. Now that we are passing from the Cheka to state political courts we must say at this congress that there is no such thing as above-class courts. Our courts must be elected, proletarian courts; and they must know what it is that we are permitting. They must clearly understand what state capitalism is.

This is the political slogan of the day and not a controversy about what the German professors meant by state capitalism and what we mean by it. We have gone through a great deal since then, and it is altogether unseemly for us to look back.

The degree to which Comrade Preobrazhensky goes off the political track is shown by what he said about an Economic Bureau and about the programme.[11] What a magnificent thing

---

11   At the congress E. A. Preobrazhensky suggested that another organ of the Central Committee, an Economic Bureau, should be set up in addition to the Political Bureau and the Organising Bureau. He accused the Central Committee of violating that part of the Party programme dealing with bourgeois specialists, which stated that while creating a comradely atmosphere for the work of these people and showing concern for their material welfare no political concessions should be made to them and their counter-revolutionary impulses should be curbed. He alleged that the CC had made a political concession to the professors who had taken part in the strikes at institutions of higher learning in Moscow, Kazan, Petrograd and other cities in 1921-2. One of their basic demands was that the new Rules of Institutions of Higher Learning, drawn up by the Central Administration of Vocational and Political Schools and Institutions of Higher Learning and endorsed in the autumn of 1921 by the Council of People's Commissars, should be revised. They objected to the Workers' Faculties at institutions of higher learning and to the procedure, laid down in the new rules, of forming the boards of these institutions with the participation of representatives of the students, trade unions and the Central Administration of Vocational and Political Schools and Institutions of Higher Learning. They demanded that the latter right be transferred to the teachers' boards, and also made a number of economic demands. The Central Administration of Vocational and Political Schools and Institutions of Higher Learning, which was at that time headed by Preobrazhensky, made the mistake of insisting on stern measures, including detention, against the striking instructors. The same stand was taken by the Communist cells and Workers' Faculties of some institutions of higher learning. The Political Bureau of the CC, RCP(B) took this question

our programme is, but how frightfully we garble it! How is that possible? Because some people read it word for word and line by line, and beyond that they will not look. They pick out a passage and say: 'There was a controversy over this.' Some say that the line of the Workers' Faculties and of the Communist local cells was correct, but the line of those who said: 'Go easy, treat those specialists more carefully', was wrong. True, the Communist cells are splendid and so are the Workers' Faculties, but they are not infallible; they are not saints ...

Yes, the Communist cells are the representatives of our Party, and the Workers' Faculties are the representatives of our class; but the fact that they make mistakes and that we must correct them is an elementary truism. How they are to be corrected I do not know, because I did not attend the meetings of the Central Committee at which this question was discussed. But I do know that the Workers' Faculties and the Communist cells overdo things in the line they have taken against the professors. After our Central Committee has examined this question in all its aspects and has decided that things have been overdone and that a more cautious line must be adopted towards these professors, who are the representatives of an alien class,

---

up several times. In view of the need for a flexible approach to specialists, it rectified the mistake of the Central Administration of Vocational and Political Schools and Institutions of Higher Learning, instructing A. V. Lunacharsky, M. N. Pokrovsky and other leading officials of the People's Commissariat of Public Education to examine the teachers' demands and, without making any fundamental, political concessions, to reach agreement with them. In February 1922 the Political Bureau set up a commission consisting of representatives of the People's Commissariat of Public Education, the Central Committee of the Trade Union of Public Education Workers and teachers to examine the economic position of institutions of higher learning and recognise the need nor new rules of Institutions of Higher Learning. After repeated conferences between the teachers and the commission, and a number of other measures that were taken by the People's Commissariat of Public Education on instructions from the Party CC, the strikes were stopped.

Comrade Preobrazhensky comes along, takes out the programme and says: 'No political concessions to this stratum; that would be an infringement of the programme.'

If we start guiding the Party in this way we shall inevitably go under. And this is not because Comrade Preobrazhensky has wrong ideas about politics in general, but because he approaches everything from the angle of what is his strongest point; he is a theoretician whose mind is restricted by what is customary and usual; he is a propagandist whose mind is taken up with measures directed to the purpose of propaganda. Everybody is aware of and appreciates this strong point of his, but when he approaches things from the political and administrative angle the result is simply monstrous. Set up an Economic Bureau?! But everybody has just said, everybody has agreed, and we have complete unanimity on the point (and this is very important, for action depends upon this unity) that the Party machinery must be separated from the Soviet government machinery.

It is terribly difficult to do this; we lack the men! But Preobrazhensky comes along and airily says that Stalin has jobs in two commissariats.[12] Who among us has not sinned in this way? Who has not undertaken several duties at once? And how can we do otherwise? What can we do to preserve the present situation in the People's Commissariat of Nationalities, to handle all the Turkestan, Caucasian, and other questions? These are all political questions! They have to be settled. These are questions that have engaged the attention of European states for hundreds of years, and only an infinitesimal number of them have been settled in democratic

---

12   J. V. Stalin was People's Commissar of Nationalities from the time the People's Commissariat of Nationalities was set up on 26 October (8 November) 1917 to its dissolution in July 1923. From March 1919 he was also people's commissar of state control, and after the reorganisation of this commissariat in February 1920, he was people's commissar of workers' and peasants' inspection until 25 April 1922.

republics. We are settling them; and we need a man to whom the representatives of any of these nations can go and discuss their difficulties in all detail. Where can we find such a man? I don't think Comrade Preobrazhensky could suggest any better candidate than Comrade Stalin.

The same thing applies to the Workers' and Peasants' Inspection. This is a vast business; but to be able to handle investigations we must have at the head of it a man who enjoys high prestige, otherwise we shall become submerged in and overwhelmed by petty intrigue.

Comrade Preobrazhensky proposes that an Economic Bureau should be set up; but if we do that all our talk about separating Party activities from Soviet government activities will be just hot air. Comrade Preobrazhensky proposes what appears to be a splendid scheme: on the one hand the Political Bureau, then the Economic Bureau, and then the Organising Bureau. But all this is very fine only on paper; in actual practice it is ridiculous! I positively cannot understand how, after Soviet power has been in existence for five years, a man who has an intuition for vital politics can make and insist upon such a proposal.

What is the difference between the Organising Bureau and the Political Bureau? You cannot draw a hard and fast line between a political question and an organisation question. Any political question may be an organisation question, and vice versa. Only after established practice had shown that questions could be transferred from the Organising Bureau to the Political Bureau was it possible to organise the work of the Central Committee properly.

Has anybody ever proposed anything different? No, because no other rational solution can be proposed. Political questions cannot be mechanically separated from organisation questions. Politics are conducted by definite people; but if other people are going to draft documents, nothing will come of it.

You know perfectly well that there have been revolutions in which parliamentary assemblies drafted documents which were put into effect by people from another class. This led to friction, and they were kicked out. Organisation questions cannot be separated from politics. Politics are concentrated economics.

Comrade Kosior complained about the Central Committee and mentioned names (I have written them all down). I am not personally familiar with the subject, and so I cannot answer; but if you, as the Party congress, are interested, it is your duty to elect a commission to investigate every case and subject Kosior and the persons concerned to examination in the third degree. The whole point here is that if the Central Committee is deprived of the right to distribute forces, it will be unable to direct policy. Although we make mistakes when we transfer people from one place to another, nevertheless, I take the liberty of asserting that all the time it has been functioning, the Political Bureau of the Central Committee has made the minimum of mistakes. This is not self-praise. The activities of the Political Bureau are tested not by commissions, not by people appointed by our Party, but by the whiteguards, by our enemies; and the proof is the results of its policy, in which no serious mistakes have been committed.

Comrade Osinsky's strong point is that if he undertakes anything he pursues it with energy and vigour. We must do all we can to cultivate this strong point of his and to curb his weak points (even if Osinsky raises a howl – he is such a vigorous fellow – this must be done; otherwise, as a worker, he will be done for). We on the Central Committee have taken measures which, I think, will combine his weak points with his strong ones.

If I wanted to polemicise with Comrade Osinsky – which I do not want to do – I would say that the weightiest evidence that could be brought against him is the speech he delivered here today. I would have it printed and posted up on a board. … There was once a man …

A deputy people's commissar and a leading figure in one of the most important people's commissariats, and foremost among those who can draw up a platform on any question, this man proposes that we should adopt the cabinet system.[13] I assert that this man is absolutely done for … I will not go into this in detail, or polemicise; what interests me most is that Comrade Osinsky's vast energy should be directed into proper channels. If Comrade Osinsky does not, in a comradely way, heed the advice that has been often given to him by the Central Committee, and for which I have been largely responsible, and if he does not moderate his zeal in this matter, he will inevitably find himself in the mire, as he found himself today.

This is very unpleasant for a man who is fond of displaying his character; and it is quite legitimate for a man gifted with a strong character to want to display it. Would to God that everybody had such a character to display. But the Central Committee must see to it that this character is displayed for a useful purpose. The Central Committee must see to it that this talk about a cabinet is cut short, even if the man who undergoes this circumcision, so to speak, complains about it. This will be beneficial. He must put a curb on his talents to prevent himself from landing in the mire; and he must consult comrades in the other people's commissariats and adhere to the general line. Has any one of our commissariats done anything without controversy? No.

---

13   N. Osinsky (V. V. Obolensky), speaking at the congress, proposed that a 'cabinet' of commissars be set up. His suggestion was that it should be formed not by the All-Russia Central Executive Cornmittee but unilaterally by its chairman, who would be responsible to the ARCEC. While Osinsky spoke Lenin made the following entry in his note book: '(*Set up a cabinet!*) one member should form the cabinet' (*Lenin Miscellany XIII*, 1930, p. 22).

'Improvement of the system of administration and the psychological mobilisation of the masses.' This is sheer murder! If the congress were to adopt this politically reactionary point of view it would be the surest and best method of committing suicide.

'Improvement of the system of administration'?! Pray God that we succeed, at least, in getting out of the muddle that we are in today.

We have no system?! For five years we have been spending our best efforts in the endeavour to create this system! This system is a tremendous step forward.

The machinery of state is faulty! Do we know what the trouble is? We do not! But Comrade Osinsky talks as if he does. Why, he can sit down and in ten minutes devise a whole system of administration. It will be harmful and a political mistake if his zeal is not curbed. In other channels, however, the zeal he is displaying now will be very useful.

Well, that's one illustration. And then Comrades Preobrazhensky and Osinsky bore out in their comments what I said about the most important thing, and Comrade Larin proved it still more thoroughly. Look what he did. He hurled accusations at me and laughed and jested very merrily.

He does this magnificently; this is his strong point. If Comrade Larin could display this strong point of his in some field other than that of state activities he would be a thousand times more useful for our republic; for he is a very capable man and has a vivid imagination. This quality is extremely valuable; it is wrong to think that only poets need imagination. That is a silly prejudice! It is needed even in mathematics; it would have been impossible to discover the differential and integral calculus without imagination. Imagination is a very valuable asset; but Comrade Larin has a little too much of it. I would say, for example, that if Comrade Larin's stock of imagination were divided equally among all the members of the RCP,

there would be very good results. [*Laughter. Applause.*] But
until we can perform this operation, Comrade Larin must be
kept away from state, administrative, planning and economic
affairs. Otherwise, we shall have the same thing occurring as
in the old Supreme Economic Council, when Comrade Rykov
had not yet recovered, and affairs were directed and documents
signed by 'Y. Larin' on behalf of the entire Supreme Economic
Council. Things were run badly not because Comrade Larin
displayed his worst qualities, but on the contrary; it was
because he displayed his best qualities – and nobody can have
even a shadow of doubt about his devotion and knowledge of
affairs. Nevertheless, things were run badly.

This is exactly what I said. True, all these are copybook
maxims. As for copybook maxims, even Kamkov poked fun
at me for this at the Congress of the Socialist-Revolutionaries.
He said: 'Today, Lenin is preaching: "Thou shalt not steal";
and tomorrow he will add: "Thou shalt not commit adul-
tery." This is all that Lenin's wisdom amounts to.' I heard
this from Kamkov, the Socialist-Revolutionary, as far back
as 1918. And if Kamkov, who backed these arguments with
artillery, made no impression on anyone, what impression can
Comrade Larin's jokes make? Now we must concentrate all
our attention on the major problems of our New Economic
Policy. Here Comrade Larin tried to divert the Party on to
the wrong road. If he were engaged with matters on which he
could usefully display his numerous talents, where he could
be of great benefit to the younger generation, and where he
would not play such a trick as he played in the State Planning
Commission, it would be entirely different. If he were engaged
in such work he would make an impression on the younger
generation – I think I am speaking plainly enough – and we
should not have the confusion that he has caused here.[14]

---

14 At the congress Y. Larin alleged that an authorised body of the
State Planning Commission had proposed that at the Genoa Conference

I said that Comrade Kamenev proposed on the Political Bureau that a resolution be adopted to the effect that it would be useful to import food and that canned goods be purchased with Soviet currency. Larin sat here, heard this perfectly well, and remembering it perfectly well, said as soon as he got on to the platform: 'Lenin forgot, owing to ill health – we shall forgive him this time – that the permission of the Political Bureau has to be obtained for disbursements from the gold reserve.' Had Comrade Kamenev proposed that we should take money out of the gold reserve and give it to French profiteers in exchange for canned goods we would not have listened to him. We did not offer a single gold kopek for the canned goods, we offered Soviet paper currency and – just imagine – it was accepted. Wolfson even assured me yesterday that these canned goods were of good quality (although they have not arrived yet); but I shall not believe him until we have tasted them, because here they may try to cheat us. The point is, however, that Comrade Larin garbled the facts; we did not spend a single gold kopek; we spent 160,000 million Soviet paper roubles.

Of course, it would be ridiculous and absurd to think that Comrade Larin did this with malicious intent. No, that is not the point. The point is that his imagination soars a trillion kilometres high and, as a consequence, he mixes everything up.

Then he went on to say that the State Planning Commission had proposed to lease out three-fourths of our railways. It is a good thing that he said this at the Party congress, where Krzhizhanovsky immediately refuted him. It does not often happen like that. You think that talk of this sort is heard

---

the Soviet delegation should offer to lease (as a concession) three-quarters of the country's railways, the Petrograd–Rybinsk waterway, the iron and steel plants in the Urals with a railway network of 3,000 *versts*, and the power engineering industry. This allegation was refuted by G. M. Krzhizhanovsky.

only at Party congresses? Inquire at the Central Control Commission and they will tell you how they examined the case of the Moscow Debating Club, and what brought up the case of the Moscow Debating Club,[15] where Comrades Larin and Ryazanov – [*Ryazanov from his seat*: 'I said nothing about the gold reserve there; worse things were said.'] I was not in Moscow and took no part in the investigation of this case, I merely had a brief report – [*Ryazanov*: 'Don't believe every rumour.'] I learned this from a conversation I had with Comrade Solts; it is not a rumour, but a conversation I had with a man whom our supreme body, the Party congress, had appointed to the Central Control Commission. It was he who told me; and what he told me cannot rouse the slightest doubt. One must be very thoughtless to call this a rumour. The Central Control Commission investigated the affair of the Debating Club and was obliged to state unanimously that it was not being run properly. What is wrong is quite clear to me. Today, Larin, in passing, carried away by his own eloquence, went to the length of saying that a proposal had been made to lease out three-fourths of our railways, but that the Central Committee had put the matter right. Krzhizhanovsky said that nothing of the kind had happened; the Central Committee had put nothing right; Larin had simply muddled up his facts. This is constantly happening.

---

15 The Debating Club at the Moscow Committee of the RCP(B) was organised in August 1921. Similar clubs were opened in various parts of Moscow. They debated Party and Soviet development, the Soviet Republic's economic policy and other problems. However, the Debating Club soon began to be used by opposition groups as a forum for propagandising their views. On 20 February 1922, the Central Committee of the RCP(B) examined the question of the Debating Club on the basis of a report from the Central Control Commission and instructed the Moscow Committee to reconsider the composition of the club's board and to organise its work in conformity with the Party's tasks.

For four years we have been unable to put a useful worker like Larin to really useful work and to relieve him of work where he causes harm, in spite of himself.

The situation is rather unnatural, I think. We have the dictatorship of the proletariat, a reign of terror, victory over all the armies in the world, but no victory over Larin's army! Here we have suffered utter defeat! He is always doing what he has no business to do. His vast knowledge and his ability to enthuse people would be of real benefit to the younger generation, which is groping in the dark. We are unable to utilise his knowledge, and this gives rise to friction and resistance. Here the Political Bureau, the Organising Bureau of the Central Committee and the plenary meetings of the Central Committee, which are accused of enjoying too much authority, turn out to have insufficient authority, or prestige, to distribute all the comrades properly.

We must think this question over and discuss it seriously. This is the pivot of our work, and we must set things right here. If we do, we shall emerge from our difficulties. We shall achieve this by rectifying things, but not by talking about the new tasks of the Agrarian Programme as Osinsky and Larin did. I wrote a review of this programme for the Central Committee. I shall not discuss it now; every member of the Party interested in the subject has a right to go to the Secretariat and read it there. Please do so. If we divert the efforts of Larin and Osinsky into the proper channels and curb their misguided zeal, enormous benefit will accrue.

In conclusion I shall say a few words about Shlyapnikov. I intended to speak about him at greater length, but 99 per cent of this subject has been covered by Trotsky and Zinoviev, who on instructions of the Central Committee replied to the Statement of the Twenty-Two at the meeting of the Communist International.[16]

16 This anti-Party statement was sent on 26 February 1922 to the

First, Comrade Shlyapnikov pretended not to understand why I referred to machine guns and panic-mongers; and he jokingly said that he had been tried lots of times. Of course, comrades, it is not a bad thing to make a joke. One cannot speak at a big meeting without cracking a joke or two, because one's audience gets weary. One must be human. But there are certain things that one must not joke about; there is such a thing as Party unity.

At a time when we are completely surrounded by enemies; when the international bourgeoisie is sufficiently astute to shift Milyukov to the left, to supply the Socialist-Revolutionaries with money for the publication of all sorts of newspapers and to incite Vandervelde and Otto Bauer to launch a campaign against the trial of the Socialist-Revolutionaries and to

---

Presidium of the Extended Plenary Meeting of the Comintern Executive Committee by a group of members of the former Workers' Opposition (A. G. Shlyapnikov, S. P. Medvedyev, A. M. Kollontai, G. I. Myasnikov and others, which continued to exist as a faction despite the resolution 'On Party Unity' passed by the Tenth Congress of the RCP(B). The statement claimed that 'matters were unsatisfactory with regard to a united front in our country', that the leading Party bodies were ignoring the requirements and interests of the workers and that a split was impending in the Party. The Comintern Executive Committee appointed a commission consisting of Clara Zetkin, Marcel Cachin, Jacob Friis, Vasil Kolarov, Karl Krejbich, Umberto Terracini and Arthur McManus to look into the Statement of the Twenty-Two. On 4 March, on the basis of the report of this commission, a plenary meeting of the Comintern Executive Committee, with four abstentions, passed a resolution rejecting the accusations in the statement and censured the stand of the twenty-two as running counter to the decisions of the Tenth Congress of the RCP(B). The Eleventh Congress of the RCP(B) appointed a commission of nineteen persons to examine the Statement of the Twenty-Two. On 2 April, on the basis of the report of this commission, a closed session of the congress adopted a special resolution 'On Certain Members of the Former Workers' Opposition', in which it stigmatised the anti-Party behaviour of members of the Workers' Opposition group, and warned the leaders of the group that they would be expelled from the Party if they renewed their factional activity.

howl that the Bolsheviks are brutes; when all these people, who have studied politics for ages and have thousands of millions of gold roubles, francs, etc., at their disposal, are arrayed against us, for Comrade Shlyapnikov to crack jokes and to say: 'I have been tried by the Central Committee,' and so forth, is a deplorable thing, comrades. The Party congress must draw definite conclusions. We do not arrange trials at the Central Committee for nothing! Comrade Shlyapnikov was tried by the Central Committee, and we were short of three votes to expel him from the Party.[17] The members of the Party gathered at this Congress should interest themselves in the matter and read the minutes of that meeting of the Central Committee. This is no laughing matter!

You have a legitimate right to appeal to the Communist International. But a long time before that appeal was lodged a large majority of the Central Committee was in favour of expelling Comrade Shlyapnikov; only the necessary two-thirds vote was lacking. You cannot trifle with a thing like that! It will do you no harm to know that at the meeting of the communist group at the Metalworkers' Congress Comrade Shlyapnikov openly advocated a split.

Comrade Trotsky has already dealt with the significance of Comrade Kollontai's pamphlet.

If we trifle with things like this it will be utterly hopeless to expect that we shall hold on in the difficult situation in which we now find ourselves. I have indicated the three conditions under which it will be possible for us to hold on: first, that there shall be no intervention; second, that the financial crisis shall not be too severe; and third, that we shall make no political mistakes.

---

17 On a motion proposed by Lenin, the joint sitting of the plenary meeting of the Central Committee and the Central Control Commission, on 9 August 1921, examined the question of expelling A. Shlyapnikov from the Central Committee and from the Party for anti-Party activity.

One of the speakers stated that I said political complications. No, I said political mistakes. If we make no political mistakes, I say, 99 per cent of the Party membership will be with us, and so also will the non-Party workers and peasants, who will understand that this is the time to learn.

I remember that in the article he wrote on the anniversary of the Red Army Comrade Trotsky said: 'A year of tuition.' This slogan applies equally to the Party and to the working class. During this period we have rallied around us a vast number of heroic people who have undoubtedly made the turn in world history permanent. But this does not justify our failure to understand that we now have ahead of us a 'year of tuition'.

We are standing much more firmly on our feet today than we stood a year ago. Of course, even today the bourgeoisie may attempt another armed intervention, but they will find it much more difficult than before; it is much more difficult today than it was yesterday.

To ensure ourselves the opportunity to learn we must make no political mistakes. We must waste no time playing with the unity of the Party, as Comrade Shlyapnikov is doing. We cannot afford games of that kind! We know that the conflict within the Party is costing us a great deal. Comrades, we must not forget this lesson! Concerning the past year, the Central Committee has every right to say that at the opening of this congress there was less factional strife in the Party, it was more united than last year. I do not want to boast that all factionalism in the Party has vanished. But it is an incontrovertible fact that there is less factionalism in the Party today. This has been proved.

You know that the present Workers' Opposition is only a wreck of the former Workers' Opposition. Compare the signatures appended to the Statement of the Twenty-Two with those appended to the platform that was issued before the Tenth Congress. You will find that many of those signatures are missing. We must tell those people who legitimately used their right to appeal to the Communist International that they had no right to appeal on behalf of Myasnikov. The Myasnikov case came up last summer;[18] I was not in Moscow at the time, but I wrote Myasnikov a long letter, which he inserted in his pamphlet. I saw that he was a capable man and that it was worthwhile having a talk with him; but this man must be told that if he comes out with criticism of this sort it will not be tolerated.

He writes a letter saying: 'Collect all the discontented in the district.' Yes, it is not a very difficult matter to collect all the discontented in a district. Take the speeches that Shlyapnikov delivers here, and which Comrade Medvedyev delivers elsewhere. [*Medvedyev from his seat*: 'Where did you obtain your information?'] I obtained my information from the bodies appointed by the Congress of the RCP: the Organising Bureau of the Central Committee, the Secretariat of the Central Committee, and the Central Control Commission.

---

18   In Motovilikha District, Perm Gubernia, G. I. Myasnikov organised an anti-Party group which opposed the Party's policy. On 29 July 1921, the Organising Bureau of the CC, RCP(B) examined Myasnikov's statements in the Perm organisation, found that they were directed against the Party and set up a commission to investigate Myasnikov's activities. On 22 August, acting on the basis of the report of this commission, the Organising Bureau found Myasnikov's theses incompatible with Party interests, prohibited him from speaking of his theses at official Party meetings, recalled him from the Perm organisation and placed him at the disposal of the Central Committee. Myasnikov disobeyed the Central Committee, returned to Motovilikha and continued his anti-Party activities. At the same time, he tried to organise an anti-Party group in Petrograd. After investigating his activities, the CC, RCP(B) commission proposed that he should be expelled from the Party for repeated violations of Party discipline and for organising a special anti-Party group in defiance of the Tenth Party Congress decision on Party unity. On 20 February 1922, the Political Bureau approved the commission's decision on Myasnikov's expulsion from the Party, with the provision that he should have the right to apply for Party membership in a year (see *Eleventh Congress of the RCP(B). Verbatim Report*, Moscow, 1961, pp. 748–9).

Make inquiries there, if you like, and you will learn what sort of speeches Comrade Medvedyev delivers. If we do not put a stop to this sort of thing we shall be unable to maintain the unity which, perhaps, is our greatest asset. We must ruthlessly expose our mistakes and discuss them. If we clearly understand this – and we are beginning to understand it at this congress – there is not the slightest doubt that we shall be able to overcome them. [*Tumultuous applause.*]

4. *Speech in Closing the Congress, 2 April*
Comrades, we have reached the end of our congress.

The first difference that strikes one in comparing this congress with the preceding one is the greater solidarity, the greater unanimity and greater organisational unity that have been displayed.

Only a small part of one of the sections of the opposition that existed at the last congress has placed itself outside the Party.

On the trade union question and on the New Economic Policy no disagreements, or hardly any disagreements, have been revealed in our Party.

The radically and fundamentally 'new' achievement of this congress is that it has provided vivid proof that our enemies are wrong in constantly reiterating that our Party is becoming senile and is losing its flexibility of mind and body.

No. We have not lost this flexibility.

When the objective state of affairs in Russia, and all over the world, called for an advance, for a supremely bold, swift and determined onslaught on the enemy, we made that onslaught. If necessary, we shall do it again and again.

By that we raised our revolution to a height hitherto unparalleled in the world. No power on earth, no matter how much evil, hardship and suffering it may yet cause millions and hundreds of millions of people, can annul the major gains of our revolution, for these are no longer our but historic gains.

But when in the spring of 1921 it turned out that the vanguard of the revolution was in danger of becoming isolated from the masses of the people, from the masses of the peasants, whom it must skilfully lead forward, we unanimously and firmly decided to retreat. And on the whole, during the past year we retreated in good revolutionary order.

The proletarian revolutions maturing in all advanced countries of the world will be unable to solve their problems unless they combine the ability to fight heroically and to attack with the ability to retreat in good revolutionary order. The experience of the second period of our struggle, i.e., the experience of retreat, will in the future probably be just as useful to the workers of at least some countries, as the experience of the first period of our revolution, i.e., the experience of bold attack, will undoubtedly prove useful to the workers of all countries.

Now we have decided to halt the retreat.

This means that the entire object of our policy must be formulated in a new way.

The central feature of the situation now is that the vanguard must not shirk the work of educating itself, of remoulding itself; must not be afraid of frankly admitting that it is not sufficiently trained and lacks the necessary skill. The main thing now is to advance as an immeasurably wider and larger mass, and only together with the peasantry, proving to them by deeds, in practice, by experience, that we are learning, and that we shall learn to assist them, to lead them forward. In the present international situation, in the present state of the productive forces of Russia, this problem can be solved only very slowly, cautiously, in a businesslike way, and by testing a thousand times in a practical way every step that is taken.

If voices are raised in our Party against this extremely slow and extremely cautious progress, these voices will be isolated ones.

The Party as a whole has understood – and will now prove by deeds that it has understood – that at the present time its work must be organised exactly along these lines, and since we have understood it, we shall achieve our goal.

I declare the Eleventh Congress of the Russian Communist Party closed.

27 March–2 April 1922

Memo Combating Dominant-Nation Chauvinism

I declare war to the death on dominant-nation chauvinism. I shall eat it with all my healthy teeth as soon as I get rid of this accursed bad tooth.

It must be *absolutely* insisted that the Union Central Executive Committee should be *presided over* in turn by a:

Russian,
Ukrainian,
Georgian, etc.

Absolutely!

Yours,
Lenin

6 October 1922

'Last Testament'
Letters to Congress

Letter to Congress

I.

I would urge strongly that at this congress a number of changes be made in our political structure.

I want to tell you of the considerations to which I attach most importance.

At the head of the list I set an increase in the number of Central Committee members to a few dozen or even a hundred. It is my opinion that without this reform our Central Committee would be in great danger if the course of events were not quite favourable for us (and that is something we cannot count on).

Then, I intend to propose that the congress should on certain conditions invest the decisions of the State Planning Commission with legislative force, meeting, in this respect, the wishes of Comrade Trotsky – to a certain extent and on certain conditions.

As for the first point, i.e., increasing the number of CC members, I think it must be done in order to raise the prestige of the Central Committee, to do a thorough job of improving our administrative machinery and to prevent conflicts between small sections of the CC from acquiring excessive importance for the future of the Party.

It seems to me that our Party has every right to demand from the working class 50 to 100 CC members, and that it could get them from it without unduly taxing the resources of that class.

Such a reform would considerably increase the stability of our Party and ease its struggle in the encirclement of hostile states, which, in my opinion, is likely to, and must, become much more acute in the next few years. I think that the stability of our Party would gain a thousandfold by such measure.

23 December 1922
Dictated to M. V.

II.
Continuation of the notes.
24 December 1922

By stability of the Central Committee, of which I spoke above, I mean measure against a split, as far as such measures can at all be taken. For, of course, the whiteguard in *Russkaya Mysl* (it seems to have been S.S. Oldenburg) was right when, first, in the whiteguards' game against Soviet Russia he banked on a split in our Party, and when, second, he banked on grave differences in our Party to cause that split.

Our Party relies on two classes and therefore its instability would be possible and its downfall inevitable if there were no agreement between those two classes. In that event this or that measure, and generally all talk about the stability of our CC, would be futile. No measure of any kind could prevent a split in such a case. But I hope that this is too remote a future and too improbable an event to talk about.

I have in mind stability as a guarantee against a split in the immediate future, and I intend to deal here with a few ideas concerning personal qualities.

I think that from this standpoint the prime factors in the question of stability are such members of the CC as Stalin and Trotsky. I think relations between them make up the greater part of the danger of a split, which could be avoided, and this purpose, in my opinion, would be served, among other things, by increasing the number of CC members to 50 or 100.

Comrade Stalin, having become secretary general, has unlimited authority concentrated in his hands, and I am not sure whether he will always be capable of using that authority with sufficient caution. Comrade Trotsky, on the other hand, as his struggle against the CC on the question of the people's commissariat of communications has already proved, is distinguished not only by outstanding ability. He is personally perhaps the most capable man in the present CC, but he has displayed excessive self-assurance and shown excessive pre-occupation with the purely administrative side of the work.

These two qualities of the two outstanding leaders of the present CC can inadvertently lead to a split, and if our Party does not take steps to avert this, the split may come unexpectedly.

I shall not give any further appraisals of the personal qualities of other members of the CC. I shall just recall that the October episode with Zinoviev and Kamenev [See *Complete* Works, Vol. 26, pp. 216–19] was, of course, no accident, but neither can the blame for it be laid upon them personally, any more than non-Bolshevism can upon Trotsky.

Speaking of the young CC members, I wish to say a few words about Bukharin and Pyatakov. They are, in my opinion, the most outstanding figures (among the youngest ones), and the following must be borne in mind about them: Bukharin is not only a most valuable and major theorist of the Party; he is also rightly considered the favourite of the whole Party, but his theoretical views can be classified as fully Marxist only with great reserve, for there is something scholastic about him (he has never made a study of the dialectics, and, I think, never fully understood it).

25 December. As for Pyatakov, he is unquestionably a man of outstanding will and outstanding ability, but shows too

much zeal for administrating and the administrative side of the work to be relied upon in a serious political matter.

Both of these remarks, of course, are made only for the present, on the assumption that both these outstanding and devoted Party workers fail to find an occasion to enhance their knowledge and amend their one-sidedness.

Dictated to M.V.

Addition to the above letter

Stalin is too rude and this defect, although quite tolerable in our midst and in dealing among us Communists, becomes intolerable in a secretary general. That is why I suggest that the comrades think about a way of removing Stalin from that post and appointing another man in his stead who in all other respects differs from Comrade Stalin in having only one advantage, namely that of being more tolerant, more loyal, more polite and more considerate to the comrades, less capricious, etc. This circumstance may appear to be a negligible detail. But I think that from the standpoint of safeguards against a split and from the standpoint of what I wrote above about the relationship between Stalin and Trotsky it is not a [minor] detail, but it is a detail which can assume decisive importance.

Taken down by L.F.
4 January 1923

III.
Continuation of the notes.
26 December 1922

The increase in the number of CC members to 50 or even 100 must, in my opinion, serve a double or even a treble purpose: the more members there are in the CC, the more men will be trained in CC work and the less danger there will be of a split due to some indiscretion. The enlistment of many workers to the CC will help the workers to improve our administrative machinery, which is pretty bad. We inherited it, in effect, from the old regime, for it was absolutely impossible to reorganise it in such a short time, especially in conditions of war, famine, etc. That is why those 'critics' who point to the defects of our administrative machinery out of mockery or malice may be calmly answered that they do not in the least understand the conditions of the revolution today. It is altogether impossible in five years to reorganise the machinery adequately, especially in the conditions in which our revolution took place. It is enough that in five years we have created a new type of state in which the workers are leading the peasants against the bourgeoisie; and in a hostile international environment this in itself is a gigantic achievement. But knowledge of this must on no account blind us to the fact that, in effect, we took over the old machinery of state from the tsar and the bourgeoisie and that now, with the onset of peace and the satisfaction of the minimum requirements against famine, all our work must be directed towards improving the administrative machinery.

I think that a few dozen workers, being members of the CC, can deal better than anybody else with checking, improving and remodeling our state apparatus. The Workers' and Peasants' Inspection on whom this function devolved at the beginning proved unable to cope with it and can be used only as an 'appendage' or, on certain conditions, as an assistant to these members of the CC. In my opinion, the workers admitted to the Central Committee should come preferably not from among those who have had long service in Soviet bodies (in this part of my letter the term 'workers' everywhere includes peasants), because those workers have already acquired the very traditions and the very prejudices which it is desirable to combat.

The working-class members of the CC must be mainly workers of a lower stratum than those promoted in the last five years to work in Soviet bodies; they must be people closer to being rank-and-file workers and peasants, who, however, do not fall into the category of direct or indirect exploiters. I think that by attending all sittings of the CC and all sittings of the Political Bureau, and by reading all the documents of the CC, such workers can form a staff of devoted supporters of the Soviet system, able, first, to give stability to the CC itself, and second, to work effectively on the renewal and improvement of the state apparatus.

Dictated to L.F.

VII.
Continuation of the notes.
29 December 1922

In increasing the number of its members, the CC, I think, must also, and perhaps mainly, devote attention to checking and improving our administrative machinery, which is no good at all. For this we must enlist the services of highly qualified specialists, and the task of supplying those specialists must devolve upon the Workers' and Peasants' Inspection.

How are we to combine these checking specialists, people with adequate knowledge, and the new members of the CC? This problem must be resolved in practice.

It seems to me that the Workers' and Peasants' Inspection (as a result of its development and of our perplexity about its development) has led all in all to what we now observe, namely to an intermediate position between a special people's commissariat and a special function of the members of the CC; between an institution that inspects anything and everything and an aggregate of not very numerous but first-class

inspectors, who must be well paid (this is especially indis-
pensable in our age when every thing must be paid for and
inspectors are directly employed by the institutions that pay
them better).

If the number of CC members is increased in the appropriate way, and they go through a course of state management
year after year with the help of highly qualified specialists and
of members of the Workers' and Peasants Inspection who are
highly authoritative in every branch – then, I think, we shall
successfully solve this problem which we have not managed to
do for such a long time.

To sum up, 100 members of the CC at the most and not
more than 400–500 assistants, members of the Workers'
and Peasants' Inspection, engaged in inspecting under their
direction.

Dictated to M.V.

On Education (Pages from a Diary)

The recent publication of the report on literacy among the population of Russia, based on the census of 1920 (*Literacy in Russia*, issued by the Central Statistical Board, Public Education Section, Moscow, 1922), is a very important event.

Below I quote a table from this report on the state of literacy among the population of Russia in 1897 and 1920.

	Literates per thousand males		Literates per thousand females		Literates per thousand population	
	1897	1920	1897	1920	1897	1920
1. European Russia	326	422	136	255	229	330
2. North Caucasus	241	357	56	215	150	281
3. Siberia (Western)	170	307	46	134	108	218
Overall average	318	409	131	244	223	319

At a time when we hold forth on proletarian culture and the relation in which it stands to bourgeois culture, facts and figures reveal that we are in a very bad way even as far as bourgeois culture is concerned. As might have been expected, it appears that we are still a very long way from attaining universal literacy, and that even compared with tsarist times (1897) our progress has been far too slow. This should serve as a stern warning and reproach to those who have been soaring in the empyreal heights of 'proletarian culture'. It shows what a vast amount of urgent spadework we still have to do to reach the standard of an ordinary Western European civilised country. It also shows what a vast amount of work we have to do today to achieve, on the basis of our proletarian gains, anything like a real cultural standard.

We must not confine ourselves to this incontrovertible but too theoretical proposition. The very next time we revise our quarterly budget we must take this matter up in a practical way as well. In the first place, of course, we shall have to cut down the expenditure of government departments other than the People's Commissariat of Education, and the sums thus released should be assigned for the latter's needs. In a year like the present, when we are relatively well supplied, we must not be chary in increasing the bread ration for schoolteachers.

Generally speaking, it cannot be said that the work now being done in public education is too narrow. Quite a lot is being done to get the old teachers out of their rut, to attract them to the new problems, to rouse their interest in new methods of education, and in such problems as religion.

But we are not doing the main thing. We are not doing anything – or doing far from enough – to raise the schoolteacher to the level that is absolutely essential if we want any culture at all, proletarian or even bourgeois. We must bear in mind the semi-Asiatic ignorance from which we have not yet extricated ourselves, and from which we cannot extricate ourselves without strenuous effort – although we have every opportunity to do so, because nowhere are the masses of the people so interested in real culture as they are in our country; nowhere are the problems of this culture tackled so thoroughly and consistently as they are in our country; in no other country is state power in the hands of the working class which, in its mass, is fully aware of the deficiencies, I shall not say of its culture, but of its literacy; nowhere is the working class so ready to make, and nowhere is it actually making, such sacrifices to improve its position in this respect as in our country.

Too little, far too little, is still being done by us to adjust our state budget to satisfy, as a first measure, the requirements of elementary public education. Even in our People's Commissariat of Education we all too often find disgracefully inflated staffs in some state publishing establishment, which is contrary to the concept that the state's first concern should not be publishing houses but that there should be people to read, that the number of people able to read is greater, so that book publishing should have a wider political field in future Russia. Owing to the old (and bad) habit, we are still devoting much more time and effort to technical questions, such as the question of book publishing, than to the general political question of literacy among the people.

If we take the Central Vocational Education Board, we are sure that there, too, we shall find far too much that is superfluous and inflated by departmental interests, much that is ill-adjusted to the requirements of broad public education. Far from everything that we find in the Central Vocational Education Board can be justified by the legitimate desire first of all to improve and give a practical slant to the education of our young factory workers. If we examine the staff of the Central Vocational Education Board carefully we shall find very much that is inflated and is in that respect fictitious and should be done away with. There is still very much in the proletarian and peasant state that can and must be economised for the purpose of promoting literacy among the people; this can be done by closing institutions which are playthings of a semi-aristocratic type, or institutions we can still do without and will be able to do without, and shall have to do without, for a long time to come, considering the state of literacy among the people as revealed by the statistics.

Our schoolteacher should be raised to a standard he has never achieved, and cannot achieve, in bourgeois society. This is a truism and requires no proof. We must strive for this state of affairs by working steadily, methodically and persistently to raise the teacher to a higher cultural level, to train him thoroughly for his really high calling and – mainly, mainly and mainly – to improve his position materially.

We must systematically step up our efforts to organise the schoolteachers so as to transform them from the bulwark of the bourgeois system that they still are in all capitalist countries without exception, into the bulwark of the Soviet system, in order, through their agency, to divert the peasantry from alliance with the bourgeoisie and to bring them into alliance with the proletariat.

I want briefly to emphasise the special importance in this respect of regular visits to the villages; such visits, it is true, are already being practised and should be regularly promoted. We should not stint money – which we all too often waste on the machinery of state that is almost entirely a product of the past historical epoch – on measures like these visits to the villages.

For the speech I was to have delivered at the Congress of Soviets in December 1922 I collected data on the patronage undertaken by urban workers over villagers. Part of these data was obtained for me by Comrade Khodorovsky, and since I have been unable to deal with this problem and give it publicity through the congress, I submit the matter to the comrades for discussion now.

Here we have a fundamental political question – the relations between town and country – which is of decisive importance for the whole of our revolution. While the bourgeois state methodically concentrates all its efforts on doping the urban workers, adapting all the literature published at state expense and at the expense of the tsarist and bourgeois parties for this purpose, we can and must utilise our political power to make the urban worker an effective vehicle of communist ideas among the rural proletariat.

I said 'communist', but I hasten to make a reservation for fear of causing a misunderstanding, or of being taken too literally. Under no circumstances must this be understood to mean that we should immediately propagate purely and strictly communist ideas in the countryside. As long as our countryside lacks the material basis for communism, it will be, I should say, harmful, in fact, I should say, fatal, for communism to do so.

That is a fact. We must start by establishing contacts between town and country without the preconceived aim of implanting communism in the rural districts. It is an aim which cannot be achieved at the present time. It is inopportune, and to set an aim like that at the present time would be harmful, instead of useful, to the cause.

But it is our duty to establish contacts between the urban workers and the rural working people, to establish between them a form of comradeship which can easily be created. This is one of the fundamental tasks of the working class which holds power. To achieve this we must form a number of associations (Party, trade union and private) of factory workers, which would devote themselves regularly to assisting the villages in their cultural development.

Is it possible to 'attach' all the urban groups to all the village groups, so that every working-class group may take advantage regularly of every opportunity, of every occasion to serve the cultural needs of the village group it is 'attached' to? Or will it be possible to find other forms of contact? I here confine myself solely to formulating the question in order to draw the comrades' attention to it, to point out the available experience of Western Siberia (to which Comrade Khodorovsky drew my attention) and to present this gigantic, historic cultural task in all its magnitude.

We are doing almost nothing for the rural districts outside our official budget or outside official channels. True, in our country the nature of the cultural relations between town and village is automatically and inevitably changing. Under capitalism the town introduced political, economic, moral, physical, etc., corruption into the countryside. In our case, towns are automatically beginning to introduce the very opposite of this into the countryside. But, I repeat, all this is going on automatically, spontaneously, and can be improved (and later increased a hundredfold) by doing it consciously, methodically and systematically.

We shall begin to advance (and shall then surely advance a hundred times more quickly) only after we have studied the question, after we have formed all sorts of workers' organisations – doing everything to prevent them from becoming bureaucratic – to take up the matter, discuss it and get things done.

2 January 1923

On Cooperation
(Apropos of N. Sukhanov's Notes)

It seems to me that not enough attention is being paid to the cooperative movement in our country. Not everyone understands that now, since the time of the October revolution and quite apart from the NEP (on the contrary, in this connection we must say – because of the NEP), our cooperative movement has become one of great significance. There is a lot of fantasy in the dreams of the old cooperators. Often they are ridiculously fantastic. But why are they fantastic? Because people do not understand the fundamental, the rock-bottom, significance of the working-class political struggle for the overthrow of the rule of the exploiters. We have overthrown the rule of the exploiters, and much that was fantastic, even romantic, even banal, in the dreams of the old cooperators is now becoming unvarnished reality.

Indeed, since political power is in the hands of the working class, since this political power owns all the means of production, the only task, indeed, that remains for us is to organise the population in cooperative societies. With most of the population organising cooperatives, the socialism which in the past was legitimately treated with ridicule, scorn and contempt by those who were rightly convinced that it was necessary to wage the class struggle, the struggle for political power, etc., will achieve its aim automatically. But not all comrades realise how vastly, how infinitely, important it is now to organise the population of Russia in cooperative societies. By adopting the NEP we made a concession to the peasant as a trader, to the principle of private trade; it is precisely for this reason (contrary to what some people think) that the cooperative movement is of such immense importance. All we actually need under the NEP is to organise the population of Russia in cooperative societies on a sufficiently large scale, for we have now found the degree of combination of private interest, of private commercial interest, with state supervision and control of this interest, that degree of its subordination to the common interests which was formerly the stumbling block for very many socialists. Indeed, the power of the state over all large-scale means of production, political power in the hands of the proletariat, the alliance of this proletariat with the many millions of small and very small peasants, the assured proletarian leadership of the peasantry, etc. – is this not all that is necessary to build a complete socialist society out of cooperatives, out of cooperatives alone, which we formerly ridiculed as huckstering and which from a certain aspect we have the right to treat as such now, under the NEP? Is this not all that is necessary to build a complete socialist society? It is still not the building of socialist society, but it is all that is necessary and sufficient for it.

It is this very circumstance that is underestimated by many of our practical workers. They look down upon cooperative societies, failing to appreciate their exceptional importance, first, from the standpoint of principle (the means of production are owned by the state), and, second, from the standpoint of transition to the new system by means that are the *simplest, easiest and most acceptable to the peasant.*

But this again is of fundamental importance. It is one thing to draw out fantastic plans for building socialism through all sorts of workers' associations, and quite another to learn to build socialism in practice in such a way that *every* small peasant could take part in it. That is the very stage we have now reached. And there is no doubt that, having reached it, we are taking too little advantage of it.

We went too far when we reintroduced the NEP, but not because we attached too much importance to the principle of free enterprise and trade – we went too far because we lost sight of the cooperatives, because we now underrate cooperatives, because we are already beginning to forget the vast importance of the cooperatives from the above two points of view.

I now propose to discuss with the reader what can and must at once be done practically on the basis of this 'cooperative' principle. By what means can we, and must we, start at once to develop this 'cooperative' principle so that its socialist meaning may be clear to all?

Cooperation must be politically so organised that it will not only generally and always enjoy certain privileges, but that these privileges should be of a purely material nature (a favourable bank rate, etc.). The cooperatives must be granted state loans that are greater, if only by a little, than the loans we grant to private enterprises, even to heavy industry, etc.

A social system emerges only if it has the financial backing of a definite class. There is no need to mention the hundreds of millions of rubles that the birth of 'free' capitalism cost. At present we have to realise that the cooperative system is a social system we must now give more than ordinary assistance, and we must actually give that assistance. But it must be it assistance in the real sense of the word, i.e., it will not be enough to interpret it to mean assistance for any kind of cooperative trade; by assistance we must mean aid to cooperative trade in which *really large masses of the population actually take part*. It is certainly a correct form of assistance to give a bonus to peasants who take part in cooperative trade; but the whole point is to verify the nature of this participation, to verify the awareness behind it, and to verify its quality. Strictly speaking, when a cooperator goes to a village and opens a cooperative store, the people take no part in this whatever;

but at the same time guided by their own interests they will hasten to try to take part in it.

There is another aspect to this question. From the point of view of the 'enlightened' European there is not much left for us to do to induce absolutely everyone to take not a passive, but inactive part in cooperative operations. Strictly speaking, there is '*only*' one thing we have left to do and that is to make our people so 'enlightened' that they understand all the advantages of everybody participating in the work of the cooperatives, and organises participation. '*Only*' the fact. There are now no other devices needed to advance to socialism. But to achieve this 'only', there must be a veritable revolution – the entire people must go through a period of cultural development. Therefore, our rule must be: as little philosophising and as few acrobatics as possible. In this respect the NEP is an advance, because it is adjustable to the level of the most ordinary peasant and does not demand anything higher of him. But it will take a whole historical epoch to get the entire population into the work of the cooperatives through the NEP. At best we can achieve this in one or two decades. Nevertheless, it will be a distinct historical epoch, and without this historical epoch, without universal literacy, without a proper degree of efficiency, without training the population sufficiently to acquire the habit of book reading, and without the material basis for this, without a certain sufficiency to safeguard against, say, bad harvests, famine, etc. – without this we shall not achieve our object. The thing now is to learn to combine the wide revolutionary range of action, the revolutionary enthusiasm which we have displayed, and displayed abundantly, and crowned with complete success – to learn to combine this with (I'm almost inclined to say) the ability to be an efficient and capable trader, which is quite enough to be a good cooperator. By ability to be a trader I mean the ability to be a cultured trader. Let those Russians, or peasants, who imagine that since they trade they are good traders, get that well into their heads. This does not follow that all. They do trade, but that is far from being cultured traders. They now trade in an Asiatic manner, but to be a good trader one must trade in the European manner. They are a whole epoch behind in that.

In conclusion: a number of economic, financial and banking privileges must be granted to the cooperatives – this is the way our socialist state must promote the new principle on which the population must be organised. But this is only the general outline of the task; it does not define and depict in detail the entire content of the practical task, i.e., we must find what form of 'bonus' to give for joining the cooperatives (and the terms on which we should give it), the form of bonus by which we shall assist the cooperative sufficiently, the form of bonus that will produce the civilised cooperator. And given social ownership of the means of production, given the class victory of the proletariat over the bourgeoisie, the system of civilised cooperators is the system of socialism.

4 January 1923

II

Whenever I wrote about the New Economic Policy I always quoted the article on state capitalism which I wrote in 1918.[1] This has more than once aroused doubts in the minds of certain young comrades but their doubts were mainly on abstract political points.

It seemed to them that the term 'state capitalism' could not be applied to a system under which the means of production were owned by the working class, a working class that held political power. They did not notice, however, that I use the

---

1 V.I. Lenin, '"Left-Wing" Childishness and the Perry-Bourgeois Mentality', *Collected Works*, Vol. 27, Progress Publishers, 1972, pp. 323–34.

term 'state capitalism', *first*, to connect historically our present position with the position adopted in my controversy with the so-called Left Communists; also, I argued at the time that state capitalism would be superior to our existing economy. It was important for me to show the continuity between ordinary state capitalism and the unusual, even very unusual, state capitalism to which I referred in introducing the reader to the New Economic Policy. *Second*, the practical purpose was always important to me. And the practical purpose of our New Economic Policy was to lease out concessions. In the prevailing circumstances, concessions in our country would unquestionably have been a pure type of state capitalism. That is how I argued about state capitalism.

But there is another aspect of the matter for which we may need state capitalism, or at least a comparison with it. It is a question of cooperatives.

In the capitalist state, cooperatives are no doubt collective capitalist institutions. Nor is there any doubt that under our present economic conditions, when we combine private capitalist enterprises – but in no other way than nationalised land and in no other way than under the control of the working-class state – with enterprises of the consistently socialist type (the means of production, the land on which the enterprises are situated, and the enterprises as a whole belonging to the state), the question arises about a third type of enterprise, the cooperatives, which were not formally regarded as an independent type differing fundamentally from the others. Under private capitalism, cooperative enterprises differ from capitalist enterprises as collective enterprises differ from private enterprises. Under state capitalism, cooperative enterprises differ from state capitalist enterprises, first, because they are private enterprises, and, second, because they are collective enterprises. Under our present system, cooperative enterprises differ from private capitalist enterprises because they are collective enterprises, but do not differ from socialist enterprises if the land on which they are situated and the means of production belong to the state, i.e., the working class.

This circumstance is not considered sufficiently when cooperatives are discussed. It is forgotten that owing to the special features of our political system, our cooperatives acquire an altogether exceptional significance. If we exclude concessions, which, incidentally, have not developed on any considerable scale, cooperation under our conditions nearly always coincides fully with socialism.

Let me explain what I mean. Why were the plans of the old cooperators, from Robert Owen onwards, fantastic? Because they dreamed of peacefully remodelling contemporary society into socialism without taking account of such fundamental questions as the class struggle, the capture of political power by the working class, the overthrow of the rule of the exploiting class. That is why we are right in regarding as entirely fantastic this 'cooperative' socialism, and as romantic, and even banal, the dream of transforming class enemies into class collaborators and class war into class peace (so-called class truce) by merely organising the population in cooperative societies.

Undoubtedly we were right from the point of view of the fundamental task of the present day, for socialism cannot be established without a class struggle for the political power and a state.

But see how things have changed now that the political power is in the hands of the working class, now that the political power of the exploiters is overthrown and all the means of production (except those which the workers' state voluntarily abandons on specified terms and for a certain time to the exploiters in the form of concessions) are owned by the working class.

Now we are entitled to say that for us the mere growth of

cooperation (with the 'slight' exception mentioned above) is identical with the growth of socialism, and at the same time we have to admit that there has been a radical modification in our whole outlook on socialism. The radical modification is this; formerly we placed, and had to place, the main emphasis on the political struggle, on revolution, on winning political power, etc. Now the emphasis is changing and shifting to peaceful, organisational, 'cultural' work. I should say that emphasis is shifting to educational work, were it not for our international relations, were it not for the fact that we have to fight for our position on a world scale. If we leave that aside, however, and confine ourselves to internal economic relations, the emphasis in our work is certainly shifting to education.

Two main tasks confront us, which constitute the epoch – to reorganise our machinery of state, which is utterly useless, and which we took over in its entirety from the preceding epoch; during the past five years of struggle we did not, and could not, drastically reorganise it. Our second task is educational work among the peasants. And the economic object of this educational work among the peasants is to organise the latter in cooperative societies. If the whole of the peasantry had been organised in cooperatives, we would by now have been standing with both feet on the soil of socialism. But the organisation of the entire peasantry in cooperative societies presupposes a standard of culture, and the peasants (precisely among the peasants as the overwhelming mass) that cannot, in fact, be achieved without a cultural revolution.

Our opponents told us repeatedly that we were rash in undertaking to implant socialism in an insufficiently cultured country. But they were misled by our having started from the opposite end to that prescribed by theory (the theory of pedants of all kinds), because in our country the political and social revolution preceded the cultural revolution, that very cultural revolution which nevertheless now confronts us.

This cultural revolution would now suffice to make our country a completely socialist country; but it presents immense difficulties of a purely cultural (for we are illiterate) and material character (for to be cultured we must achieve a certain development of the material means of production; we must have a certain material base).

6 January 1923

Our Revolution
(Apropos of N. Sukhanov's Notes)

I have lately been glancing through Sukhanov's notes on the revolution. What strikes one most is the pedantry of all our petty-bourgeois democrats and of all heroes of the Second International. Apart from the fact that they are all extremely fainthearted, that when it comes to the minutest deviation from the German model [of socialism] even the best of them fortified themselves with reservations – apart from this characteristic, which is common to all petty-bourgeois democrats and has been abundantly manifested by them throughout the revolution, what strikes one is their slavish imitation of the past.

They all call themselves Marxists, but their conception of Marxism is impossibly pedantic. They have completely failed to understand what is decisive in Marxism, namely its revolutionary dialectics. They have even absolutely failed to understand Marx's plain statements that in times of revolution the utmost flexibility is demanded,[1] and have even failed to notice, for instance, the statements Marx made in his letters – I think it was in 1856 – expressing the hope of combining the peasant war in Germany, which might create a revolutionary situation, with the working-class movement[2] – they avoid even this plain statement and walk around and about it like a cat around a bowl of hot porridge.

Their conduct betrays them as cowardly reformists who are afraid to deviate from the bourgeoisie, let alone break with

---

1 A reference to Marx's *The Civil War in France* and his letter to Kugelmann dated 12 April 1871.

2 See the letter of Marx and Engels of 16 April 1856.

them, at the same time they disguised their cowardice with the wildest rhetoric and braggadocio. But what strikes one in all of them even from the purely theoretical point of view is their utter inability to grasp the following Marxist considerations: up to now they have seen capitalism and bourgeois democracy in Western Europe follow a definite path of development, and cannot conceive that this path can be taken as a model only *mutatis mutandis*, only with certain amendments (quite insignificant from the standpoint of the general development of world history).

First – the revolution connected with the first imperialist world war. Such revolution was bound to reveal new features, or variations, resulting from the war itself; the world has never seen such a war in such a situation. We find that since the war the bourgeoisie of the wealthiest countries have to this day been unable to restore 'normal' bourgeois relations. Yet our reformists – petty bourgeois who make a show of being revolutionaries – believed, and still believe, that normal bourgeois relations are the limit (thus far shalt thou go and no farther). And even their conception of 'normal' is extremely stereotyped and narrow.

Second, they are complete strangers to the idea that while the development of world history as a whole follows general laws it is by no means precluded, but, on the contrary, is presumed, that certain periods of development may display peculiarities in either the form or the sequence of this development. For instance, it has not even occurred to them that because Russia stands on the borderline between civilised countries and the countries which this war has for the first time definitely brought into the orbit of civilisation – all the oriental, non-European countries – she could and was, indeed, bound to reveal certain distinguishing features; although these, of course, are in keeping with the general line of world development, they distinguish her revolution from those which took place in the Western European countries and introduce certain partial innovations as the revolution moves on to the countries of the East.

Infinitely stereotyped, for instance, is the argument they learned by rote during the development of Western European social democracy, namely that we are not yet ripe for socialism, but as certain 'learned' gentleman among them put it, the objective economic premises for socialism do not exist in our country. Does it not occur to any of them to ask: what about the people that found itself in a revolutionary situation such as that created during the first imperialist war? Might it not, influenced by the hopelessness of its situation, fling itself into a struggle that would offer it at least some chance of securing conditions for the further development of civilisation that were somewhat unusual?

'The development of the productive forces of Russia has not yet attained the level that makes socialism possible.' All the heroes of the Second International, including, of course, Sukhanov, beat the drums about this proposition. They keep harping on this incontrovertible proposition in a thousand different keys, and think that it is the decisive criterion of our revolution.

But what if the situation, which drew Russia into the imperialist world war that involved every more or less influential Western European country and made her a witness of the eve of the revolutions maturing or partly already begun in the East, gave rise to circumstances that put Russia and her development in a position which enabled us to achieve precisely that combination of a 'peasant war' with the working-class movement suggested in 1856 by no less a Marxist than Marx himself as a possible prospect for Prussia?

What if the complete hopelessness of the situation, by stimulating the efforts of the workers and peasants tenfold, offered us the opportunity to create the fundamental requisites of civilisation in a different way from that of the Western European countries? Has that altered the general line of development of world history? Has that altered the basic relations between the basic classes of all the countries that are being, or have been, drawn into the general course of world history?

If a definite level of culture is required for the building of socialism (although nobody can say just what that definite 'level of culture' is, for it differs in every Western European country), why cannot we begin by first achieving the prerequisites for that definite level of culture in a revolutionary way, and *then*, with the aid of the workers' and peasants' government and Soviet system, proceed to overtake the other nations?

16 January 1923

II

You say that civilisation is necessary for the building of socialism. Very good. But why could we not first create such prerequisites of civilisation in our country by the expulsion of the landowners and the Russian capitalists, and then start moving toward socialism? Where, in what books, have you read that such variations of the customary historical sequence of events are impermissible or impossible?

Napoleon, I think, wrote: *'On s'engage et puis ... on voit.'* rendered freely this means: 'First engage in a serious battle and then see what happens.' Well, we did first engage in a serious battle in October 1917, and then saw such details of development (from the standpoint of world history they were certainly details) as the Brest peace, the New Economic Policy, and so forth. And now there can be no doubt that in the main we have been victorious.

Our Sukhanovs, not to mention social democrats still farther to the right, never even dream that revolutions cannot be made any other way. Our European philistines never even dream that the subsequent revolutions in oriental countries, which possess much vaster populations in a much vaster diversity of social conditions, will undoubtedly display even greater distinctions than the Russian revolution.

It need hardly be said that a textbook written on Kautskian lines was a very useful thing in its day. But it is time, given that, to abandon the idea that it foresaw all the forms of development of subsequent world history. It would be timely to say that those who think so are simply fools.

17 January 1923

How We Should Reorganise the Workers' and Peasants' Inspection Recommendation to the Twelfth Party Congress

It is beyond question that the Workers' and Peasants' Inspection is an enormous difficulty for us, and that so far this difficulty has not been overcome. I think that the comrades who try to overcome the difficulty by denying that the Workers' and Peasants' Inspection is useful and necessary are wrong. But I do not deny that the problem presented by our state apparatus and the task of improving it is very difficult, that it is far from being solved, and is extremely urgent.

With the exception of the People's Commissariat of Foreign Affairs, our state apparatus is to a considerable extent a survival of the past and has undergone hardly any serious change. It has only been slightly touched up on the surface, but in all other respects it is a most typical relic of our old state machine. And so, to find a method of really renovating it, I think we ought to turn for experience to our Civil War.

How did we act in the more critical moment of the Civil War?

We concentrated our best Party forces in the Red Army; we mobilised the best of our workers; we looked for new forces at the deepest roots of our dictatorship.

I am convinced that we must go to the same source to find the means of reorganising the Workers' and Peasants' Inspection. I recommend that our Twelfth Party Congress adopt the following plan of reorganisation, based on some enlargement of our Central Control Commission.

The plenary meetings of the Central Committee of our Party are already revealing a tendency to develop into a kind of supreme Party conference. They take place, on the average, not more than once in two months, while the routine work is conducted, as we know, on behalf of the Central Committee by our Political Bureau, our Organising Bureau, our Secretariat, and so forth. I think we ought to follow the road we have thus far taken to the end and definitely transform the plenary meetings of the Central Committee into supreme Party conferences convened once in two months jointly with the Central Control Commission.

The Central Control Commission should be combined with the main body of the reorganised Workers' and Peasants' Inspection along the following lines.

I propose that the congress should elect seventy-five to a hundred new members to the Central Control Commission. They should be workers and peasants, and should go through the same Party screening as ordinary members of the Central Committee, because they are to enjoy the same rights as the members of the Central Committee.

On the other hand, the staff of the Workers' and Peasants' Inspection should be reduced to three or four hundred persons, specially screened for conscientiousness and knowledge of our state apparatus. They must also undergo a special test as regards their knowledge of the principles of scientific organisation of labour in general, and of administrative work, office work, and so forth, in particular.

In my opinion, such a union of the Workers' and Peasants' Inspection with the Central Control Commission will be beneficial to both these institutions. On the one hand, the Workers' and Peasants' Inspection will thus obtain such high authority that it will certainly not be inferior to the People's Commissariat of Foreign Affairs. On the other hand, our Central Committee, together with the Central Control Commission, will definitely take the road of becoming a supreme Party conference, which in fact it has already taken, and along which it should proceed to the end so as to be able to fulfil its functions properly in two respects: in respect to *its own* methodical, expedient and systematic organisation of work, and in respect to maintaining contacts with the broad masses through the medium of the best of our workers and peasants.

I foresee an objection that, directly or indirectly, may come from those spheres which make our state apparatus antiquated, i.e., from those who urge that its present, utterly impossible, indecently pre-revolutionary form be preserved (incidentally, we now have an opportunity which rarely occurs in history of ascertaining the period necessary for bringing about radical social changes; we now see clearly *what* can be done in five years, and what requires much more time). The objection I foresee is that the change I propose will lead to nothing but chaos. The members of the Central Control Commission will wander around all the institutions, not knowing where, why or to whom to apply, causing disorganisation everywhere and distracting employees from their routine work, etc., etc.

I think that the malicious source of this objection is so obvious that it does not warrant a reply. It goes without saying that the Presidium of the Central Control Commission, the people's commissar of the Workers' and Peasants' Inspection and his collegium (and also, in the proper cases, the Secretariat of our Central Committee) will have to put in years of persistent effort to get the Commissariat properly organised, and to get it to function smoothly in conjunction with the Central Control Commission. In my opinion, the people's commissar of the Workers' and Peasants' Inspection, as well as the whole collegium, can (and should) remain and guide the work of the entire Workers' and Peasants' Inspection, including the work of all the members of the Central Control Commission who will be 'placed under his command'. The three or four hundred employees of the Workers' and Peasants' Inspection that are to remain, according to my plan, should, on the one hand, perform purely secretarial functions for the other members of the Workers' and Peasants' Inspection and for the supplementary members of the Central Control Commission; and, on the other hand, they should be highly skilled, specially screened, particularly reliable, and highly paid, so that they may be relieved of their present truly unhappy (to say the least) position of Workers' and Peasants' Inspection officials.

I am sure that the reduction of the staff to the number I have indicated will greatly enhance the efficiency of the Workers' and Peasants' Inspection personnel and the quality of all its work, enabling the People's Commissar and the members of the collegium to concentrate their efforts entirely on organising work and on systematically and steadily improving its efficiency, which is so absolutely essential for our workers' and peasants' government, and for our Soviet system.

On the other hand, I also think that the people's commissar of the Workers' and Peasants' Inspection should work partly combining and partly coordinating those higher institutions for the organisation of labour (the Central Institute of Labour, etc.), of which there are now no fewer than twelve in our republic. Excessive uniformity and a consequent desire to unity will be harmful. On the contrary, what is needed here is a reasonable and expedient mean between combining all these institutions and properly delimiting them, allowing for a certain independence in each of them.

Our own Central Committee will undoubtedly gain no less from this reorganisation than the Workers' and Peasants' Inspection. It will gain because its contacts with the masses will be greater and because the regularity and effectiveness of its work will improve. It will then be possible (and necessary) to institute a stricter and more responsible procedure of preparing for the meetings of the Political Bureau, which should be attended by a definite number of members of the Central Control Commission determined either for a definite period or by some organisation plan.

In distributing work to the members of the Central Control Commission, the people's commissar of the Workers' and Peasants' Inspection, in conjunction with the Presidium of the Central Control Commission, should impose on them the duty either of attending the meetings of the Political Bureau for the purpose of examining all the documents pertaining to matters that come before it in one way or another; or of devoting their working time to theoretical study, to the study of scientific methods of organising labour; or of taking a practical part in the work of supervising and improving our machinery of state, from the higher state institutions to the lower local bodies, etc.

I also think that in addition to the political advantages accruing from the fact that the members of the Central Committee and the Central Control Commission will, as a consequence of this reform, be much better informed and better prepared for the meetings of the Political Bureau (all the documents relevant to the business to be discussed at these meetings should be sent to all the members of the Central Committee and the Central Control Commission not later than the day before the meeting of the Political Bureau, except in absolutely urgent cases, for which special methods of informing the members of the Central Committee and the Central Control Commission and of settling these matters must be devised), there will also be the advantage that the influence of purely personal and incidental factors in our Central Committee will diminish, and this will reduce the danger of a split.

Our Central Committee has grown into a strictly centralised and highly authoritative group, but the conditions under which this group is working are not commensurate with its authority. The reform I recommend should help to remove this defect, and the members of the Central Control Commission, whose duty it will be to attend all meetings of the Political Bureau in a definite number, will have to form a compact group which should not allow anybody's authority without exception, neither that of the secretary general [Stalin] nor of any other member of the Central Committee, to prevent them from putting questions, verifying documents, and, in general, keeping themselves fully informed of all things and exercising the strictest control over the proper conduct of affairs.

Of course, in our Soviet Republic, the social order is based on the collaboration of two classes: the workers and peasants, in which the 'Nepmen', i.e., the bourgeoisie, are now permitted to participate on certain terms. If serious class disagreements arise between these classes, a split will be inevitable. But the grounds for such a split are not inevitable in our social system, and it is the principal tasks of our Central Committee and Central Control Commission, as well as of our Party as a whole, to watch very closely over such circumstances as may cause a split, and to forestall them, for in the final analysis the fate of our Republic will depend on whether the peasant masses will stand by the working class, loyal to their alliance, or whether they will permit the 'Nepmen', i.e., the new bourgeoisie, to drive a wedge between them and the working class, to split them off from the working class. The more clearly we see this alternative, the more clearly all our workers and peasants understand it, the greater are the chances that we shall avoid a split which would be fatal for the Soviet Republic.

23 January 1923

Better Fewer, but Better

In the matter of improving our state apparatus, the Workers' and Peasants' Inspection should not, in my opinion, either strive after quantity or hurry.[1] We have so far been able to devote so little thought and attention to the efficiency of our state apparatus that it would now be quite legitimate if we took special care to secure its thorough organisation, and concentrated in the Workers' and Peasants' Inspection a staff of workers really abreast of the times, i.e., not inferior to the best Western European standards. For a socialist republic this condition is, of course, too modest. But our experience of the first five years has fairly crammed our heads with mistrust and scepticism. These qualities assert themselves involuntarily when, for example, we hear people dilating at too great length and too flippantly on 'proletarian' culture. For a start, we should be satisfied with real bourgeois culture; for a start we should be glad to dispense with the crude types of pre-bourgeois culture, i.e., bureaucratic culture or serf culture, etc. In matters of culture, haste and sweeping measures are most harmful. Many of our young writers and Communists should get this well into their heads.

Thus, in the matter of our state apparatus we should now draw the conclusion from our past experience that it would be better to proceed more slowly.

Our state apparatus is so deplorable, not to say wretched, that we must first think very carefully how to combat its defects, bearing in mind that these defects are rooted in the

---

1 This text is the second part of Lenin's letter to the Twelfth Congress, 'How We Should Reorganise the Workers' and Peasants' Inspection'.

past, which, although it has been overthrown, has not yet been overcome, has not yet reached the stage of a culture that has receded into the distant past. I say culture deliberately, because in these matters we can only regard as achieved what has become part and parcel of our culture, of our social life, our habits. We might say that the good in our social system has not been properly studied, understood and taken to heart; it has been hastily grasped at; it has not been verified or tested, corroborated by experience, and not made durable, etc. Of course, it could not be otherwise in a revolutionary epoch, when development proceeded at such breakneck speed that in a matter of five years we passed from tsarism to the Soviet system.

It is time we did something about it. We must show sound scepticism for too rapid progress, for boastfulness, etc. We must give thought to testing the steps forward we proclaim every hour, take every minute and then prove every second that they are flimsy, superficial and misunderstood. The most harmful thing here would be haste. The most harmful thing would be to rely on the assumption that we know at least something, or that we have any considerable number of elements necessary for the building of a really new state apparatus, one really worthy to be called socialist, Soviet, etc.

No, we are ridiculously deficient of such an apparatus, and even of the elements of it, and we must remember that we should not stint time on building it, and that it will take many, many years.

What elements have we for building this apparatus? Only two. First, the workers who are absorbed in the struggle of socialism. These elements are not sufficiently educated. They would like to build a better apparatus for us, but they do not know how. They cannot build one. They have not yet developed the culture required for this; and it is culture that is required. Nothing will be achieved in this by doing things in a rush, by assault, by vim or vigour, or, in general, by any of the best human qualities. Second, we have elements of knowledge, education and training, but they are ridiculously inadequate compared with all other countries.

Here we must not forget that we are too prone to compensate (or imagine that we can compensate) our lack of knowledge by zeal, haste, etc.

In order to renovate our state apparatus we must at all costs set out, first, to learn; second, to learn; and third, to learn, and then see to it that learning shall not remain a dead letter, or a fashionable catchphrase (and we should admit in all frankness that this happens very often with us), that learning shall really become part of our very being, that it shall actually and fully become a constituent element of our social life. In short, we must not make the demands that were made by bourgeois Western Europe, but demands that are fit and proper for a country which has set out to develop into a socialist country.

The conclusion to be drawn from the above is the following: we must make the Workers' and Peasants' Inspection a really exemplary institution, an instrument to improve our state apparatus.

In order that it may attain the desired high level, we must follow the rule: 'Measure your cloth seven times before you cut.'

For this purpose, we must utilise the very best of what there is in our social system, and utilise it with the greatest caution, thoughtfulness and knowledge, to build up the new People's Commissariat.

For this purpose, the best elements that we have in our social system – such as, first, the advanced workers, and, second, the really enlightened elements for whom we can vouch that they will not take the word for the deed, and will not utter a single word that goes against their conscience – should not shrink from admitting any difficulty and should not shrink from any struggle in order to achieve the object they have seriously set themselves.

We have been bustling for five years trying to improve our state apparatus, but it has been mere bustle, which has proved useless in these five years, or even futile, or even harmful. This bustle created the impression that we were doing something, but in effect it was only clogging up our institutions and our brains.

It is high time things were changed.

We must follow the rule: better fewer, but better. We must follow the rule: better get good human material in two or even three years than work in haste without hope of getting any at all.

I know that it will be hard to keep to this rule and apply it under our conditions. I know that the opposite rule will force its way through a thousand loopholes. I know that enormous resistance will have to be put up, that devilish persistence will be required, that in the first few years at least work in this field will be hellishly hard. Nevertheless, I am convinced that only by such effort shall we be able to achieve our aim; and that only by achieving this aim shall we create a republic that is really worthy of the name of Soviet, socialist, and so on, and so forth.

Many readers probably thought that the figures I quoted by way of illustration in my first article ['How We Should Reorganise the Workers' and Peasants' Inspection'] were too small. I am sure that many calculations may be made to prove that they are. But I think that we must put one thing above all such and other calculations, i.e., our desire to obtain really exemplary quality.

I think that the time has at last come when we must work in real earnest to improve our state apparatus, and in this there can scarcely be anything more harmful than haste. That is why I would sound a strong warning against inflating the

figures. In my opinion, we should, on the contrary, be especially sparing with figures in this matter. Let us say frankly
that the People's Commissariat of the Workers' and Peasants'
Inspection does not at present enjoy the slightest authority.
Everybody knows that no other institutions are worse organised than those of our Workers' and Peasants' Inspection, and
that under present conditions nothing can be expected from
this people's commissariat. We must have this firmly fixed in
our minds if we really want to create within a few years an
institution that will, first, be an exemplary institution; second,
win everybody's absolute confidence; and third, prove to all
and sundry that we have really justified the work of such a
highly placed institution as the Central Control Commission.
In my opinion, we must immediately and irrevocably reject
all general figures for the size of office staffs. We must select
employees for the Workers' and Peasants' Inspection with particular care and only on the basis of the strictest test. Indeed,
what is the use of establishing a people's commissariat which
carries on anyhow, which does not enjoy the slightest confidence, and whose word carries scarcely any weight? I think
that our main object in launching the work of reconstruction
that we now have in mind is to avoid all this.

The workers whom we are enlisting as members of the Central
Control Commission must be irreproachable Communists, and
I think that a great deal has yet to be done to teach them the
methods and objects of their work. Furthermore, there must
be a definite number of secretaries to assist in this work, who
must be put to a triple test before they are appointed to their
posts. Lastly, the officials whom in exceptional cases we shall
accept directly as employees of the Workers' and Peasants'
Inspection must conform to the following requirements:

First, they must be recommended by several Communists.

Second, they must pass a test for knowledge of our state
apparatus.

Third, they must pass a test in the fundamentals of the theory of our state apparatus, in the fundamentals of management, office routine, etc.

Fourth, they must work in such close harmony with the members of the Central Control Commission and with their own secretariat that we could vouch for the work of the whole apparatus.

I know that these requirements are extraordinarily strict, and I am very much afraid that the majority of the 'practical' workers in the Workers' and Peasants' Inspection will say that these requirements are impracticable, or will scoff at them. But I ask any of the present chiefs of the Workers' and Peasants' Inspection, or anyone associated with that body, whether they can honestly tell me the practical purpose of a people's commissariat like the Workers' and Peasants' Inspection. I think this question will help them recover their sense of proportion. Either it is not worth while having another of the numerous reorganisations that we have had of this hopeless affair, the Workers' and Peasants' Inspection, or we must really set to work, by slow, difficult and unusual methods, and by testing these methods over and over again, to create something really exemplary, something that will win the respect of all and sundry for its merits, and not only because of its rank and title.

If we do not arm ourselves with patience, if we do not devote several years to this task, we had better not tackle it at all.

In my opinion we ought to select a minimum number of the higher labour research institutes, etc., which we have baked so hastily, see whether they are organised properly, and allow them to continue working, but only in a way that conforms to the high standards of modern science and gives us all its benefits. If we do that it will not be utopian to hope that within a few years we shall have an institution that will be able to perform its functions, to work systematically and steadily on improving our state apparatus, an institution backed by the trust of the working class, of the Russian Communist Party, and the whole population of our republic.

The spadework for this could begin at once. If the People's Commissariat of the Workers' and Peasants' Inspection accepted the present plan of reogranisation, it could not take the preparatory steps and work methodically until the task is completed, without haste, and not hesitating to alter what has already been done.

Any half-hearted solution would be extremely harmful in this matter. A measure for the size of the staff of the Workers' and Peasants' Inspection based on any other consideration would, in fact, be based on the old bureaucratic considerations, on old prejudices, on what has already been condemned, universally ridiculed, etc.

In substance, the matter is as follows:

Either we prove now that we have really learned something about state organisation (we ought to have learned something in five years), or we prove that we are not sufficiently mature for it. If the latter is the case, we had better not tackle the task.

I think that with the available human material it will not be immodest to assume that we have learned enough to be able to systematically rebuild at least one people's commissariat. True, this one people's commissariat will have to be the model for our entire state apparatus.

We ought to at once announce a contest in the compilation of two or more textbooks on the organisation of labour in general, and on management in particular. We can take as a basis the book already published by Yermansky, although it should be said in parentheses that he obviously sympathises with Menshevism and is unfit to compile textbooks for the Soviet system.

We can also take as a basis the recent book by Kerzhentsev, and some of the other partial textbooks available may be useful too.

We ought to send several qualified and conscientious people to Germany, or to Britain, to collect literature and to study this question. I mention Britain in case it is found impossible to send people to the USA or Canada.

We ought to appoint a commission to draw up the preliminary programme of examinations for prospective employees of the Workers' and Peasants' Inspection; ditto for candidates to the Central Control Commission.

These and similar measures will not, of course, cause any difficulties for the people's commissar or the collegium of the Workers' and Peasants' Inspection, or for the Presidium of the Central Control Commission.

Simultaneously, a preparatory commission should be appointed to select candidates for membership of the Central Control Commission. I hope that we shall now be able to find more than enough candidates for this post among the experienced workers in all departments, as well as among the students of our Soviet higher schools. It would hardly be right to exclude one or another category beforehand. Probably preference will have to be given to a mixed composition for this institution, which should combine many qualities, and dissimilar merits. Consequently, the tasks of drawing up the list of candidates will entail a considerable amount of work. For example, it would be least desirable for the staff of the new people's commissariat to consist of people of one type, only of officials, say, or for it to exclude people of the propagandist type, or people whose principal quality is sociability or the ability to penetrate into circles that are not altogether customary for officials in this field, etc.

I think I shall be able to express my idea best if I compare my plan with that of academic institutions. Under the guidance of their presidium, the members of the Central Control Commission should systematically examine all the papers and documents of the Political Bureau. Moreover, they should divide their time correctly between various jobs in investigating the routine in our institutions, from the very small and privately owned offices to the highest state institutions. And lastly, their functions should include the study of theory, i.e., the theory of organisation of the work they intend to devote themselves to, and practical work under the guidance of other comrades or of teachers in the higher institutes for the organisation of labour.

I do not think, however, that they will be able to confine themselves to this sort of academic work. In addition, they will have to prepare themselves for work which I would not hesitate to call training to catch, I will not say rogues, but something like that, and working out special ruses to screen their movements, their approach, etc.

If such proposals were made in Western European government institutions they would rouse frightful resentment, a feeling of moral indignation, etc.; but I trust that we have not become so bureaucratic as to be capable of that. The NEP has not yet succeeded in gaining such respect as to cause any of us to be shocked at the idea somebody may be caught. Our Soviet Republic is of such recent construction, and there are such heaps of the old lumber still lying around, that it would hardly occur to anyone to be shocked at the idea that we should delve into them by means of ruses, by means of investigations sometimes directed to rather remote sources or in a roundabout way. And even if it did occur to anyone to be shocked by this, we may be sure that such a person would make himself a laughing stock.

Let us hope that our new Workers' and Peasants' Inspection will abandon what the French call *pruderie*, which we may call ridiculous primness, or ridiculous swank, and which plays entirely into the hands of our Soviet and Party bureaucracy. Let it be said in parentheses that we have bureaucrats in our Party offices as well as in Soviet offices.

When I said above that we must study and study hard in institutes for the higher organisation of labour, etc., I did not by any means imply 'studying' in the schoolroom way, nor did I confine myself to the idea of studying only in the schoolroom way. I hope that not a single genuine revolutionary will suspect me of refusing, in this case, to understand 'studies' to include resorting to some semi-humorous trick, cunning device, piece of trickery or something of that sort. I know that in the staid and earnest states of Western Europe such an idea would horrify people and that not a single decent official would even entertain it. I hope, however, that we have not yet become as bureaucratic as all that and that in our midst the discussion of this idea will give rise to nothing more than amusement.

Indeed, why not combine pleasure with utility? Why not resort to some humorous or semi-humorous trick to expose something ridiculous, something harmful, something semi-ridiculous, semi-harmful, etc.?

It seems to me that our Workers' and Peasants' Inspection will gain a great deal if it undertakes to examine these ideas, and that the list of cases in which our Central Control Commission and its colleagues in the Workers' and Peasants' Inspection achieved a few of their most brilliant victories will be enriched by not a few exploits of our future Workers' and Peasants' Inspection and Central Control Commission members in places not quite mentionable in prim and staid textbooks.

How can a Party institution be amalgamated with a Soviet institution? Is there not something improper in this suggestion?

I do not ask these questions on my own behalf, but on behalf of those I hinted at above when I said that we have bureaucrats in our Party institutions as well as in the Soviet institutions.

But why, indeed, should we not amalgamate the two if this is in the interests of our work? Do we not all see that such an amalgamation has been very beneficial in the case of the People's Commissariat of Foreign Affairs, where it was brought about at the very beginning? Does not the Political Bureau discuss from the Party point of view many questions, both minor and important, concerning the 'moves' we should make in reply to the 'moves' of foreign powers in order to forestall their, say, cunning, if we are not to use a less respectable term? Is not this flexible amalgamation of a Soviet institution with a Party institution a source of great strength in our politics? I think that what has proved its usefulness, what has been definitely adopted in our foreign politics and has become so customary that it no longer calls forth any doubt in this field, will be at least as appropriate (in fact, I think it will be much more appropriate) for our state apparatus as a whole. The functions of the Workers' and Peasants' Inspection cover our state apparatus as a whole, and its activities should affect all and every state institution without exception: local, central, commercial, purely administrative, educational, archival, theatrical, etc. – in short, all without any exception.

Why, then, should not an institution, whose activities have such wide scope, and which moreover requires such extraordinary flexibility of forms, be permitted to adopt this peculiar amalgamation of a Party control institution with a Soviet control institution?

I see no obstacles to this. What is more, I think that such an amalgamation is the only guarantee of success in our work. I think that all doubts on this score arise in the dustiest corners of our government offices, and that they deserve to be treated with nothing but ridicule.

Another doubt: is it expedient to combine educational activities with official activities? I think that it is not only expedient, but necessary. Generally speaking, in spite of our revolutionary attitude towards the Western European form of state, we have allowed ourselves to become infected with a number of its most harmful and ridiculous prejudices; to some extent we have been deliberately infected with them by our dear bureaucrats, who counted on being able again and again to fish in the muddy waters of these prejudices. And they did fish in these muddy waters to so great an extent that only the blind among us failed to see how extensively this fishing was practised.

In all spheres of social, economic and political relationships we are 'frightfully' revolutionary. But as regards precedence, the observance of the forms and rites of office management, our 'revolutionariness' often gives way to the mustiest routine. On more than one occasion, we have witnessed the very interesting phenomenon of a great leap forward in social life being accompanied by amazing timidity whenever the slightest changes are proposed.

This is natural, for the boldest steps forward were taken in a field which was long reserved for theoretical study, which was promoted mainly, and even almost exclusively, in theory. The Russian, when away from work, found solace from bleak bureaucratic realities in unusually bold theoretical constructions, and that is why in our country these unusually bold theoretical constructions assumed an unusually lopsided character. Theoretical audacity in general constructions went hand in hand with amazing timidity as regards certain very minor reforms in office routine. Some great universal agrarian revolution was worked out with an audacity unexampled in any other country, and at the same time the imagination failed when it came to working out a tenth-rate reform in office routine; the imagination, or patience, was lacking to apply to this reform the general propositions that produced such brilliant results when applied to general problems.

That is why in our present life reckless audacity goes hand

in hand, to an astonishing degree, with timidity of thought even when it comes to very minor changes.

I think that this has happened in all really great revolutions, for really great revolutions grow out of the contradictions between the old, between what is directed towards developing the old, and the very abstract striving for the new, which must be so new as not to contain the tiniest particle of the old.

And the more abrupt the revolution, the longer will many of these contradictions last.

The general feature of our present life is the following: we have destroyed capitalist industry and have done our best to raze to the ground the medieval institutions and landed proprietorship, and thus created a small and very small peasantry, which is following the lead of the proletariat because it believes in the results of its revolutionary work. It is not easy for us, however, to keep going until the socialist revolution is victorious in more developed countries merely with the aid of this confidence, because economic necessity, especially under the NEP, keeps the productivity of labour of the small and very small peasants at an extremely low level. Moreover, the international situation, too, threw Russia back and, by and large, reduced the labour productivity of the people to a level considerably below pre-war. The Western European capitalist powers, partly deliberately and partly unconsciously, did everything they could to throw us back, to utilise the elements of the Civil War in Russia in order to spread as much ruin in the country as possible. It was precisely this way out of the imperialist war that seemed to have many advantages. They argued somewhat as follows: 'If we fail to overthrow the revolutionary system in Russia, we shall, at all events, hinder its progress towards socialism.' And from their point of view they could argue in no other way. In the end, their problem was half-solved. They failed to overthrow the new system created by the revolution, but they did prevent it from at once taking the step forward that would have justified the forecasts of the socialists, that would have enabled the latter to develop the productive forces with enormous speed, to develop all the potentialities which, taken together, would have produced socialism; socialists would thus have proved to all and sundry that socialism contains within itself gigantic forces and that mankind had now entered into a new stage of development of extraordinarily brilliant prospects.

The system of international relationships which has now taken shape is one in which a European state, Germany, is enslaved by the victor countries. Furthermore, owing to their victory, a number of states, the oldest states in the West, are in a position to make some insignificant concessions to their oppressed classes – concessions which, insignificant though they are, nevertheless heard the revolutionary movement in those countries and create some semblance of 'class truce'.

At the same time, as a result of the last imperialist war, a number of countries of the East, India, China, etc., have been completely jolted out of the rut. Their development has definitely shifted to general European capitalist lines. The general European ferment has begun to affect them, and it is now clear to the whole world that they have been drawn into a process of development that must lead to a crisis in the whole of world capitalism.

Thus, at the present time we are confronted with the question: shall we be able to hold on with our small and very small peasant production, and in our present state of ruin, until the Western European capitalist countries consummate their development towards socialism? But they are consummating it not as we formerly expected. They are not consummating it through the gradual 'maturing' of socialism, but through the exploitation of some countries by others, through the exploitation of the first of the countries vanquished in the imperialist war combined with the exploitation of the whole of the East.

On the other hand, precisely as a result of the first imperialist war, the East has been definitely drawn into the revolutionary movement, has been definitely drawn into the general maelstrom of the world revolutionary movement.

What tactics does this situation prescribe for our country? Obviously the following. We must display extreme caution so as to preserve our workers' government and to retain our small and very small peasantry under its leadership and authority. We have the advantage that the whole world is now passing to a movement that must give rise to a world socialist revolution. But we are labouring under the disadvantage that the imperialists have succeeded in splitting the world into two camps; and this split is made more complicated by the fact that it is extremely difficult for Germany, which is really a land of advanced, cultured, capitalist development, to rise to her feet. All the capitalist powers of what is called the West are pecking at her and preventing her from rising. On the other hand, the entire East, with its hundreds of millions of exploited working people, reduced to the last degree of human suffering, has been forced into a position where its physical and material strength cannot possibly be compared with the physical, material and military strength of any of the much smaller Western European states.

Can we save ourselves from the impending conflict with these imperialist countries? May we hope that the internal antagonisms and conflicts between the thriving imperialist countries of the East will give us a second respite as they did the first time, when the campaign of the Western European counter-revolution in support of the Russian counter-revolution broke down owing to the antagonisms in the camp of the counter-revolutionaries of the West and the East, in the camp of the Eastern and Western exploiters, in the camp of Japan and the USA?

I think the reply to this question should be that the issue

depends upon too many factors, and that the outcome of the struggle as a whole can be forecast only because in the long run capitalism itself is educating and training the vast majority of the population of the globe for the struggle.

In the last analysis, the outcome of the struggle will be determined by the fact that Russia, India, China, etc. account for the overwhelming majority of the population of the globe. And during the past few years it is this majority that has been drawn into the struggle for emancipation with extraordinary rapidity, so that in this respect there cannot be the slightest doubt what the final outcome of the world struggle will be. In this sense, the complete victory of socialism is fully and absolutely assured.

But what interests us is not the inevitability of this complete victory of socialism, but the tactics which we, the Russian Communist Party, we the Russian Soviet government, should pursue to prevent the Western European counter-revolutionary states from crushing us. To ensure our existence until the next military conflict between the counter-revolutionary imperialist West and the revolutionary and nationalist East, between the most civilised countries of the world and the orientally backward countries which, however, comprise the majority, this majority must become civilised. We, too, lack enough civilisation to enable us to pass straight on to socialism, although we do have the political requisites for it. We should adopt the following tactics, or pursue the following policy, to save ourselves.

We must strive to build up a state in which the workers retain leadership of the peasants, in which they retain the confidence of the peasants, and by exercising the greatest economy remove every trace of extravagance from our social relations.

We must reduce our state apparatus to the utmost degree of economy. We must banish from it all traces of extravagance, of which so much has been left over from tsarist Russia, from its bureaucratic capitalist state machine.

Will not this be a reign of peasant limitations?

No. If we see to it that the working class retains its leadership over the peasantry, we shall be able, by exercising the greatest possible thrift in the economic life of our state, to use every saving we make to develop our large-scale machine industry, to develop electrification, the hydraulic extraction of peat, to complete the Volkhov Power Project, etc.[2]

In this, and in this alone, lies our hope. Only when we have done this shall we, speaking figuratively, be able to change horses, to change from the peasant, *muzhik* horse of poverty, from the horse of an economy designed for a ruined peasant country, to the horse which the proletariat is seeking and must seek – the horse of large-scale machine industry, of electrification, of the Volkhov Power Station, etc.

That is how I link up in my mind the general plan of our work, of our policy, of our tactics, of our strategy, with the functions of the reorganised Workers' and Peasants' Inspection. This is what, in my opinion, justifies the exceptional care, the exceptional attention that we must devote to the Workers' and Peasants' Inspection in raising it to an exceptionally high level, in giving it a leadership with Central Committee rights, etc., etc.

And this justification is that only by thoroughly purging our government machine, by reducing to the utmost everything that is not absolutely essential in it, shall we be certain of being able to keep going. Moreover, we shall be able to keep going not on the level of a small-peasant country, not on the level of universal limitation, but on a level steadily advancing to large-scale machine industry.

---

2 The Volkhov Power Project was the first of the big hydroelectric power stations the Soviet Union built on the River Volkhov. Its construction began in 1918, but made little progress until after the Civil War ended in 1920. It was commissioned in 1926.

These are the lofty tasks that I dream of for our Workers' and Peasants' Inspection. That is why I am planning for it the amalgamation of the most authoritative Party body with an 'ordinary' people's commissariat.

2 March 1923

To Comrade Stalin

Top secret
Personal

Copy to Comrades Kamenev and Zinoviev

Dear Comrade Stalin:

You have been so rude as to summon my wife to the telephone and use bad language. Although she had told you that she was prepared to forget this, the fact nevertheless became known through her to Zinoviev and Kamenev. I have no intention of forgetting so easily what has been done against me, and it goes without saying that what has been done against my wife I consider having been done against me as well. I ask you, therefore, to think it over whether you are prepared to withdraw what you have said and to make your apologies, or whether you prefer that relations between us should be broken off.[1]

Respectfully yours,
Lenin

5 March 1923

---

1   After Lenin, with the permission of his doctors, had, on 21 December 1922, dictated a letter to Trotsky on the foreign trade monopoly, Joseph Stalin, whom a CC Plenum decision of 18 December had made personally responsible for the observance of the medical regimen ordered for Lenin, used offensive language against Nadezhda Krupskaya and threatened to take the case to the Control Commission for having taken down the said letter. On 23 December 1922, Krupskaya sent Kamenev a letter asking for protection from 'the gross interference in my personal life, offensive language and threats'. Nadezhda Krupskaya apparently told Lenin of this

fact in early March 1923. Having learned about this Lenin dictated the document here published.

Maria Ulyanova later wrote in a letter to the presidium of the July (1926) joint plenum of the Central Committee and the Central Control Commission of the RCP(B), at which the question had been raised by G. Y. Zinoviev, one of the leaders of the 'new opposition', that Stalin had offered his apologies.

To P. G. Mdivani,
F. Y. Makharadze and Others

Top secret

Comrades Mdivani, Makharadze and others

Copy to Comrades *Trotsky and Kamenev*

Dear Comrades:

I am following your case with all my heart. I am indignant over Orjonikidze's rudeness and the connivance of Stalin and Dzerzhinsky. I am preparing for you notes and a speech.[1]

Respectfully yours,
Lenin

6 *March 1923*

---

1 Lenin was unable to prepare the letter and the speech on the 'Georgian question'. On 10 March 1923, there was an acute deterioration in his condition. This letter is the last document dictated by Lenin.

Afterword: Lenin Navigating in Uncharted Territories

by Slavoj Žižek

Those who follow obscure spiritual–cosmological specula-
tions will have surely heard of one of the most popular topics
in the field: when three planets (usually the Earth, the moon
and the sun) find themselves on the same axis, some cataclys-
mic event will take place. The whole order of the universe is
momentarily thrown out of joint and has to restore its balance
(as was supposed to happen in 2012). Does something like
this not hold for the year 2017, when we celebrate not only
the centenary of the October Revolution but also the 150th
anniversary of the first edition of Marx's *Capital* (1867) and
the 50th anniversary of the so-called Shanghai Commune,
when, at the climactic moment of the Cultural Revolution,
the residents of Shanghai decided to take Mao's call literally and seize power directly, overthrowing the Communist
Party (which is why Mao quickly decided to restore order by
sending the army to quash them)? Do these three events not
mark the three stages of the communist movement? *Capital*
outlined the theoretical foundations of the communist revolution; the October Revolution was the first successful attempt
to overthrow the bourgeois state and build a new social and
economic order; while the Shanghai Commune represents the
most radical attempt to realize the most daring aspect of the
communist vision – the abolishment of state power and the
imposition of direct people's power organized as a network of
local communes. It was this radical idea that already motivated

Lenin in his preparatory theoretical work for the Revolution. In *The State and Revolution*, he outlined his vision of the workers' state where every *kukharka* (not simply a cook, and especially not a great *chef*, but more a modest woman servant in the kitchen of a wealthy family) will have to learn how to rule; where everyone, even the highest administrators, will be paid the same worker's wages; where all administrators will be directly elected by their local constituencies, which will have the right to recall them at any moment; where there will be no standing army. How this vision turned into its opposite immediately after the Revolution is the stuff of numerous critical analyses; but what is perhaps much more interesting is the fact that Lenin proposes as the normative ground of this 'utopian' vision an almost Habermasian notion of 'the elementary rules of social intercourse'. In communism, this permanent normative base of human intercourse will finally rule in a non-distorted way. Only in a communist society,

> freed from capitalist slavery, from the untold horrors, savagery, absurdities, and infamies of capitalist exploitation, [will] people … gradually become accustomed to observing the elementary rules of social intercourse that have been known for centuries and repeated for thousands of years in all copy-book maxims. They will become accustomed to observing them without force, without coercion, without subordination, without the special apparatus for coercion called the state.[1]

A page or so later, Lenin again states that 'we know that the fundamental social cause of excesses, which consist in the violation of the rules of social intercourse, is the exploitation of the people'.[2] Does this mean that revolution is normatively

---

1 V.I. Lenin, *The State and Revolution*, Chicago: Haymarket, 2014, p. 127.
2 Ibid.

grounded in some set of universal rules that function to define an eternal 'human nature'? (And perhaps there is an echo of this preoccupation with the 'elementary rules of social inter-course' even in Lenin's critical remarks, from the last months of his life, on Stalin's brutal manners.) In another passage of *The State and Revolution*, Lenin seems to claim almost the opposite – surprisingly, he grounds the (in)famous differ-ence between the lower and higher stages of communism in a different relation to human nature. In the first, lower, stage, we are still dealing with the same 'human nature' as in the entire history of exploitation and class struggle; but what will happen in the second, higher, stage is that 'human nature' itself will be changed:

> We are not utopians, we do not indulge in 'dreams' of dispens-ing at once with all administration, with all subordination; these anarchist dreams ... serve only to postpone the socialist revolution until human nature has changed. No, we want the socialist revolution with human nature as it is now, with human nature that cannot dispense with subordination, control and 'managers' ... The united workers themselves ... will hire their own technicians, managers and bookkeepers, and pay them all, as, indeed, every state official, ordinary workmen's wages.[3]

The interesting point here is that the passage from the lower to the higher stage does not rely primarily on the development of productive forces (beyond scarcity) but on the change in human nature. In this sense the Chinese communists, in their most radical moment, were right: there can be a communism of poverty (if we change human nature) and a socialism of (relative) prosperity ('goulash communism'). When the situ-ation is most desperate, as it was in Russia during the Civil War of 1918–20, there is always the millenarian temptation to

---

3   Ibid.

see in this utter misery a unique opportunity to pass directly to communism. Platonov's *Chevengur* has to be read against this background ... In what are these oscillations and tensions of Lenin grounded? Let us turn to Jean-Claude Milner's perspicuous analysis of the imbroglios of modern European revolutions which culminated in Stalinism. Milner's starting point is the radical gap that separates exactitude (factual truth, accuracy) and truth (the Cause to which we are committed):

> When one admits the radical difference between exactitude and truth, only one ethical maxim remains: never oppose the two. Never make of the inexact the privileged means of the effects of truth. Never transform these effects into by-products of the lie. Never make the real into an instrument of the conquest of reality. And I would allow myself to add: never make revolution into the lever of an absolute power.[4]

The role of proverbs in justifying this claim to absolute power is significant in the communist tradition, from Mao's 'Revolution is not a dinner party' to the legendary Stalinist 'You cannot make an omelette without breaking eggs.' The preferred saying among the Yugoslav communists was more obscene: 'You cannot sleep with a girl without leaving some traces.' But the point is always the same: endorsing brutality with no constraints. For those for whom God exists (in the guise of the big Other of History whose instruments they are), everything is permitted ... However, the theological reference can also function in the opposite way: not in the fundamentalist sense of directly legitimizing political measures as an imposition of the divine will, whose instruments are the revolutionaries, but in the sense that the theological dimension serves as a kind of safety valve, a mark of the

---

4 Jean-Claude Milner, *Relire la révolution*, Lagrasse: Verdier, 2016, p. 246.

openness and uncertainty of the situation which prevents political agents from conceiving of their acts in terms of self-transparency – 'God' means that we should always bear in mind that the outcome of our acts will never fit our expectations. This imperative to 'mind the gap' refers not only to the complexity of the situation in which we intervene; it concerns above all the utter ambiguity of the exercise of our own will.

Was this short circuit between truth and exactitude not Stalin's own basic axiom (which, of course, had to remain unspoken)? Truth is not only allowed to ignore exactitude – it is allowed to refashion it arbitrarily. Perhaps the peculiarity of some Russian words can be a guide in this matter: often, in Russian, there are two words for (what appears to us Westerners) the same term, one designating the ordinary meaning and the other a more ethically charged 'absolute' use. There is, for example, *istina*, the common notion of truth as adequacy to the facts, and (the usually capitalized) *Pravda*, the absolute Truth designating also the ethically committing ideal Order of the Good. There is also *svoboda*, the ordinary freedom to do what one wants within the existing social order, and *volja*, the more metaphysically charged absolute drive to follow one's will to the point of self-destruction – as the Russians like to say, in the West, you have *svoboda*, but we have *volja*. There is *gosudarstvo*, the state in its ordinary administrative aspects, and *derzhava*, the state as the unique agency of absolute power. (Applying the well-known Benjamin–Schmitt distinction, one may venture the claim that the difference between *gosudarstvo* and *derzhava* is that between constituted and constituting power: *gosudarstvo* is the state administrative machine running its course as prescribed by legal regulations, while *derzhava* is the agent of unconditional power.) There are *intellectuals*, educated people, and *intelligentsia*, intellectuals charged with and dedicated to a special mission to reform society. (Along the same lines, there is already in Marx an implicit distinction between the 'working class', a simple category of social Being, and the 'proletariat', a category of Truth, the revolutionary Subject proper.)

Is this opposition ultimately not that elaborated by Alain Badiou between Event and the positivity of mere Being? *Istina* is the mere factual truth (correspondence, adequacy), while *Pravda* designates the self-relating Event of truth; *svoboda* is the ordinary freedom of choice, while *volja* is the resolute Event of freedom ... In Russian, this gap is directly inscribed, appears as such, and thus renders visible the radical *risk* involved in every Truth-Event: there is no ontological guarantee that *Pravda* will succeed in asserting itself at the level of facts (covered by *istina*). And, again, it seems as if the awareness of this gap itself is inscribed in the Russian language in the unique expression *avos* or *na avos*, which means something like 'on our luck', and which articulates the hope that things will turn out OK when one makes a risky radical gesture without being able to discern all its possible consequences – something like Napoleon's *on s'engage, et puis on le verra*, often quoted by Lenin.

So where does Lenin stand here? Milner locates him at the edge, bringing the tension to its extreme: while Lenin remained fully committed to that Marxist orthodoxy which views revolution as part of the global historical reality, in his political practice he exercised to the utmost a stance of openness and improvisation, passing from revolutionary terror to a partial opening to capitalism. In the process, the Bolsheviks 'committed all possible mistakes', as Lenin himself put it. Milner writes:

> During the French Revolution itself, it is easy to recognise the moments in which the most rational and the most courageous among the revolutionaries despaired. Most of them were com-

petent and cultured, but no historical precedent in history, no scientific discovery, and no philosophical argument could help them. The same can be said about Lenin. Whoever has read his works cannot but admire his intelligence, his encyclopedic culture and his ability to invent new political concepts. Nonetheless, his own writings show a growing uncertainty about the situation that he himself had created. Right or wrong, the NEP was not only a turning point; it implied a severe self-criticism, bordering on renegading. At least, it proved that Lenin had been confronted by his own lack of knowledge in the field of political economy, where, as a Marxist, he was the most sure of himself; he was indeed discovering a new political country. He was encountering the very difficulty that Saint-Just had announced.[5]

In his practice, Lenin was thus effectively acting as the captain of a vessel lost in a stormy sea, finding its way through uncharted territory. Although he tried to develop a theoretical framework for this practice – that of a complex overdetermined totality in which the exception *is* the law and allows for a revolution in the 'weakest link' of the capitalist system – the tension became more and more palpable. So what did Stalin do here? He 'chose the easy way in preferring the absolute solitude of S_1 which leads to absolute opportunism. No party, no family, no allies except circumstantial ones, but also no predetermined theory of social forms, no accepted criteria for rationality, no ethical rules.'[6]

But perhaps Milner's reading is a little bit too narrow here. At a certain level, Stalin's break with Lenin was purely discursive, the violent imposition of a radically different subjective economy. The gap, still palpable in Lenin, between

---

5   Jean-Claude Milner, 'The Prince and the Revolutionary', available at crisiscritique.org.
6   Ibid.

general principles ('historical laws') regulating reality and improvised pragmatic decisions is simply disavowed, and the two extremes directly coincide: on the one hand, we get total pragmatic opportunism; on the other, this opportunism is legitimized by a new Marxist orthodoxy that proposes a general ontology. Marxism thus becomes a 'world view' allowing us access to objective reality and its laws; an operation that brings a new and false sense of security: our acts are 'ontologically' covered, part of an 'objective reality' regulated by laws known only to us, the communists. But the price paid for this ontological security is terrible: exactitude, to which Lenin was still committed, disappears; facts can be voluntarily manipulated and retroactively changed – events and persons become non-events and non-persons. In other words, in Stalinism, the Real of politics, in the form of brutal subjective interventions which violate the texture of reality, returns with a vengeance, although in the guise of its opposite: the respect for objective knowledge.

What Milner seems to neglect here, then, is the crucial fact that the Real of the 'absolute solitude of S_1' (the arbitrary interventions of the Master), 'which leads to absolute opportunism', *has to appear as its exact opposite*, the reign of 'objective knowledge' – in Lacanese, Stalinism is the supreme case of the full reign of the 'University discourse' whose agent is knowledge, not the Master. The only way to sustain the full harmony between S_1 and S_2, between the abyss of the Master's arbitrary decisions and knowledge, is to subordinate (factual) knowledge to the Master's arbitrariness – and, again, that's why the Stalinist discourse has to change the facts retroactively. In Stalinism, there are no 'renegades' (agents who were once on the right path but later deviated from it), as Kautsky was for Lenin; once Trotsky began to oppose Stalin and was denounced as a traitor, it had to be proven that he *was always already a traitor*. It is this readiness to accept sudden radical changes in the Party line, without demanding any argumentation, that characterizes a true Stalinist. He doesn't just faithfully follow the shifts in the Party line – first the Social Democrats are our enemies, then we are ordered to build a Popular Front with them; first Hitler is our ultimate enemy, then we conclude a pact with him – he treats his obedience to these arbitrary shifts as the ultimate proof of his fidelity to the Cause. In other words, within the Stalinist universe, the lack of argumentation for such shifts is not a sign of weakness but a proof of strength – one should follow the new line not in spite of not understanding the reasons for it but *because* we don't understand them. Here is how Milner recapitulates his argument:

> I do not hesitate to qualify Lenin's policy as delusional: in October 1917, he made a decision, without any clear notion of what his decision implied; moreover, his doctrine precluded the possibility of learning anything new from an event. According to him, audacity is taught by the right doctrine; it cannot add anything to that doctrine. In other words, it cannot teach anything new. Lenin's conviction is the exact opposite of Saint-Just's saying. It is delusional because it denies the alterity between S_1 and S_2. In his own devious way, Stalin sided with Saint-Just; at least, he understood intuitively that a revolution has something to do with the real, rather than with the imaginary mixture of past events and past assessments that is called 'reality.' Lenin and all true Marxist–Leninists treated the revolution as a reality. More generally, they seem to have had no sense of the real difference between the real and reality. Stalin is but the symptom of what happens when the real comes back in a world that denies it: it destroys all reality.[7]

---

7 Ibid.

Milner outlines in detail the gap that separates the French Revolution from the two (or three) later paradigms of the ideal revolution (October, Chinese and, for some, Cuban), as well as the gap that separates it from the American War of Independence. The American 'Revolution', celebrated as a model by Hannah Arendt, was mired in compromises (slavery, etc.); in a way it was finished only in 1865, and maybe not even until the 1960s, so it was logical that it lacked the universal appeal of the French Revolution. For the later communist revolutions which as a rule referred to the French Revolution as their model, the latter implied a fundamentally different stance towards the 'big Other': communist revolutions were grounded in a clear vision of historical reality ('scientific socialism'), of its laws and tendencies, so that, in spite of all its unpredictable turns, the revolution was fully located in this process of historical reality. As they liked to say, socialism should be built in each country according to its particular conditions, but in accordance with the general laws of history. In theory, revolution was thus deprived of the dimension of subjectivity proper, of the radical cuts of the real into the texture of 'objective reality' – in clear contrast to the French Revolution, whose most radical figures perceived it as an open process lacking any support in a higher Necessity. Saint-Just wrote in 1794: 'Ceux qui font des révolutions ressemblent au premier navigateur instruit par son audace' ('Those who make revolutions resemble a first navigator, who has audacity alone as a guide').[8] Here is Milner's reading of these lines:

> In Saint-Just's analogy, the explorer discovers what no one has seen before. There is no previous map of the political regions that he enters. This ignorance is particularly true of those who do not participate in the exploration. They cannot see what

---

8 Louis Antoine de Saint-Just, 'Rapport sur les factions de l'étranger', in *Œuvres complètes*, Paris: Gallimard, 2004, p. 695.

the revolutionaries see. Of course, the latter do not occupy a higher position than the former. Nevertheless their political perceptions are radically different. Moreover, there is no previous theoretical or practical science of revolution that could be common to the revolutionaries and their non-revolutionary counterparts. Consequently no one but revolutionaries themselves may express a judgment on their choices. The parallel with Descartes is striking, but Saint-Just's analogy entails yet another consequence. Revolutionary reality is compared to an undiscovered part of the earth. To suppose that it is possible to draw up a map of a revolution before its occurrence would be self-contradictory. Saint-Just would have rejected Lenin's *The State and Revolution* as a masterpiece in science fiction. Indeed, the whole program of Marxism-Leninism is rejected in advance. Such is the paradox of what is commonly called 'the revolutionary tradition'. It supposes that several revolutions in history share a set of features and that this set defines an ideal type of revolution, the most prominent source of such features being the French Revolution. But, as one of the main participants of that historical sequence, Saint-Just would have unflinchingly opposed such a conception. In his view, every revolution is a type in itself.[9]

From this basic difference, a whole series of others follow. Critics like to identify Terror as the common thread of revolutions, but for the Jacobins, terror was a strictly constrained instrument that was also to be used against itself: they unleashed state terror to regulate and contain the popular terror (the 'September massacres' of 1792) with the motto: 'Let us be terrible so that the people will not have to be'. The Jacobin trials were far from the Stalinist show trials: many of the accused were proclaimed innocent, and the guilt of the accused was as a rule actual (for example, today we know

---

9   Milner, 'The Prince and the Revolutionary'.

that Danton was financed by the British). The Jacobins' entire mode of operation was public – not secret plots but speeches in the National Assembly – and this was also how they lost power (after a simple vote in the Assembly). Robespierre 'wanted the revolution to finish as soon as possible; as his doctrine foresaw it, he was ready to accept that his own death will be necessary in order to stop the internal wars'.[10] In contrast to the Stalinist revolutionary who acts as a 'subject supposed to know' (Lacan), the Jacobin revolutionary 'is a revolutionary only to the exact extent to which he is not supposed to know. More precisely, he is the subject-supposed-not-to-know constitutive of the revolutionary gesture.'[11] In this sense, revolution is not part of objective reality: it implies a subjective gesture and as such an eruption of the Real in historical reality.

This, of course, does not mean that Robespierre's position is not without its own antagonist tensions. When Milner says that Robespierre 'believed what he said – and we know this was his symptom',[12] we should take the word 'symptom' here in the strict psychoanalytic sense, not just as a term synonymous with 'a sign of some deep feature'. Robespierre's very sincerity (believing what he was saying) paradoxically becomes a sign of something he desperately tried to avoid or even repress, something that returns as a compromise formation uniting contradictory features. And we should not be afraid of a recourse to Marxism in order to discern this tension: what Robespierre's egalitarianism, his dedication to the axiom of equality, ignores is the full extent to which political equality is the very form of economic inequality, of economic class struggle.

We navigate today in uncharted territories, with no global cognitive map – but what if this is hope, an opening to avoid

---

10 Milner, *Relire la révolution*, p. 129.
11 Ibid., p. 128.
12 Ibid., p. 129.

totalitarian closure, like Saint-Just for Milner?[13] What if we read the couple Lenin/Trotsky as a repetition of the couple Robespierre/Saint-Just – who are, or could be, today's Lenin and Trotsky?

---

13   Milner, 'The Prince and the Revolutionary'.

Sources

Chapter titles in quotation marks were chosen by the author; all others are descriptive designations of untitled pieces.

To M.F. Sokolov. 16 May 1921. *Collected Works*, Vol. 35, trans. Andrew Rothstein, Moscow: Progress Publishers, 1976, pp. 491–3 (*Pravda* No 1, 1 January 1924). Transcribed by R. Cymbala.

To G. Myasnikov. 5 August 1921. *Collected Works*, Vol. 32, trans. Yuri Sdobnikov, Moscow: Progress Publishers, 1965, pp. 504–9. Transcribed by David Walters and R. Cymbala.

'New Times and Old Mistakes in a New Guise'. 20 August 1921. *Collected Works*, Vol. 33, trans. David Skvirsky and George Hanna, Moscow: Progress Publishers, 1965, pp. 21–9 (*Pravda* No 190, 28 August 1921). Transcribed by David Walters and R. Cymbala.

'Notes of a Publicist: On Ascending a High Mountain; the Harm of Despondency; the Utility of Trade; Attitude towards the Mensheviks, Etc.' Late February 1922. *Collected Works*, Vol. 33, trans. David Skvirsky and George Hanna, Moscow: Progress Publishers, 1965, pp. 204–11 (*Pravda* No 87, 16 April 1924). Transcribed by David Walters and R. Cymbala.

Eleventh Congress of the RCP(B). 16 March 1922. *Collected Works*, Vol. 33, trans. David Skvirsky and George Hanna, Moscow: Progress Publishers, 1965, pp. 237–42. Transcribed by David Walters and R. Cymbala.

Memo Combating Dominant-Nation Chauvinism. 6 October 1922. *Collected Works*, Vol. 33, trans. David Skvirsky and George Hanna, Moscow: Progress Publishers, 1965, p. 372 (*Pravda* No 21, 21 January 1937). Transcribed by David Walters and R. Cymbala.

'Last Testament': Letters to Congress. *Collected Works*, Vol. 36, trans. Andrew Rothstein, Moscow: Progress Publishers, 1971, pp. 593–611. Transcribed by Brian Baggins.

On Education (Pages from a Diary). 15 December 1922. *Collected Works*, Vol. 33, trans. David Skvirsky and George Hanna, Moscow: Progress Publishers, 1965, pp. 462–6 (*Pravda* No 2, 4 January 1923). Transcribed by David Walters and R. Cymbala.

'On Cooperation'. 4 and 6 January 1923. *Collected Works*, Vol. 33, trans. David Skvirsky and George Hanna, Moscow: Progress Publishers, 1965, pp. 467–75 (*Pravda* Nos 115–16, 26–7 May 1923). Transcribed by David Walters and R. Cymbala.

'Our Revolution (Apropos of N. Sukhanov's Notes)'. 16 January 1923. *Collected Works*, Vol. 33, trans. David Skvirsky and George Hanna, Moscow: Progress Publishers, 1965, pp. 476–80 (*Pravda* No 117, 30 May 1923). Transcribed by Brian Baggins.

'How We Should Reorganise the Workers' and Peasants' Inspection: Recommendation to the Twelfth Party Congress'. 23 January 1923. *Collected Works*, Vol. 33, trans. David Skvirsky and George Hanna, Moscow: Progress Publishers, 1965, pp. 462–6 (*Pravda* No 16, 25 January 1923). Transcribed by Brian Baggins.

'Better Fewer, but Better'. 2 March 1923. *Collected Works*, Vol. 33, trans. David Skvirsky and George Hanna, Moscow: Progress Publishers, 1965, pp. 487–502 (*Pravda* No 49, 4 March 1923). Transcribed by Brian Baggins.